also by Martin Brayne

The Greatest Storm
Harry Peckham's Tour (ed.)

To Elaine
with thanks + best wishes

Gone

to the

Continent

The British in Calais, 1760-1860

Martin Brayne

Martin Brayne

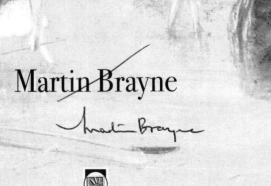

Queen Anne's Fan

First published in 2016 by

Queen Anne's Fan PO Box 883 • Canterbury • Kent • CT1 3WJ

© Copyright Martin Brayne 2016

ISBN 978-0-9573639-1-5

A CIP record of this book can be obtained from the British Library.

Set in New Baskerville 11 on 12pt.

www.queenannesfan.com

Printed in England

Queen Anne's Fan

CONTENTS

ACKNOWLEDGEMENTS

In a sense my greatest debt is to a long-dead and little-known eighteenth century barrister, Harry Peckham. It was in researching his life (he died in 1787) that I first came across the Hôtel d'Angleterre in Calais where he had stayed for a couple of nights in 1769 and which, I later discovered, was one and the same as Dessein's hotel made famous by Laurence Sterne in his novel *A Sentimental Journey* published in the year prior to Peckham's trip. My fascination with the English in Calais, in fact and fiction, had begun.

My subsequent researches have left me further indebted to a considerable number of people for whose friendly assistance I am enormously grateful. The availability of so much information online means that one no longer needs to visit as many libraries and archives as was once the case but nothing can beat physical contact with the real thing and I am especially thankful to the Librarians of the Portico Library, Manchester, the Royal Geographical Society, and the Archives Municipales de Calais. I would particularly mention Mme Geneviève Van Goethen and her staff in Calais, especially Grégory Boyer. I must also thank Natacha Haffringues and Anthony Cadet at the Musée des Beaux Arts, Calais and, collectively, for their website, Les Amis du Vieux Calais. My thanks are also due to Stephen Black and

Richard Lander, both descendants of Britons who lived in Calais and subsequently emigrated to Australia. Dick Ayres, Dick Bateman, Roy and Pat Creamer, Pamela Eagan, Bill Grove, Mike Harris, Katherine McClung-Oakes, Pietro Micheli, Peter Searby, John Sharp, Jennifer Soan, Katharine Solomon Ian Richardson and Iain Taylor have all, in different ways, helped me. James Thornely, who drew the maps, provided an especially helpful service and I must pay particular thanks to Martin Lloyd of Queen Anne's Fan whose assistance and encouragement have been invaluable and to my wife, Ann, who has once more been tolerant of an obsession. The remaining errors are all my own.

PREFACE

The British relationship to Calais, the nearest Continental town to Great Britain – has undergone a variety of fluctuations since, in 1558, it became the last English possession to be lost to the French and Mary Tudor predicted that when she was, 'dead and opened, you shall find "Calais" lying in my heart'. The present book deals with a period when the Channel port was best known to its island neighbour. An article which appeared in the *Spectator* just three years before the outbreak of the First World War looked back upon those nostalgically remembered days:

> Calais can never again be to English travellers on the Continent what it was to Sterne, to Wordsworth and to Thackeray – the pleasant threshold of a holiday abroad. It was with something of boyish gusto of enjoyment that Thackeray claimed that, 'there is no town more French than Calais'. Subjectively, the claim was just, for Calais was the first French town where an Englishman on his grand tour began his adventures of mind and body.[1]

The inauguration of a railway station at the port, the Gare Maritime, in 1848, persuaded most British travellers that they need not break their journey at Calais. From the steam packet they could now step aboard a steam train and head directly for Paris. Until that time Calais had been for almost a century much frequented, and much written about, by the British. Arriving from Dover after a voyage of rarely less than three hours, the great majority had been only too happy to seek an hotel, recover from the crossing and look, often with some amazement, about them. For those visiting the Continent for the first time, it was Calais that, as often as not, provided them with their first experience of 'abroad' and of a strange non-English-speaking, non-Protestant land from which their tastes and fashions had often emanated but with which their own nation had often been at war.

Whilst educated, Whiggish men-of-the-world may have inclined towards Francophilia and backwoods Tory squires towards a suspicion of most things French, attitudes varied

greatly. By quoting extensively from letters, diaries and
memoirs and works of fiction (novels, plays and poems) as
well as of fact, the aim here is to reflect these varying
shades of opinion and place them in a social, historical and
geographical context. When making use of unedited
material I have, when consistent with comprehension,
retained original spelling and punctuation. In this way I
seek to recapture the British experience, real and
imagined, of travelling to and living in what Thackeray
regarded as the most French of towns but what was, at the
same time, the most English town in France.

It is true, as the French historian Arlette Farge has
said, that, 'A quotation is never proof'.[2] For almost every
quotation a counter-quotation might be found and, 'The
quotation has so much charm that it can be difficult to
resist... it has the charm of aptness and exoticism, with the
colourfulness of language of another era....' But the case I
would make is that the traveller, whether writing in a
journal, sending a letter home, writing a book or newspaper
article, inevitably adopts a point of view and, in attempting
to gauge the British experience of Calais, that is exactly
what one wishes to recapture. If, as a consequence, this
book is more anthological than, in an academic sense,
historical, it may be less important but not, perhaps, totally
without interest or merit.

All manner of folk visited Calais. In addition to, 'the
arrivals and departures of Regents, Dauphins, Field
Marshalls and Hidalgoes,' recorded in the visitors' books
of the most fashionable hotels, many lesser mortals –
diplomats and soldiers, merchants, sailors and pleasure-
seekers – called briefly on their way to Paris or Brussels, Italy
or the Rhineland. There were others who had no ambition
to travel further unless, in the fullness of time, to return
home. These were those, numbering in the thousands by the
middle of the nineteenth century, who were seeking refuge
from the then much shorter arm of the British legal system.
Most were debtors. There were others who were endeavoring
to reduce the cost of living. The biggest single group, and

one which increased exponentially in size during the period covered by this book, was that of tourists. In the years prior to the upheavals of the French Revolution, these were mostly drawn from the upper classes and, although they might be aiming to go no further than Paris, many would be on one version or another of the Grand Tour. After Waterloo, and especially after the introduction of cheap steam packet excursions, the trippers were often of an altogether more democratic nature, often disparagingly referred to by their socially superior fellow travellers as 'cockneys'.

In 1760 there was only one inn of any significance in the town – the Lion d'Argent – but it was soon joined by another, L'Hôtel d'Angleterre, as often as not referred to by the name of its proprietor, Pierre Dessin and eventually becoming known as *l'auberge des rois*. As the cross-Channel trade increased so, of course, did the supply of accommodation and Dessin's was not always their first choice. Mariana Starke, in her pioneering Continental Guide, expressed a preference for the Hôtel Royal (formerly the Kingston) kept by Mr Roberts, an Englishman whose wines were, 'particularly good'.[3] Miss Starke conceded that L'Hôtel Dessin and L'Hôtel de Bourbon were 'likewise good inns'. This latter was run by a M. Rignolle who, 'from the humble station of a barber in London had raised himself to an innkeeper in Calais'.[4] By 1842, Francis Hervé, who claimed he had visited many of the town's numerous hotels, was of the opinion that the Bourbon, by then kept by M. Derhorter whose civility, 'cannot anywhere be surpassed', was 'the most comfortable and economical. For the nobility and those with equipages Dessin's was still the favourite, 'and has been since time immemorial'.[5] Other hotels included Meurice's, the successor of which still exists, the Crown and the Diligence, both in the rue de la Mer.[6]

Such grand hotels were not for the indigent who would seek to make a home in a cheap, rented apartment. One such was that at 27 rue Française in which Emma Hamilton spent her last, miserably impecunious days.[7] Charles Dickens envisaged another – 'A dead sort of place, with dead walls over the way and a dead gateway at the side, where a pendant bell-handle produced two dead tinkles' – the depressing residence in which Arthur Clennam discovers Miss Wade and Tattycoram in *Little Dorrit*.

Whilst not comparable with Paris or Florence, Calais is a significant location in English literature. Although it was not the only packet station through which British travellers entered the Continent – Hellevoetsluis, Ostend, Boulogne, Dieppe and Le Havre might also be used – it was certainly the one most frequently to inspire the literary imagination. This is doubtless because poets and novelists, like the population in general, were most likely themselves to have entered France there, at least until the 1830s when it was overtaken by Boulogne. Calais also had something of romance about it which was not possessed by its rivals: not only had it been the last English enclave in France but, since during the reign of Mary's father, Henry VIII, Froissart's *Chronicles* had been translated into English, the story of the Burghers of Calais had been well-known in England. Then in 1768 Laurence Sterne's best-selling novel, *A Sentimental Journey* was published. The opening chapters take place at the inn which he spelt 'Dessein's' and, as we shall see, this played a key role in establishing Calais as a place considered worthy of a literary setting.

In addition to Sterne, Wordsworth and Thackeray who have already been mentioned, there can be added the names of Samuel Foote, Thomas Holcroft, Thomas Moore, Captain Marryat and, perhaps most memorably, Dickens himself.

For much of the first sixty years covered here Britain and France were at war, making travel between the two countries impossible. When Sterne first visited in 1762, the Seven Years' War had not ended and officially did not do so for another year but he was fortunate in being able to travel with a diplomatic party. In 1778 hostilities again broke out (lasting until 1783) when France allied itself with the Americans fighting for independence. After a decade of peace, the French Revolutionary Wars broke out and were followed by the Napoleonic Wars, lasting from 1793 to 1814 with just a short period of peace – the Peace of Amiens – between 25 March 1802 and 18 May 1803. After Napoleon had been exiled to Elba and the Bourbon monarchy restored there was, as in 1802, another mad rush to the Continent, which came to an abrupt end with Bonaparte's return and the Hundred Days, themselves terminated by Waterloo. With the second, more successful restoration of the monarchy, the flow of British travellers through Calais was resumed; the Belgian battlefield being added to the number of Continental attractions. The next forty years were ones of uninterrupted Franco-British peace. Even during the war-riven first sixty years after *A Sentimental Journey* was published a remarkable amount of travel literature featuring Calais issued from the press. In the words of Colonel Francis Hall, whose own *Travels in France in 1818* prompted him to assert that, 'A man must have considerable courage to write Travels in France, especially if he begins by Calais',

The public has... banqueted on Travels, Agricultural, Philosophical and Political; on Visits and Visitations, from Six Months to Six Weeks; on Letters and Observations; on 'Reflections during a Residence', and 'Notes during an Abode'; on 'Walks in, round and about Paris'; on 'Sketches of Scenery' and 'Scenic Delineations'; on journeys voluntary and forced; on Excursions on Horseback and on Foot; by Old Routes and new Routes and Unusual Routes.[8]

There is, thus, no shortage of material with which to assess the nature of the British experience of travelling to and living in, for however short a period, a place which invariably made a lasting impression. Since the *Spectator* article was written, the devastation of two World Wars and subsequent rebuilding, the construction of the Channel Tunnel and a new railway station, Calais-Fréthun, and the growth of hypermarkets are just some of the developments which have further changed the appearance and nature of a town which had once figured far more prominently in the lives of British travellers than it does today.

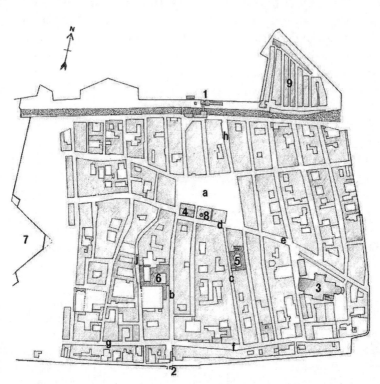

1 Porte du Havre	a Place d'Armes/Grande
2 Porte Royale	Place
3 Notre-Dame	b rue Royale
4 Hôtel de Ville	c rue Neuve
5 Lion d'Argent	d rue des Boucheries
6 Hôtel d'Angleterre	e rue Nôtre Dame
(Dessein's)	f rue des Maréchaux
7 La Citadelle	g rue Française
8 Tour de Guet	h rue de la Tête d'Or
9 Courgain	j rue de la Comédie

ill.1

CALAIS

Based on the '*plan cadastral*' of 1834

1

The Shock of Abroad

The present-day traveller between England and France is unlikely to see much of Calais. He may observe it briefly from the air, noting the white wake of a ferry silently heading for the harbour entrance far below. Even the motorist disembarking from the boat, or emerging from the Tunnel, will get little more than a distant glimpse of the extravagantly Flemish tower of the Hotel de Ville before by-passing the town en route for the Loire, the Dordogne and *Toutes Directions*.

Such has been the case since the introduction in the 1860s of the first boat trains – the forerunners of the *Flèche d'Or* – which whisked their passengers away from the quay-side at Calais-Maritime in great billows of smoke, steam and excitement, giving them little opportunity to visit the town or stroll upon the once famous sands.[1] Calais, nevertheless, had been the traditional point of arrival for British tourists visiting the Continent and, for all but the most world-weary of travellers prior to the building of the railway, it had been a place of romance; a place where they encountered, often for the first time, the wonders of *la différence* between themselves and what that influential arbiter of eighteenth century manners Joseph Addison had called 'that Fantastick Nation'.[2]

Mary Wordsworth was not alone in finding, 'The first shock of difference of country... very picturesque'.[3] The impact of this culture shock still resonates to this day in hundreds of letters and journals, although these flights of literary contrast – as often as not hastily confirmed prejudices involving English neatness and French squalor, Protestant reason and Catholic emotion, British reserve and

Gallic *politesse* – were not always expressed with the colourful economy of William Beckford who on a Sunday in 1819 wrote:

> They're singing and drumming in every street, all the shops are open, and all the people have a gaiety and primitive Frenchiness, dancing and shitting with zest and talking all the time – nothing Anglican about it....[4]

In 1785 the young Edward Nares, a future Regius Professor of Modern History at Oxford, travelled to France,

> The moment we disembarked on the pier head at Calais, we seemed to be in a New World – nothing could be greater than the contrast between the English and the French shores ...Monks were to be seen in all the streets, in the habits of their order, with their feet bare or in sandals. The carriages, carts, horses and even dogs were different.[5]

The young Irish woman Katherine Wilmot was one of the many who rushed across the Channel in anticipation of the Treaty of Amiens; arriving at Calais on the afternoon of 29 November 1801, she and her friends:

> ...were soon put into good humour, by the contemplation of novelty, which struck our senses in every direction and such a quick hocus pocus metamorphosis from what we had left in England a few hours before.
> Every man in a cock'd hat, three colour'd cockade and gold ear-rings, savage black whiskers and frequently a muff on his arm. Indeed this was the costume of every ragged poltroon. The grisettes, pretty and smartly adorned with sparkling crosses, necklaces, ear-rings and every shining decoration, with close caps upon their round rosy cheeks, and an air of courtesy and ease...[6]

Katherine's fellow countryman John Mayne was one of those who made for France when peace was next declared, following the first fall of Napoleon in 1814. Having spent three weeks, prior to embarkation, at Dover, where they had seen many Frenchmen, he and his travelling companions, 'did not experience in a very high degree the surprise usually felt by those whose change from England to France is more abrupt.' Nevertheless, 'women of the lower class and children, shops, posting carriages, horses and drivers were novel and produced infinite diversion'.[7]

And such effusions were by no means confined to the pens of out-going travellers. The need to await a packet, or for favourable winds, often confined returning tourists to Calais for a day or two, providing ample opportunity for reflection upon Continental experience. Even those who had seen Paris, the Alps and Italy would often find something to say, very often to its credit, of Calais. Horace Walpole, writing to his friend Richard West in 1739 from Rome itself, declared, 'We did not cry out Lord! half so much as at Calais which to this hour I look upon as one of the most surprising cities of the universe.'[8]

The portrait painter John Hoppner aimed to explain the fascinating difference. According to his friend and fellow artist Joseph Farington:

Hoppner observed that nothing could be more striking than the sudden change from a people of one appearance to that of another than was seen by crossing the Sea from Dover to Calais. He thought the French in their appearance much more picturesque than the English from the variety which is seen among them. In England every one aims at an appearance of substantial propriety, which brings them nearer to an equality. In France to please their own fancies is more their object than to imitate, which causes such whimsical mixtures of dress to be seen everywhere. Poverty obliges them also to be content that a portion of finery shall be mixed with meanness producing very odd contrasts.[9]

The feature of the town which was most likely to be the subject of favourable comment by English travellers was Dessin's (or Dessein's) Hotel; officially called the *Hotel d'Angleterre*. The original owner, Pierre Dessin, was immortalised as 'Monsieur. Dessein' in Laurence Sterne's picaresque travel story of 1768, *A Sentimental Journey through*

France and Italy. Sterne's more familiar spelling will be used here except when quoting from those who have employed the alternative. In the nineteenth century the hotel passed into the hands of the related family of Quillac, or Quillacq, who also became owners of another hotel, *Le Lion d'Argent.*

Whilst based upon a real journey and featuring such real and identifiable persons as Yorick (Sterne himself), Dessein, the Monk (Father Lorenzo), Smelfungus (Tobias Smollett) and Mundungus (Samuel Sharp), *A Sentimental Journey* is a work of fiction.[10] But although it was the first such work in which Dessein's hotel would appear, it was by no means the last, albeit that it was, almost certainly, the *sine qua non*; for whether Samuel Foote, Thackeray, Dickens, Captain Marryat or James Fenimore Cooper and even Barbara Cartland would have found the hotel half so romantic without Yorick's example is unlikely.

Similarly, of Sterne himself, for as Robert Bell Calton put it:

> ...the spirit of the author of *Tristram Shandy* hovers in the corridors of the house, as you fancy you are following in his footsteps; flits about the festooned casements to your dormitory and more hallows the hostelrie of Monsieur Dessin than do all the chronicled arrivals and sojourns of 'Regents, Dauphins, Field Marshals and Hidalgoes' of their fleeting and evanescent hour![11]

The founder of the hotel was Pierre Quillacq (1726-93), known as Dessin. A Gascon from Castets in the Landes, he had leased the *Lyon d'Argent,* or Grandsire's Inn, from Louis-Guillaume Grandsire.[12] This was the inn, catering especially for English travellers, to which a huge rib of beef is being delivered, whilst undernourished Frenchmen, including soldiers of the garrison, look on with envy in Hogarth's famous picture of 1748, *The Gate of Calais,* also known as 'Roast Beef of Old England'.[13]

According to Sterne's American biographer Wilbur L. Cross, prior to taking the lease Dessein had been, 'a favourite waiter at the Silver Lion with the English passing through Calais, and had assumed his peculiar name from a compliment of one of them, who remarked, *"Il a du dessein, ce gaillard "*.[14]

By 1764 it was Grandsire who was envious of Dessein who, despite the disruption to trade caused by the Seven Years War, was making a great success of his business and proving an intractable tenant. Grandsire in consequence appears to have set up the sign of the Lion opposite Dessein's establishment in the Rue Neuve. The tenant endeavoured to minimise the damage to his trade by publishing an account of Grandsire's treachery – as he saw it – in the *London Chronicle*. Matters came to a head with first the burning down of the *Lyon d'Argent* on 25 September 1764 and then another fire a month later at the rival establishment. The probability seems to be that both fires were the result of arson and that the fire-raiser was none other than Dessein himself. Certainly he took great advantage of the disaster by soliciting, especially from his English customers, subscriptions to underwrite his loss. To Grandsire's chagrin – vented in the pages of the *Public Advertiser* – he used these funds not to re-build the burnt-out inn but to acquire a fine new building in the Rue Royale – the *Hotel d'Angleterre*. Further subscriptions rolled in when, in March of the following year, under the patronage of Lord Shelburne, Dessein appeared at Tom Davies's bookshop in Russell Street, Covent Garden, to further promote the new hotel.[15]

Poor Grandsire! When Horace Walpole's friend William Cole, who had stopped at the hotel on previous occasions, arrived at the *Lyon d'Argent* on 17 October 1765 he discovered, 'Mr Grandsire, the Landlord, just laid up with a broken Leg'! Furthermore, on his return in December, Cole revealed that his, 'Chaise was consigned by Mr Pascal to Mr Dessein at the Hotel D'Angleterre, who was his Correspondent for Carriages between Calais and Paris' and consequently decided to remain at Dessein's inn, which he describes as, 'new built, & was a fine large Quadrangle, with most sumptuous Apartments & elegantly furnished'.[16]

In the same month as Cole reported Grandsire's

broken leg, a great portion of luck was added to Dessein's enterprise with the arrival at his lavishly appointed new establishment of an English celebrity at the height of his fame, the creator of the still incomplete but partially published, *Tristram Shandy*, Laurence Sterne. Sterne would perhaps not have chosen to be the making of the Dessein fortune for when he had first visited France, three years before, he had stayed at the *Lyon d'Argent* and, although he instructed Mrs Sterne, who followed him across the Channel, to stay at the Cross Keys at Dover and, 'at Calais the *Lyon d'Argent*', he was careful to point out that there the master – Dessein – was 'a Turk in grain', an out-and-out rogue.[17] If Sterne's experience was the same as that of his eponymous hero this judgement must have been based on the most fleeting acquaintance for, according to Tristram, 'it was dusky in the evening when I landed and dark as pitch in the morning when I set out'.

It was October 1765 when Sterne arrived at Dessein's on his second trip across the Channel. If *A Sentimental Journey*, the literary fruit of his travels, is to be relied upon to provide at least the outline of the author's actual journey, the packet sailed at nine in the morning and by three he was consuming fricasseed chicken and a bottle of Burgundy at Dessein's.

Because the events which overtook the Sentimental Traveller in Calais figure so strongly in the imaginations of so many of the future guests of M. Dessein and his successors, it might be helpful to recapitulate them here, without, of course, attempting to reproduce Sterne's inimitable style and sense of humour.

The newly-arrived, always anxious Traveller has no sooner started upon the chicken than he begins to contemplate the possibility that he may die of indigestion in the night and that, as a foreigner, all of his possessions will be forfeit to the King of France. He drinks the King's health, 'to satisfy my mind that I bore him no spleen' and then there is the encounter with the Franciscan Father Lorenzo who comes to the hotel begging for the support of his convent.

At once Yorick decides – for, 'no man cares to have his virtues the sport of contingencies'– not to give as much as a single sou. No sooner had the humble mendicant presented his courteous plea than he was assailed, not impolitely yet brutally nonetheless, by the full force of English Pragmatism – 'the unfortunate of our own country, surely, have the first rights; and I have left thousands in distress upon our shore' etc. The poor Franciscan, a model of meekness and Christian resignation, retreated and, 'my heart smote me the moment he shut the door.'

Discontented with his behaviour, Yorick takes himself outside to examine the chaises, one of which he hopes to hire for the continuation of his journey. Comfortably accommodating but one person a chaise in France is known as a *désobligeante* and spying an old one in the corner of the yard he climbs in and summons Dessein who, however, has gone to church. He draws the curtains so as not to be seen by – or perhaps not to have his conscience pricked by seeing – the Monk and the Lady with whom he is now in conversation, and settles down to write a Preface to his travels. Despite the see-saw motion of the ancient vehicle he waxes philosophical on the nature of travellers – Idle, Inquisitive, Splenetic etc. – until interrupted by two of his fellow countrymen. '"We were wondering," said one who, I found, was an Inquistive Traveller, "what could occasion its motion".'

'As an Englishman does not travel to see Englishmen', he retreats to his room on the passage to which he meets Dessein, returned from vespers and anxious to, 'put me in mind of my wants' and allows himself to be taken to the coach-house – or *remise* – to inspect the hotelier's full range of vehicles. At the door to the *remise* they are met, to Yorick's embarrassment, by the Lady who had been chatting to the Monk. Here Dessein 'diabled' the coach-house key, 'above fifty times' before accepting that it was the wrong one and, leaving Yorick and the Lady accidentally hand-in-hand, went off to find the right one. 'Now a colloquy of five minutes, in such a situation, is worth one of as many ages' and so it proves; in the words of the Lady herself, *'C'est bien comique'*.

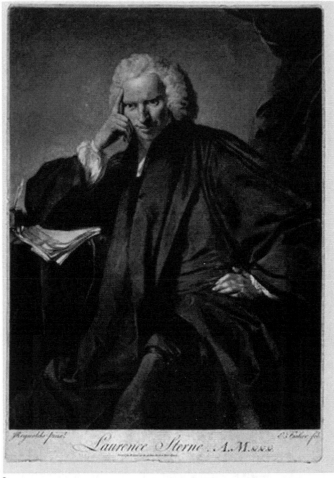

ill:2

Reynold's portrait of Laurence Sterne.
A copy was hung over the fireplace of 'Sterne's Room'
in Dessein's Hotel

M. Dessein, his hotel, the Monk, the *désobligeante* and the *remise* all become objects of the greatest interest to future travellers. Of particular interest was Sterne's own room. The words 'This is Sterne's Room' were displayed over the doorway to Room No. 31 and in the chamber itself a mezzotint of Reynolds' famous portrait of the writer hung above the chimney-piece. Percy Fitzgerald, Sterne's Victorian biographer had his doubts:

Many years ago a traveller halting at Dessin's was shown 'No. Thirty-one', and the Sir Joshua mezzotint over the chimney piece, and yet was sceptical. The outside of the house was over grown with vine-leaves, and shrewdly suspecting there might be some record of the date of erection cut on the stone, he sent up a man to cut away the vine leaves, an operation which led to the discovery of a tablet, A.D. 1770 just two years too late for the credit of 'Sterne's Room'.[18]

The waiter, however, in no way disconcerted, offered to fix on another room in the house and called it Sterne's! To this Fitzgerald added the following note - 'I am inclined to doubt the story, as the building always looked much later than the date mentioned', yet the sceptic's discovery would appear to fit Fitzgerald's own explanation:

About a year after Sterne's death, the famous inn, or a portion of it, was burnt. The chamber in which the sentimental traveller drank to the king of France, and grew agitated over the *droit d'aubaine*, and the window from which he had curiously scanned the 'Janatones' of Calais (not connected with the fishing interest) tripping across the Place, were all swept away in the conflagration.

However, as there appears to be no confirmation of this latter fire we must assume that Fitzgerald confuses it with that of 1764 which led to the building of the new hotel. But even those who doubted the authenticity of 'Sterne's Room' had no doubt that the true Shandean spirit still resided Chez Dessein.

The Dessein dynasty itself was in no doubt that Sterne had contributed hugely to the making of the family's fortune. The dramatist Frederic Reynolds recalled visiting the hotel in 1782 and being told by Pierre Dessein himself, 'Your Countryman, Monsieur Sterne, von great, von vary great man, and he carried me vid him to posterity. He gain moche money by his Journey of Sentiment – mais moi – make more through de means of dat, than he, by all his ouvrages reunies – Ha, ha!'[19] This was no idle boast, for within three weeks of the publication of *A Sentimental Journey* Laurence Sterne was dead. The Dessein family by contrast would continue to reap the benefits of his visit for decades.

This is not to suggest that all of the hotel's guests were literary tourists – although the arrival of Sir Walter Scott at the height of his fame certainly burnished the literary laurels – for it was in its day a remarkably comfortable hotel and attracted many of Calais' more prosperous visitors and, especially after the restoration of the monarchy in France, members of royal families so that it became known as *L'Auberge des Rois*.[20]

Calais, and even the *Hotel d'Angleterre*, attracted another rather different type from across the Straits of Dover; fugitives from the English legal system. This was a role the town had long fulfilled but whilst earlier refugees had often been Catholics fleeing religious persecution, by Dessein's day they were more likely to be escapees from the gloomy prospect of the Marshalsea, the King's Bench or some other debtors' prison. Robert Bell Calton explained things:

> The close proximity to England, with its artificial and fearfully extravagant mode of life among its more gay or exalted classes, has long made even the dreary sands of Calais appear as a fragrant delta to the drifting lordlings of creation as they struck out for this as the nearest point of refuge.'[21]

Lady Harriet Cavendish, the daughter of Georgiana Devonshire, put it like this:

> Calais is peopled with English slight sinners and heavy debtors, the needy and the greedy ...a sort of purgatory for half-condemned souls.[22]

Throughout the eighteenth and most of the nineteenth centuries there was no effective extradition treaty between

England and France. A clause in the Treaty of Amiens (1802) allowed for the removal of accused persons from one jurisdiction to the other but the rapid resumption of hostilities consigned the entire treaty to the flames of war. Forty years elapsed before Sir Robert Peel's ministry took up the matter with the government of Louis-Philippe, leading to the signing of an extradition treaty in 1843.[23] It was hopelessly ineffective and the two countries continued to harbour one another's outlaws until the early 1870s.[24] This did not, however, mean that the French allowed refugees from the British legal system to roam their country at will. Unless they could obtain a passport, issued at a port of entry, they were confined to that port. Thus Beau Brummell, who sought sanctuary from his British creditors in 1816 remained immured within the walls of the town until his appointment as British consul at Caen in 1830 released him, temporarily, from his French debts and permanently from Calais.[25]

In addition to being beyond the reach of the British courts, Calais had the advantage of a much lower cost of living than London. It was possible to live there in a modest way for a fraction of the amount required to maintain an equivalent household in England but whilst some reconciled themselves to such a retired existence, others, failing perhaps to recognise the true nature of their plight or hoping to meet some benevolent, or feeble-minded, fellow countryman on whom they could sponge, turned up at Dessein's. The hotel seems, however, to have had good intelligence as to the creditworthiness of their guests and their stay, whilst sometimes spectacular, was invariably short.

Thus for a hundred years Dessein's hotel was something of a honey pot for English travellers. The literary and the louche, the respectable and the royal were greeted by successive generations of the Dessein/Quillacq family. Although Arthur Young claimed that the *Hotel de Henri IV* at Nantes was superior,[26] the more commonly held view was that of Philip Thicknesse whose only complaint was that the hotel deceived the unsuspecting tourist:

After all, it must be confessed that Mons. Dessein's l'Hotel d'Angleterre at Calais, is not only the first inn strangers of fashion generally go to, but that it is the first and best inn in France. Dessein is the decoy-duck, and ought to have a salary from the French government; he is already sure of a good one from the English.[27]

A later literary visitor to Dessein's hotel was the novelist William Makepeace Thackeray. He greatly admired Sterne's literary gifts but accused him of hypocrisy and licentiousness. In a short story published in *The Roundabout Papers* [*see* Appendix 1] he dreams of an encounter with Sterne's ghost.

2

"WHAT A CURSED THING IT IS TO LIVE IN AN ISLAND!"

'How charming and very like Twickenham Ferry
Is crossing over to Calais, I vow'
(song: *The Calais Packet*)

The distance from the north turret of Dover Castle to the spire of the church of Notre Dame at Calais was measured by triangulation, as part of a remarkable example of Anglo-French co-operation, in 1787. It was found to be twenty six miles and some additional yards.[1] Not a great distance but negotiating it could be fraught.

Before setting off for France the British tourist would have a number of decisions to make and preparations to see to. Would he take his own vehicle, hire one on arrival or travel by stage? Between which ports would he sail? What belongings would he need to take with him? Would he travel on a British or a French passport?

Of these questions the one that seems strangest to us is this last for there was at this time no internationally recognised procedure with respect to passports. Practice varied from country to country: the United Kingdom was one of the most relaxed of nations in this regard, France one of the most demanding. People could enter and leave British territory and move about as they wished without being required to present 'papers'. In France by contrast, although the antiquary Dawson Turner seems to have exaggerated a little when, in 1820, he asserted that 'No Frenchman can quit his arrondissement unprovided with a passport' – anybody leaving their own *département* or canton needed one.[2] Foreigners certainly required one and they were regularly checked and stamped upon entry into a major city or garrison town.[3]

The very word 'bureaucracy' comes from the French *bureaucratie* and one of the earliest examples of its use that *The Oxford English Dictionary* supplies is from John Stuart Mill who, in 1837 wrote of, 'That vast network of administrative tyranny... that system of bureaucracy, which leaves no free agent in all France, except the man at Paris who pulls the wires.' Something of the British contempt for French bureaucracy is to be detected in the words of the lawyer Harry Peckham who the day before he left Paris for Calais and home in 1769:

Was fully employed in hiring a coach for which I gave six guineas to Mr Paschall, in obtaining an order from the Post-Master General to be furnished on the road with six horses, in getting a passport from our Ambassador to return without molestation, and in obtaining another passport signed by the King of France and countersigned by the Duke of Choiseul, to permit a poor Englishman to return to his country after having spent all of the money he had brought with him.[4]

The poet Thomas Campbell, although he had travelled on the Continent at least twice before, forgot that this was required when arranging to travel to Germany in 1820. From Bonn, he wrote to his friend and fellow poet Samuel Rogers:

My dear Rogers – I dare say you thought me a sad fellow for leaving England without seeing you, but I assure you it was from misfortune and not neglect. On the morning of the day which I meant to have devoted to you, I was asked by a friend if I had a passport. The thought of such a thing being necessary had never occurred to my recollection, but my friend had just been conversing with a Prussian baron, who had mentioned that in the present state of things it was indispensable. I find that he was right. But the time that I had allotted to a conversation with you was spent in a vain application to the Foreign Office and, in the next place, in hunting out the Dutch ambassador, who was more civil to me than the clerks of our own State office.[5]

So ignorant were British travellers of the French passport requirements that the credulity of the readers of *A Sentimental Journey* would not have been too greatly imposed upon by the notion of its hero, Yorick, arriving in Paris (via Calais) without a passport. Equally, they would not have been surprised by French pettiness in demanding one. Threatened with the Bastille, Yorick decides to plead his case to the Minister for Foreign Affairs, Choiseul, in person. After a ludicrous misunderstanding he is granted a passport, albeit that:

> As the passport was directed to all lieutenant governors, governors, and commandants of cities, generals of armies, justiciaries, and all other officers of justice, to let Mr Yorick, the king's jester, and his baggage, travel quietly along – I own the triumph of obtaining the passport was not a little tarnisd'd by the figure I cut in it.[6]

Seventeenth century royal decrees of 1623 and 1669 had sought to regulate the internal movement of the population of France by requiring that passports be carried.[7] For a short time during the Revolution, in the spirit of *Liberté* and of *laissez-faire, laissez passer,* these regulations were done away with but a rise in crime rates and vagrancy was attributed to an over-enthusiasm for this ideal and controls were rapidly re-introduced.[8] The insistence upon *'papiers'* thereafter endured despite their failure to undo the most notorious runaways in French history. It was not their papers, which were apparently 'in order', but the fact that Louis XVI and his queen were recognised by a veteran cavalryman that led to the failure of the flight to Varennes.[9]

The curious thing, to those of us accustomed to the beady-eyed scrutiny of the officers of the Border Agency, is that British citizens could, and very frequently did, travel on a French passport. This is because a passport issued by the French Embassy in London was valid in France, was cheaper than one issued by the Foreign Office and in some respects was easier to obtain. It was not until the 1850s that the increased demand brought about a more efficient method of issuing British passports – in theory, prior to that time the holder should have been personally known to the Foreign Secretary – and the cost was lowered from £2-7-6d to 7/6d.[10]

Typical of the eighteenth century attitude of the British to passports was that of the well-travelled Richard Twiss who in the summer of 1792 set out for Paris to experience the Revolution and, perhaps, the Counter-Revolution which he anticipated and who, 'sent for a passport from the Secretary of State's office, which I knew could do no harm if it did no good.'[11] He made the application, 'thinking I should have it for nothing,'

...and obtained one signed by Lord Grenville but at the same time a demand was made for two guineas and sixpence for the fees; now, as I have had passports from almost all the European nations, all and every one of which were gratis, I sent the pass back; it was however immediately returned to me, and I was told that, "A passport is never issued from that office without that fee, even if the party asking for it changes his mind." *I paid the money and that is all I shall say about the matter.*[12]

Twiss, nevertheless, took the precaution of obtaining a passport from the French Ambassador, Chauvelin, but was delighted to point out, on reaching Calais, that, 'No passport of any kind is necessary to enter France,' and there one was given to him by the magistrates, 'mentioning my age, structure, complexion etc. and this would have been a sufficient permit for my going out of France by sea or by land if the disturbances in Paris of the 10th of August, had not happened.'[13] Whilst Twiss could land on French soil without a passport, he could not have travelled beyond Calais without one; a regulation which led to a steady build-up of indigent Britons in the town.

Nor did passports have a standard format. Both French and British passports consisted of a single, pre-printed sheet of paper on to which the issuing officer entered the holder's details but the nature of the details varied greatly.[14] British passports, issued in London, tended to contain much less information than those issued by the French authorities. Thus, when William Bulwer travelled to the Continent in 1826 he obtained a passport for himself and his servant from the French Embassy in London. He, although not the servant, is described in considerable detail: he is six feet tall, twenty six years of age, has brown hair, eyebrows and eyes, his chin is round, his face oval, his nose average and his complexion ordinary. Such details were not necessarily accurate. On a passport issued to Bulwer a year before, his eyes are *'gris'* whilst on one issued when he was twenty one they had been *'bleus'*.[15]

Other evidence, however, suggests that considerable attention was given to the verbal depiction of the bearer's appearance. When in 1792 the actor James Fennell took his newly-married wife to Paris, they were preparing to depart from Dessein's when, 'I was informed that it was necessary to obtain passports'.[16] They were referred to what, in those Revolutionary days was known as the Office of Public Safety:

> And when there sate for our pictures. The height, the contour, the hair, the forehead, the eyes, noses and mouths, were minutely delineated in our passports: so extremely particular were the police officers, as to ask whether a small pimple I had on my forehead was a natural or accidental mark.[17]

Photographs on passports were not introduced, first by the USA, until 1914.[18] Bulwer was on a diplomatic mission for which reason, doubtless, his passport was 'Gratis'. If he had been travelling on a British passport between London and Paris his passport would have been taken from him at Calais and forwarded to the French capital and he would have received a temporary *laissez-passer* in exchange. As it was, he was heading for Brussels and before leaving London he had taken it to the embassy of the short-lived Kingdom of the Netherlands where it had been endorsed as, *'Bon pour Les Pays-Bas'*. In the course of a little over six weeks Bulwer travelled from Calais to Brussels and from there to Geneva (via Dijon and Lyon) from whence to Paris and then back to Calais. In addition to a dozen stamps of various authorities, the passport contains one other – that of 'Quillacq's hotel, Calais'.[19]

It is perhaps because the carrying of passports was quite unfamiliar to Britons that passports issued by the Foreign Office and by the British Embassy in Paris had affixed to them in the 1820s, a printed list of, 'Regulations required by the French Government to be observed by Foreigners in France'. These regulations may be summarised as follows:

1) No foreigners are permitted to travel or reside in France without special authorisation from the Director of Police;

2) Every foreigner, on arriving at a sea-port or frontier town, is to present himself before the local authorities, to produce his passport and deposit it in their hands;

3) If the passport be regular and there be no reason to suspect the intentions of the bearer, the local authorities are to give in exchange a French passport, bearing the words *Passe provisoire* inscribed immediately under the arms of France, for any place in the kingdom the foreigner may specify, and for which a fee of two francs is required;

4) The original passport is immediately transmitted to the police at Paris and, after being signed, is either collected by the bearer on his arrival in Paris or is forwarded to another city to which he is travelling;

5) Holders of provisional passports must travel by the route specified on that passport and report to the police at their destination within twenty four hours of their arrival;

6) The signature of the director of the police authority gives the bearer the right to stay in the country for one year;

7) No provisional passport can be given to foreigners arriving without a passport [It is for this reason that debtors and others who had left the United Kingdom without valid papers were obliged to remain at their port of arrival];

8) If the traveller is going no further than a department adjacent to that in which the seaport is located, the passport is retained by the police authorities at the port, a limited provisional passport is issued and the original passport restored to the owner on departure;

9) Couriers and members of diplomatic missions retain their passports;

10) Passports issued by members of the *Corps diplomatique* resident in Paris to the subjects of their respective sovereigns, must be countersigned by the director of police and the minister of foreign affairs. A fee of ten francs is charged.

In addition to a passport, the clothes he stood up in and, perhaps, his own carriage, with what else would the British traveller arrive at Calais? He would almost certainly require both ready cash and bills of credit which he would obtain in much the same way as did a 'Gentleman of York' who made a tour of France in 1818:

On the 28th July, we applied at the French Ambassador's office in London for passports. Having obtained them we proceeded to Herries's Bank, St James's Street and supplied ourselves with a competent number of bills of credit, which are convertible into cash by their correspondents at upwards of 150 of the principal towns of the Continent. At Thomas's, near the Royal Exchange, we procured a supply of gold and silver coin for immediate use.[20]

Mariana Starke's book, *Information and Direction to Travellers on the Continent,* the predecessor of the famous Murray Guides, provides detailed information on passports, currency, accommodation and much else including the items of baggage which the diligent traveller would be advised to take with him across the Channel. The list is remarkably comprehensive:

Leather sheets made of sheep skin or doe skin – pillows – blankets – calico sheets – pillow cases – a travelling chamber lock (easily fixed on any door in less than 5 minutes) – Bramah locks for writing desks and coach seats – a tinder box and matches – a small lantern – towels, table cloths & napkins, strong but not fine – a carving knife and fork – a silver tea-pot or a black tin tea-kettle, tea-pot, tea, sugar canisters (the three last made so as to fit into the kettle) – pen-knives, pens, razors, strops & hones – needles, thread, tape, worsted & pins – gauze – worsted stockings – flannel

– double-soled shoes and boots, which are particularly needful in order to resist the chill of brick and marble floors – clogs called Paraboues (which can be purchased from the Patentee, Davis, Tottenham Court Road, No.229) – warm pelisses, great coats & travelling caps; [From] the London & Edinburgh Dispensary, by Reece, a thermometer – a medical chest with scales, weights, an ounce and half ounce measures for liquids – a glass pestle and mortar – Shuttleworth's drop measure, an article of great importance, as the practice of administering active fluids by drops is dangerously inaccurate – tooth and hair brushes – James's powder – bark – sal volatile – sulphuric acid – pure opium – liquid laudanum – ipecacuanha – emetic tartar – prepared calomel – diluted vitriolic acid – essential oil of lavender – spirit of lavender – antinomial wine – supercarbonated kali – court – plaster and lint.

Whether such a travelling pharmaceutical store very frequently crossed the Channel we must doubt but the very extent of Miss Starke's list is a reminder of how hazardous foreign travel was perceived to be two hundred years ago. In 1828 every passenger was allowed to take one hundred weight (112 lb) of baggage on the London-Calais steam packet without incurring a surcharge. Generous as this may seem to modern air travellers, conscientious followers of Starke's advice would surely have been obliged to pay up.

Having obtained a passport, packed his bags and taken himself off to a Channel port, the voyager to France was now confronted with the crossing itself. In the eighteenth century crossing the Channel was at best uncomfortable and, not infrequently, a dangerous undertaking. The shortest route, that from Dover to Calais, tended to be preferred. However, neither of those harbours was deep enough to allow even the small sailing cutters normally employed to enter at low tide. Passengers might therefore be compelled to endure either a long wait for the incoming tide or transfer to a rowing boat in which they might be carried to the quay by local fishermen.

> ...through the surf the ride astraddle
> a Frenchman's shoulders for your saddle.[21]

These words come from a poem written by Richard 'Conversation' Sharp to a young lady preparing to make her first trip across the Channel in 1821. A similar thought was expressed in a famous comic song of the 1820s: *The Calais Packet* which includes the lines:

> *Full six hours after sailing from Dover,*
> *Safely anchored at Calais at last:*
> *All forgetting, their sufferings now over,*
> *But what's to follow is worse than the past.*
> *Can't make the pier, good lack,*
> *Carried on shore pick-a-back;*
> *Souse in the water smack. These are the joys now!*[22]

Some complained that hearing the song made them feel sea-sick all over again! Small wonder that Edward Gibbon, a seasoned cross-Channel traveller, writing from Dover in 1782 and bound for Switzerland, complained that:

> Last night the wind was so high, that the vessel could not stir from the harbour; this day it is brisk and fair. We start about one o'clock, and flattered with the hope of making Calais harbour by the same tide, in three hours and a half; but any delay will leave the disagreeable option of a tottering boat or a tossing night. What a cursed thing it is to live in an island! This step is more awkward than the whole journey.

As it was, the wind blew them to Boulogne where, 'we landed in the evening with much noise and difficulty.'[23]

Gibbon had not always been so unfortunate. On 7 March 1777 he had written to the same correspondent, his friend John Holroyd (later Lord Sheffield) – the recent success of the first volume of *The Decline and Fall* perhaps giving to his view of the world a rosier tint – to report, 'A pleasant passage, an excellent house' – Dessein's – and, 'a good dinner'.[24]

Still more euphoric was the journalist Francis William Blagdon who, taking advantage of the outbreak of peace in 1801, 'An English flag of truce' flying above Dover harbour, 'stepped off the quay into the Nancy, on board of which I was the only passenger.' At which, 'a propitious breeze sprang up... and in less than three hours wafted me to Calais pier'.[25]

Being more concerned with the sights and sensations (often unpleasant) of the crossing, than the means whereby it was accomplished, few travellers have left a good description of the packet boats themselves but an exception was the Swiss architect and industrialist, Hans Casper Escher who, in a letter addressed from Dover wrote the following surprisingly positive account:

At 11 p.m. on the night of July 31 [1814] we embarked with some 30 other passengers on the neat little packet called Lord Dundas. We quickly selected two bunks in the middle of the vessel. It is a ship that is known as a 'cutter'. Ships of this type are always used to convey passengers and dispatches. They are lighter than other ships. They are the swiftest and safest ships for crossing the English Channel. Imagine a little room with two mahogany doors at each end. The walls and the ceilings are painted white. They have bright panels and a few gilded decorations in very good taste. Couches are placed between the doors. The little beds are fixed to the walls, one on top of the other, like bookshelves in a library. Comfortable mattresses and fine cotton sheets are supplied. Muslin curtains can be drawn across each bunk. Each cabin has eight bunks. When everyone has gone to sleep and all the curtains are drawn no one would think that the cabin is a bedroom.[26]

Whether such cabin-loads of slumbering sailors were very frequently to be observed on the cross-Channel route we must doubt, although the clergyman-artist James Douglas claimed that :

When an Englishman sets out to make his tour of the Continent, he closets himself up in the post-chaise, and sleeps to Dover; nay, it frequently happens – I have seen it myself – that he slumbers his passage over in the same vehicle. When he arrives at Calais, the first thing he enquires for is Bergundy from Mr Dessin, and horses for St Omers.[27]

The American Quaker Jabez Fisher had attempted to sleep but in the end had neither slept nor sailed:

The Master of the Packet (Radcliff) told us he should go off about 1 o'clock at Night. We went down to the Sloop at $^1/_2$ past 12 o'clock. The Cabbin was full of men, Women and Children. We got into the after part of the Vessel laid ourselves down against the transom put our feet against some boards and invoked Morpheus till 3 o'clock in the Morning without success when the captain came to inform us that the wind was a head and we could not go that Night.[28]

Still less fortunate was the sardonic sportsman Colonel Peter Hawker who on 4 May 1819:

Embarked in the Lark Packet: and after being tossed without victuals, from morning till night among a mass of vomiting cockneys, was forced to return to Dover and pass a second night among the myriads of sharpers by whom you are every instant imposed on at that place.[29]

When, in 1814, Fanny D'Arblay, (the novelist Fanny Burney) and her husband made the voyage, 'our passage, though short, was so stormy, that it appeared to me an Hurricane.' [and] 'occasioned me such violent and unremitting sufferings that when I arrived I was unable to walk on shore and Mr D'Arblay hired me an escort, not a very military one – of Fishermen, to carry me by relays, on an arm chair to Dessein's.'[30] In a letter to her sister Esther she produced a variation on this tale of woe:

I was carried on to the Inn & to a great kitchen Fire, for the fury of the waves had wetted me through all my thick equipment; and then Mad^e Dessein recovered me by drops, & heaven knows what, & I began by degrees, for I was in a state nearly torpid, to comprehend the dreadful accident [her husband had been knocked over by a cart as he walked to the hotel] that had happened.[31]

Many, of course, were more fortunate. When in March 1802 the author and experienced traveller Mary Berry made the crossing she was able to enjoy:

A clear, sunny day with hardly a cloud. Went on board the Swift, Captain Blake, at Dover quay, at eleven o'clock; got to Calais harbour at ten minutes past four, and alongside the quay in ten minutes more, the same tide carrying us from one harbour to the other.[32]

Likewise a 'Gentleman of York' in 1818 who 'left Dover Harbour at five minutes past nine, and entered Calais Harbour at five minutes past twelve. The day was fine and the wind (S.W.) fair. The packet boat was the Chichester; the passage 10s 6d.'[33]

Someone who was not deterred from Continental travel, despite a miserable introduction to Gibbon's awkward 'step', was Marianne Baillie. In 1818, she, together with her husband and a male friend, set out upon the journey which was to produce *First Impressions of a Tour upon the Continent* (1819). On Monday, 9 August:

We embarked from the Ship Inn at Dover, for Calais on board the Princess Augusta packet. The passage was dreadful, the usual miseries attended us, and at the time that I am now writing this, viz. August 13th, , we are still suffering from the effects of the voyage. I will not make my readers ill by recalling the disgusting scenes which we there encountered....[34]

Perhaps because he was travelling with a future rear-admiral Sir [Edward] Thomas Troubridge, the Revd Burroughes T. Norgate was able to provide a meteorological explanation for the illness which afflicted so many of their party of eleven who crossed the Channel in May 1816:

On Thursday morning, at seven o'clock, we set sail in the Flora Packet of fifty tons, a good sailing little vessel and the wind being favourable and pretty fresh, we had a pleasant passage as far as nearly half way over the strait; but owing to there having been a very strong West wind for some days previous to our sailing, and the wind setting in very strongly from the eastward in the night, we found such a heavy swell that our passage became very rough, and the passengers for the most part were wretchedly disordered and sick. We reached Calais however at twenty minutes past ten....[35].

Whilst some endured their misery in the relative privacy of a cabin, others hoped to avoid it by staying on deck. The American Jabez Fisher, his crossing having been aborted the previous night owing to a contrary wind, eventually set sail at ten on the morning of 29 September 1776:

We had about twenty passengers. The cabin was filled with a third of them. The rest upon deck. We had not been long on the Water before Neptune received the Tribute of plenteous Sacrifices.[36]

The clerical wit Sydney Smith, together with Mrs Smith, crossed the Channel in 1835, 'because I think every wife has a right to insist upon seeing Paris' where:

We saw all the cockney sights, and dined at all the usual restaurants, and vomited as usual in the Channel which divides Albion from Gallia. Rivers are said to run blood after an engagement: the Channel is discoloured, I am sure, in a less elegant and less pernicious way by English tourists going and coming....

As for himself, eschewing the classical allusion, 'I rolled on the deck not wholly unlike a porpoise and quite as wet.'[37]

A lack of wind could result in conditions almost as trying as those of gale force. Being becalmed for hours on end in mid-Channel could leave travellers wishing they had endured a short, rough crossing. An anonymous contributor to the *New Monthly Magazine* who made the trip in August 1815 described such a journey which although it began early on a summer afternoon, ended in phosphorescent-lit darkness:

We sailed from Dover about one o'clock in the afternoon; other packets had left the harbour two hours before, whilst we were obliged to wait for the Paris mail coming from London. It was an afternoon's sailing on a lake, so smooth was the sea. Not having been in France before I looked forward with eagerness towards the shore of the new land....

The packets that had started before us, had arrived in Calais harbour about five o'clock, whilst both wind and tide failed ours at eight, four miles from Calais. Several muskets were fired, and other signals made by our captain, for the boatmen of Calais to come to our vessel. At last when it was about dark, a large boat came alongside of us. Several ladies and their friends preferred remaining in the packet all night; the boat put off with the other passengers, including myself. An old man sat at the helm of this boat, calling out frequently to the rowers, 'Tirez fort!' (pull hard) at which they often seemed affronted. The rowers when putting their oars into the water, rose from their seats and fell back upon them, as they made the pull. I imagined from the beginning that I saw the lights of Calais, but soon discovered my mistake. The water, as it was turned by the oars, emitted a silvery light, which increased in brilliancy as the night grew darker. I now perceived many such lights in different directions, and was told that they proceeded from the waves along the shore. This phenomenon soon presented itself in all its splendour as we neared the land. The waves, as they reached the shore, and were turned, emitted from their edges a brilliant light, just as if a train of gas-lights were instantaneously lighted along a line of several miles, and as suddenly extinguished, to be renewed again as rapidly. The sea continued smooth and the lights of the South Foreland were distinctly seen twinkling like a cluster of stars. Our boatmen now seemed to consult with great seriousness, about the safest place to put our boat upon the sand, which they always contrive to do in sufficient depth of water to require the assistance of their towns-men to carry passengers on shore. Now you might behold through the darkness of the night the forms of men in long procession, advancing with a strange noise towards our boat, whilst streams of light trailed from their naked legs, as they furrowed the water. I was directed by two of them near me to place my thighs on their shoulders but in our passage through the water I found that one of the men was much shorter than the other which placed me in such a situation that I could not have endured it a moment longer when they put me down on the sand. I fortunately found myself in company with two passengers who resided in Calais; these led me over the sands to a place where we had to clamber up a broken ladder to get upon the pier, and, after stumbling in the dark over the ropes with which the ships were fastened, we arrived at the Custom-house. This, by the light of only a lanthorn, appeared like a den of banditti, where several men were lying on sacks on the ground. From among these, one grotesque figure arose yawning and, being informed that we had left our baggage on board the packet, allowed us to proceed to the town and I arrived at Dessin's (now Quillacq's) hotel between eleven and twelve at night.[38]

Unsurprisingly, there were also those who boasted about what good sailors they were in contrast with their fellow passengers. One such was William Clift F.R.S., first Conservator of the Royal College of Surgeons' Hunterian Museum who, with his wife, Caroline, took a day-trip to Calais in 1839:

...the weather being very beautiful though rather blowy, we set off at a short notice by a French steam packet for Calais as Mrs C. had never been in France and we crossed the Channel which is here two or three and twenty miles wide in about three hours... I believe each of us could sail to America without being Sea-Sick which rendered the voyage to us delightful, though the Mops and Basons were travelling every minute for our less fortunate Fellow-Passengers: and the same on our return....[39]

Some were premature in boasting of the seaworthiness of their stomachs as the beauty and wit Marguerite, Countess of Blessington observed of a crossing she undertook in August 1822:

What a passage! Old Neptune seemed in a passion at our leaving his favourite isle; and assailed us with sundry waves, so judiciously applied as to drench several of the pale voyagers who, in revenge, returned the visits far more offensively. The sky was gloomy and portentous, and the sea of a dingy leaden green, except when broken up by the waves, which came like warriors on dark coursers, speeding over the dark surface.

The packet was full to overflowing, the cabins crowded and the deck thronged. As I marked the rosy cheeks and crisp curls of my fair countrywomen, and the closely buttoned coats and bluff countenances of the men, I was disposed to pity the misery that awaited them. Many of the ladies, and nearly all the males declared that they never suffered from sea-sickness but, before we had more than half crossed the channel, they had either disappeared or were seen leaning over the ship's side, intently gazing on the sea.

Various sounds of woe reached my ears, mingled with the hoarse voices of the sailors, and the loud wind that whistled through the sails and the steward was continually demanded in tones that betrayed the utter helplessness of those who uttered them. A new-married pair, proceeding to the Continent to spend the honey moon, and who entered the packet all smiles and love, were amongst the first to yield to the fearful influence of the briny element. The bridegroom had been encouraging the bride by asserting that he was so used to the sea that he heeded it not; an assurance that seemed very consolatory to her . He sat by her and supported her waist with his encircling arm, until an ejaculation of "Take me to the cabin, Henry, Oh! Oh!" broke from the lady. He attempted to descend to the cabin; but, alas! Before he had moved three paces, he reeled and cried "Steward, Steward", consigned his bride to the tenderer mercies of that useful person who, basin in hand, escorted her below; while her liege lord eased his full breast over the ship's side. Husbands left their wives and lovers their mistresses when assailed by this disgusting malady; but in all this exhibition of our national egotism, mothers, and mothers alone, resisted – they, though half dead with sickness, could still think of their children and forget their own sufferings, to alleviate those of their offspring.

What a pitiable sight did the passengers present when they rushed on deck to leave the ship! Pale faces, languid eyes, parched lips, uncurled locks, bulged bonnets and rumpled caps, frills and draperies were to be seen at every side. The poor bride's smart pink bonnet was shorn of its brightness and looked nearly as altered and faded as her cheeks, which, half shaded by her straight dark locks, betrayed the sufferings she had endured. The bridegroom met her with a rueful countenance, declaring that, 'It was very odd, quite unaccountable that he, who had crossed the sea so often, without being ill, should now have suffered so much.'

I thought she looked reproachfully at him for having deserted her in this her first trial in wedded life. Ah! fair lady, it will be well if you have not, hereafter, greater proof of man's selfishness!

A sea voyage, however short its duration, is a most unfortunate medium for judging mankind; and they who wish to preserve the illusions of love would do well to eschew this ordeal; which, like the grave, separates those whom the wily archer has united. It is difficult for a man to believe in the divinity of a beautiful woman after he has seen her heaving like a Pythoness with extended jaws, upturned eyes and ____. But for a woman who, conscious of her own helplessness, relies for succour on the man she loves, what can restore her confidence in his supposed strength and superiority, when she has beheld him – oh! Degradation of the manly character – overpowered by sickness in its most revolting shape, and heard him uttering sounds that betray at once the internal strife and the consequent probable oblivion of her very existence![40]

Sir Walter Scott was one of those who were pleased with themselves when, on 26 October 1826 he was:

Up at five, and in the packet by six. A fine passage, save at the conclusion, while we lay on and off the harbour at Calais. But the tossing made no impression on my companion or me; we ate and drank like dragons the whole way, and were able to manage a good supper and the best part of a bottle of Chablis at the classic Dessein's, who received us with much courtesy....[41]

One of Sir Walter's own heroes could hardly have coped more manfully! There is, however, a more significant connection between Scott and the history of the cross-Channel ferry service. In 1817, at the height of his productivity and fame, he had published one of his best-known novels, *Rob Roy*. Two years later, thanks to the pioneering work on steam engines of two other Scots, James Watt and William Murdoch, the Dumbarton shipbuilders Denny and Maclachlan were building a steam-driven paddle-boat intended to operate between Glasgow and Belfast. What else should they call it but *Rob Roy* and in 1820 the French Postal Administration purchased it to carry the mails from Calais to Dover. It was not, however, greeted with enthusiasm when it first arrived at Calais in June 1821. Neither pilot nor tug could be obtained and the local fishermen, who supplemented their means by carrying packet passengers to the shore, believed this source of income was at risk and threatened to cut the moorings. The mayor was obliged to intervene.[42] Doubt was also raised by those, such as the M.P. John Cam Hobhouse who believed the high pressure engine would, 'one day get it into a scrape'.[43]

Steam travel nevertheless rapidly became the preferred option although it did not invariably provide the fastest crossing. When a Dr Roberts wished to make the journey in September 1821 his diary records:

Breakfasted at eight o'clock. The Rob Roy steam vessel being engaged by Prince Esterhazy, agreed with Captain Rutten of the Chichester Packitt for a passage to Calais. Wind S.W. Sea tremendously high. Captain not very anxious for us to embark – however he said we might make Calais in three hours and get into the harbour; about ten the wind increased, at half past from the assurance of the seafaring people, the Ladies went on board but a very heavy fall of rain came on and a great swell of Sea that the Captain very strongly recommended the Ladies to disembark but that they must determine instantly as the Mail was on board and he must sail – of course we did as he recommended – but so short was the time that we could scarcely land the Ladies before the ship was under weigh and was out of harbour with all our clothes and everything belonging to us in her. We afterwards learnt that the Chichester was 7½ hours and the Rob Roy 9 hours in crossing and obliged to land the passengers in small boats.[44]

By 1822, however, there were regular steamboat services operating from both sides of the Channel. They were much the same size as the sailing cutters, approximately 15 feet wide and 80 feet in length and whilst they were, of course, less subject to the vagaries of the wind, their passengers could find the crossing quite as unpleasant. Such was the experience of the Duke of Wellington who, writing to his friend Mrs Arbuthnot from Calais on 22 August of that year said:

We arrived here after a passage of three hours and a half, and

I was not at all sick. I consider the motion of the Steam boat, however, fully equal [to] if not greater than that in a sailing pacquet. In addition to the usual motion of the Vessel occasioned by that of the Sea, there is a tremulous motion occasioned by the wheels which is very unpleasant.[45]

The same point was made, at greater length, by John M. Cobbett, who wrote to his father William, the great journalist and political campaigner, from Paris on 12 April 1824:

I must preface my account of all that happens to me in France with my departure from Dover. At 11 o'clock on Tuesday, I got into the 'Spitfire', an English steam-boat, and after six hours of tumbling and rolling about on the water, we landed at Calais. The wind was against us and so was the tide, and thus we lost so much time. A sailing vessel would not, they say, have made the same passage in even double the time; but the very unpleasant noise and disagreeable motion which attend the steam-boat makes the sailing vessel almost preferable in weather not perfectly calm. In calms the advantage of steam is undoubtedly great and the best proof of it is that there are not now more than two or three sailing vessels that ever go to Dover, and those only on extraordinary occasions. In the transporting of horses, carriages, and other things of the kind, the steam-boat is almost equal to a drawbridge, nothing but tempestuous weather ever putting an end to its exertions. The long and bad passage had made all the passengers taste fully of the sea sensations and, as I was one of them, I lost all my curiosity to see the manner of landing and disposing of passengers and goods, and surrendered myself up immediately to a little man who handed me on to the quay and assured me he was commissioner to the best inn in Calais. He took me to Roberts's, the Hotel Royale, or Kingston, but which is known by all three of these names... The dinner was just served up, and I was invited to it, which I did more for the purpose of seeing myself at a French Table d'hôte than for any inclination I had to eat anything at it. Indeed my recollection was all of the steam-boat. The paddles were still thumping in my head and, though out of the boat, I felt its jerking still and tasted its smoke.[46]

A happier experience was had by the economist David Ricardo who sailed to Calais from London (for prices *see*

APPENDIX 4) on 12 July 1822. Not all of his party was so fortunate:

Yesterday morning we embarked at the Custom House stairs at a ¹/₄ past six o'clock, on board the Talbot Steam packet, for Calais. We found a tolerably large party already assembled on the deck; but in the hope of adding to the number the Captain did not allow the steam to operate on the machinery which was to impel us forward till 7 o'clock. At that hour we commenced our rapid career, and made our way with admirable nicety through the narrow channel which the ships in the Pool had left open to us. We expected to be Calais in 12 hours from the time of starting but, owing to the strong tide and wind which set against us, we were rather more than 14 hours, and were just too late to enter the harbour, as the water had sunk too low to admit of the vessel's going over the bar. We were very well pleased with our acquatic expedition; all our fellow passengers were very obliging and good tempered and most of them preserved their good spirits and healthy appearance, notwithstanding the swell which we encountered after passing the north Foreland. The sick withdrew from the deck one after the other as they felt the uneasy sensations come over them, so that we always had the merry faces surrounding us. Mary, Mrs Ricardo and I were among the healthy; Miss Lancey, Birtha and, above all, Mrs Cleaver, who was worse than any of the party, were included in the Sick List.[47]

By 1826, thanks to the greater speed and capacity of the steam packets (on 16 July of that year the *Hero* arrived with 150 passengers) the number of people crossing the Channel had doubled. It was not all good news for Calais, however, for Boulogne was receiving an increasing proportion of the cross-Channel traffic and by 1836 more passengers were entering by that port than by the more traditional route.[48] For the cost of travel by 1828 *see* APPENDIX 4.

The next major development also involved steam power. It was the opening on 7 February 1844 of the South Eastern Railway's line from London (Bricklayers' Arms) to Dover.[49] In June of that year the directors of the company made the journey and continued across the Channel using one of a new generation of steam boats – the *Princess Mary. The Times* reported thus and in doing so reflected many of the prejudices of the day:

> To try the speed of the new vessel, and also to test the rapidity with which one may be whirled from London to Calais by the wonderful power of steam, the directors of the railway made a trip on Saturday from one place to the other, the result of which was highly satisfactory. At about 10 minutes to 8 in the morning a special train started from the Bricklayers' Arms station, which, by the way is admirably situate for all west-end travellers who may not like to rough it through the crowded streets of the city. The distance between London and Dover was done in 2 hours and 28 minutes, including a stoppage of 12 minutes at Folkestone, and in a few minutes after the arrival of the party at the Dover station, the new vessel, the Princess Mary, which handsome vessel, with great power and speed for her build. She has two of Maudslay's engines of 60 horse power each, and the improved paddles. The distance between Dover and Calais was done in two hours and ten minutes. On the arrival of the party at Calais, they partook of a luncheon at Dessein's hotel, and after having had ample time to wander through the quaint old town and wonder at the grotesque people, they again entered the vessel, which left Calais harbour at a few minutes after 4, and arrived at Dover in two hours and five minutes. The party then returned to town in a special train. Many of them breakfasted in town, lunched at Calais, dined at Dover, and were back again in London in time for the last act of the Opera.[50]

Even prior to the arrival of the railway, steam power had proved its worth. Whilst fifty years before Edward Gibbon had cursed the inconvenience of living on an island, in 1834 Sir Robert Peel saw things quite differently. Summoned to London from Rome where he was holidaying with his family, to form a new administration, he pointed out that he had encountered as much difficulty in making the journey as had Constantine when travelling from York to Rome 1500 years earlier, 'with the exception of the up-to-date advantages of a well-fitted steam packet'.[51]

Those who wrote of the crossing in their memoirs often

saw it in a more romantic light than did those who recalled it shortly after the event in diaries or letters. One such was John Ruskin, a great admirer of Calais, who looked back over some forty or more years upon, 'one of the few pleasures... quite unmixed':

Little steamers they were then; nor in the least well appointed, nor aspiring to any pride of shape or press of speed; their bits of sails worn and patched like those of an old fishing boat... The immeasurable delight to me of being able to loiter and swing about just over the bowsprit and watch the plunge of the bows, if there was the least swell or broken sea to lift them, with the hope of Calais at breakfast, and the horses' heads set straight for Mont Blanc tomorrow....[53]

For a brilliant imaginative account of the steam packet crossing from Dover to Calais by Charles Dickens – *see* APPENDIX 2.

3

"A Dozen Dirty Civil Hands…."

Whether stepping directly on to Calais Pier from the packet at high tide or from a fisherman's shoulders at low, new arrivals from Dover would probably, if sea-sickness allowed, be impressed by its length, especially after 1822 when it was extended to 900m, and by the number and appearance of the people upon it.[1]

From the sea the harbour was approached by a channel – Le Chenal – formed by parallel jetties running SSE to NNW. The more westerly of the two – la Jetée Ouest – was built out into the sea from Fort Risban which itself was constructed at the end of a line of coastal dunes extending towards Cap Blanc-Nez. Since the end of the seventeenth century the jetty had been guarded by another fort – Fort Rouge – built on wooden piles which, during wartime, was frequently the object of British attacks. The easternmost jetty – la Jetée Est – was constructed out from Le Courgain, the fishermens' quarter, and provided easiest access to the town so that it was here that packet passengers would usually step ashore.

During the hours of daylight the pier would normally be well-peopled with soldiers, fishermen, porters, agents seeking business for the hotels, impecunious British ex-patriots hoping to appeal to the good nature of disembarking acquaintances, small children begging for a sou, the merely curious and otherwise unemployed.

Soon after peace preliminaries were signed on 1 October 1801 Britons began to pour into France or, as the great French historian Albert Sorel put it – 'All the idle captives of the land of fogs shook their damp wings and prepared to take their flight towards the regions of pleasure and brightness'[2]. One of the first to arrive at Calais was John Lemaistre who, even before leaving the boat was confronted by the representatives of bureaucracy – 'As soon as the vessel entered the port, two customs-house officers came on board in a military uniform (for every fonctionnaire public has here a regimental dress) and after taking the names of the passengers, one of them returned to make his report to the municipality, while the other stayed to prevent our landing until the return of his companion...[3] when, '...At length, monsieur de la Douane returned and,

...we were permitted to touch the territory of the republic; and conducted by a guard of Bourgeois (who in their dress resembled the ragged regiment of Terence,[4] rather than the renowned warriors of France) we proceeded to the custom house, from the custom house to the municipality and from the municipality to the commissaire's.

In the meantime, he observed,

...the jetée, or pier, was crowded with spectators, the greater part of whom were military men of different ranks and different descriptions. They seemed highly amused in staring at the dresses of the ladies, and in examining the body of my carriage, which was hung on the deck of the ship....'[5]

Writing a few months later, the experienced traveller Mary Berry noted that it was, 'a shabby custom-house officer' who came aboard and, 'begged to see our passports'. He was, she thought, 'an old invalid officer or soldier'.[6] She and her fellow voyagers were required to write down their names and nationality before disembarking when, 'not the smallest rude comment was made by the crowd upon the quay' and, 'half a dozen dirty civil hands were held out to help us up the ladder'.

Very similar words were used by Fanny Burney (or Fanny d'Arblay as she was by then) when she arrived at Calais in 1802 in the company of her son, Alexander, and a little French girl Adrienne de Chavagnac. Arriving at the pier, the vessel 'was presently filled with men, who, though dirty and mean, were so civil and gentle that they could not displease'[7] Once ashore however, they were engulfed by the crowd and,

In an instant party of them rushd round me, one demanding to carry Alex, another Adrienne, another seizing my *écritoire*, another my arm, and someone, I fear, my parasol as I have never been able to find it since.

In the summer of 1818 another travel writer, the sea-sick Marianne Baillie, was similarly impressed by 'the habitual politeness of even the lowest order of French people, evinced in the alacrity with which twenty hands were held out to support me in descending from the packet, and in the commiserations which I plainly discovered in many a sun-burnt countenance for my evident indisposition'.[8]

Both of these ladies were a good deal more fortunate than 'two young Englishman' whose story was told in the *London Weekly Times* of 23 September 1827, under the title of 'A Cruel Hoax':

...crossing on Thursday from Dover [they] met with some wag at their inn there, who had just come from the French side, and were very anxious for advice as to which hotel in Calais would be best for them to put up at. The rogue into whose hands they were delivered, discovering that they were fresh upon the world, and that they knew nothing of the French language, fell in entirely with their apprehension of "great houses", such as those of Dessein and Quillacq; recommended them by all means, to go to a small hotel – not generally known to travellers, but excellently good – the sign of the *Petit Pot de Chambre!* The two victims never perceived the meaning of the words and actually, on landing at Calais (very ill, after a rough passage) answered to the enquiries of the crowd of commissaires who beset the pier – to, "what hotel would Monsieur proceed?", "The Petit Pot de Chambre"; producing moreover a card upon which their merciless Mentor had written for them the name of the house. The termination of the jest was near being serious when, fortunately, an English resident, who was standing by, interfered and finding that they were the offerers of a hoax instead of the perpetrators of one, rescued them from the inauspicious commencement to the adventures of foreign travel. But it was not without much difficulty that even this gentleman was able to convince the angry by-standers of the real state of the fact, whenthe inquirers for the *Petit Pot de Chambre* were forwarded to an actual hotel, amidst the loud laughter of the populace.[9]

Quite how true this tale is it is impossible to say but its unsophisticated humour certainly speaks to the anxiety which tourists entering a country for the first time often feel about their ability to communicate.

Some travellers were quick to put their prejudices on record. Thus the Anglophile Italian physician Augustus Bozzi Granville, arriving in 1827, observed that when he had embarked [at Dover] 'the quay was lined with a great multitude, dressed almost uniformly and well-behaved', whereas 'at our landing we had to pierce a throng that crowded the mole, vociferating in every key-note of the treble scale, variously agitated, like the paste-eels one sees through a microscope, and looking not unlike the motley group of beggars that beseige the avenue of a convent abroad on almsdays.'[10]

The American soldier Ninian Pinkney, by contrast, witnessed a silmilar scene through quite different glasses – 'Let a stranger arrive at an English or American port and he is truly a stranger' but 'let him land at any French port [he had just arrived at Calais] and almost every one who shall meet him will salute him with the complacency of hospitality.'[11] Mary Wordsworth, attending Mass at the great parish church of Notre Dame, was likewise impressed: 'These French are certainly attractive creatures, nothing surly about them'.[12]

Lemaistre was among the first of the flood of English who visited France during the Peace of Amiens, having obtained a special licence to travel to ascertain the validity of a legacy left to him in Paris. He crossed the Channel in November 1801. Still quicker off the mark was the journalist Francis Blagdon who believed himself to be the first Englishman 'not in an official character', to arrive in France since before the war, landing in Calais some weeks before Lemaistre and having been the only passenger aboard the Nancy packet. The arrival of a British boat quickly attracted attention and Blagdon was able to see that,

except the tri-coloured cockade in the hats of the military, I could not observe the smallest difference in their general appearance. Instead of crops and round wigs, which I expected to see in vogue, here were full as many powdered heads and long queues as before the revolution…. The citoyens, as far as I am able to judge, most certainly have not fattened by warfare more than JOHN BULL; their visages are as sallow and thin as formerly, though their persons are not quite as meagre as they are portrayed by Hogarth.[13]

In addition to these sights and on days when the sea breeze was not filling the air with a distinct and overwhelming scent of salt and when the more unpleasant aromas of a voyage on a crowded packet were not present, new arrivals may have detected a difference in the atmosphere. Anthony Trollope's mother, Frances, one of the most brilliant and provocative of travel writers, told this entertaining tale:

I remember being much amused last year, when landing at Calais, at the answer made by an old traveller to a novice who was making his first voyage.
"What a dreadful smell!" said the uninitiated stranger, enveloping his nose in his pocket-hand-kerchief.
"It is the smell of the continent, sir!" replied the man of experience. And so it was.[14]

It was, on the whole, a subject which, what Mrs Trollope called, 'the Improvement of English delicacy', chose to ignore. It is doubtful that this would have been the stench of bad – or no – drains, as the smell in London, culminating in the Great Stink of 1858, was as bad as anywhere. It may be that it was the smell of wreaking fish, mixed perhaps with the all-pervasive aroma of wood smoke and tobacco. A visitor in the summer of 1818 observed that, 'This country smells of tobacco and burnt wood as usual.' Ironically, just two years before the author of a French travel guide had compared

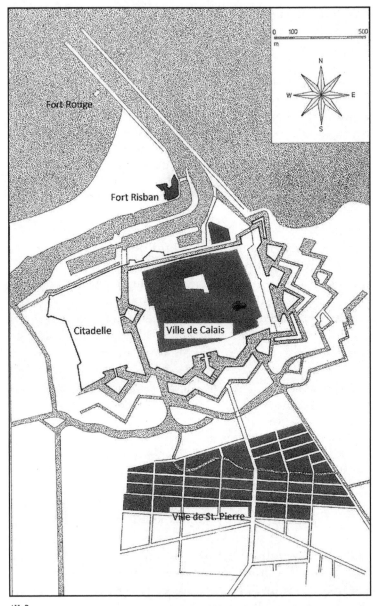

ill.3

CALAIS AND ST. PIERRE WITH FORTIFICATIONS.

Calais to an English town so great was the amount of coal
smoke it emitted, which a few years before had been
confined to kitchens and forges but was now also the
product of the drawing room.[15] The stagnant water in the
fossé, or moat, beneath the fortifications also received much
of the town's sewage and often gave off a dreadful smell.
Furthermore the following decades certainly saw a great
expansion in the use of coal as steam power was introduced
into first the cross-Channel packet boats and then the lace
factories of St. Pierre just beyond the walls of the town.

Lemaistre, having his own carriage with him, would
have been obliged to pay duty on it, amounting to a third of
its estimated value. In return he would have received a
certificate for the sum deposited and would be guaranteed
that by showing it at any frontier customs house, he would
be able to recover three-quarters of that amount, provided
it was taken out of France within three years. In addition,
there was a charge for landing or shipping a carriage which,
by 1836, amounted to 12 francs for a four-wheeled vehicle.[16]

Blagdon in 1801 thought that, 'The prospect of peace
seemed to have produced an exhilarating effect on all
ranks' and, 'satisfaction appeared in every countenance'.
Whatismore, although, 'a host of innkeeper's domestics
boarded the vessel, each vaunting the superiority of his
master's accommodation', he was freed from their
importunities by the appearance of Jean Ducroque, 'my old
landlord' who decided him in favour of the Lion d'Argent.
Prior to enjoying the comforts of M. Ducroque's establishment, however, he was summoned to the house of the
commissary for the Pas-de-Calais, M. Mengaud to whom he
had already sent a letter of introduction from the French
Commissioner for prisoners in London, Louis Guillaume
Otto. Mengaud sent him to the Town Hall, in those days in
the Place d'Armes, where his passport was made out
including, 'a minute description of my person', before being
required to present his keys for the inspection of his baggage
at the Custom-House.

The variously spelt name of Mon. Mengaud appears in a

number of early nineteenth century accounts. Pinkney, 'having seen our luggage into a wheel-barrow... waited upon the Commissary'. Unfortunately for the American, 'Mon. Mangouit' was not in his office and, 'a dirty little boy' informed him that he had gone to visit a neighbour. There he waited for three hours in a room, 'five feet in length by three in width, very dirty, without a chair, and in every respect resembling a cobler's stall'.[17] Sir John Dean Paul was also obliged to wait in 'Mon. Mangot's' office, 'about the size of a common apple-stall, and nearly as well furnished'. The commissary he characterised as, 'himself dirty and much of a coxcomb'.[18] The actor and dramatist Edmund John Eyre, who also arrived during the Peace, had a rather different observation to make of the office of 'Mons. Mangaud', 'where our passports were examined and our persons exactly noted down':

> The walls of the office were hung round with caricature prints, representing the army of England, with Pitt at their head, marching to Paris.[19]

The Revd Dawson Warren who travelled to Paris in November 1801, being unofficially attached to the diplomatic mission of his brother-in-law, the British Minister Plenipotentiary, Francis Jackson, provides a pen-portrait of the Commissary. On the morning after their arrival at Dessein's, the mission's carriages and baggage having been 'released and exempted from search by an order from Citizen Mengaud',

> We had just time to dress and breakfast when the Municipal Officers and General Ferrand, general of the District waited upon Francis to congratulate him upon his arrival. They addressed to him a great many elegant compliments which received as many elegant replies. Citizen Mengaud then made his appearance, a man 6 feet 3 inches in height with the countenance and exterior of a fierce Republican. To us however he was exceedingly civil, sat a long time in conversation with Francis, and told him many stories of his humanity to Emigrants and to strangers, whose

representations of the Commissary differ materially from the accounts he gives of himself.[20]

The *emigré* view of Mengaud was shared by those English who struggled to obtain passports after the breakdown of the Amiens' negotiations in May 1803. Shortly afterwards, however, he seems to have lost his job as William Wright recorded:

Happily for the inhabitants of Calais, M. Mengaud is stripped of a great part of his power, and will most probably lose the remainder; it is now vested in the mayor and corporation. It was a change long seriously wished for, as all persons, whether French or English, were insulted by his language, beat with his hands, cane or whip, sometimes in his office, in the street, or at the theatre, and afterwards put in prison at his pleasure, without reason or remedy.[21]

When another clergyman, the Revd Burroughes Norgate together with Sir Thomas and Lady Trowbridge and eight others arrived on their way to Paris in the year after Waterloo,

...our luggage was inspected and but little trouble given to anyone. But the ladies were ordered into a miserable little hole, where presided a most miserable looking, dirty old woman, who demanded a search, which was of course complied with.[22]

Mary Berry had had no complaints in 1802. The, 'dirty civil hands' having assisted her ashore,

...we proceeded first to one of the low small houses close by the quay, where our names and nations were again set down, and then to a sort of bureau of the custom house where we were desired to *declare* if we had anything upon us *contre les droits*; our declaration in the negative being immediately taken, we went, still with our captain, an old invalid, and M. Quillacque (the successor of M. Dessein), who had now joined us, to the Hôtel de Ville where the commissaire de police read our passports, and everyone answered to their names. Here we left our *pas* from M. Otto with a promise from the commissaire that we should have his that evening. All these ceremonies past without rudeness, impertinent questions, or delays whatever.[23]

Some, however, complained of the roughness with which the customs officials handled their baggage and some suspected that the passport officials colluded with the hoteliers to prolong a visitor's stay by delaying the issue of a provisional passport. Edmund Eyre was the victim of another ruse:

During the evening the post-master entered and politely apologizing for the unwelcome news, informed as that we must unavoidably wait two days before he could possibly provide horses for our use, as the influx of strangers was so great that they had not relays sufficient for the public service. This delay I found afterwards was a mere trick of imposition.[24]

Given the large numbers of visitors arriving at Calais at this time, it may be that the excuse was perfectly valid and that the fault lay with the London agent who had guaranteed the availability of horses. The writer of Murray's *Handbook* of 1836, who has little to say in favour of Calais, does however, advise that:

…a traveller will do well to quit it as soon as he has cleared his baggage from the custom-house, and procured the signature of the police to his passport, which, if he be pressed for time, will be done at almost any hour of the day or night… It is necessary to be aware of this, the commissioners of the hotels will sometimes endeavour to detain a stranger under pretence of not being able to get a passport signed.[25]

Many worried about having goods confiscated by the customs. A writer in the *Gentleman's Magazine* in 1820 was indignant that 'If I had had new cotton stockings they would have been seized'.[26] Needless to say, smuggling did occur. In November 1826, Emma Wedgwood (the future Mrs Charles Darwin), travelling with her two aunts, Jessie (Mrs Sismondi) and Fanny and the 21 year old Edward Drewe, wrote to her mother to announce their safe arrival at Calais, she added,

We came over with half a dozen smugglers who teased us very
much to wear plaid cloth cloaks for them, as they said they would
not take them from us but they would from them, but we would
not, as you may suppose.[27]

When Emma's aunt, Fanny Allen, clearly a lady of a
philosophical nature, next visited the Continent in 1832 she
encountered a quite different complication. Cholera was rife
in England and travellers to France were required to spend
a period in quarantine. She described the experience in
a letter to her brother-in-law Sir James Mackintosh dated
13 March:

The Quarantine was not disagreeable; it was rather more an
odd position than a disagreeable one. I do not consider the three
days there as lost days; our company were more French than
English, and I was amused at observing their diferent manner and
character. We did not suffer from cold in our station, though it was
a mere wooden shed, divided into three parts for the men, women
and our common sitting-room. The beds were excellent and our
eating not bad so that we were not to be pitied; though I must
add we enjoyed Dessein's Inn very much when we were let out of
Quarantine.[28]

The following month the following notice appeared in the
London newspaper *The Courier:*

Calais – The Nobility, Gentry and Public are respectfully
informed that the INTERIOR of FORT RISBANC having originally
been the only place established for the QUARANTINE of three
days, Messrs DESSIN, QUILLACQ, RIGNOLLE and ROBERTS
have obtained permission to fit up TEMPORARY HOTELS
OUTSIDE THE FORT, in a dry, healthy and pleasant situation
where excellent accommodations are provided. Carriages and
baggages are allowed to land.

Even without three days in quarantine, not many
travellers, especially if they had endured a rough crossing,

would have been as stoical as Fanny Allen. After being tossed about in the packet, enduring the difficulties of landing, running the gauntlet on the jetty and having their baggage searched by the *douanier*, most, like Lady Blessington, would probably have been happy to exclaim:

'Oh! the comfort of a French bed!'[29]

4

'IN EASE AND EVEN SPLENDOUR'

Mercy on us, what a bedroom! One glance at the bed suffices to show that you are now amidst the very *'fleurs des lys'* (lits?). Hang your tent-beds! How gracefully here dispose the voluminous folds of the high-hung drapery! and the bed itself – so elastic and so soft, so warmly and yet so lightly covered! The curtains, too, that throw such agreeable tinting on its surface! The matrasses are all newly combed and carded, and the pillowcases so seductively fair! No lover ever dwelt with more justifiable complacency on the charms of his mistress than does the uninitiated Englishman on the warm support of that gentle swelling cushion. On such a bed, with such enjoyment does the traveller stretch forth his limbs, wishing that he were twice as long, that he might multiply the points of pleasure by increasing those of contact! What a difference between a French and an English inn bed! The last, indeed, is too often both bed and board.

('Over the Channel', *Blackwood's Edinburgh Magazine,* Vol. 51, 1842)

By the time Queen Victoria came to the throne Dessein's was already spoken of as a place redolent with the charm of a bygone age. Although little more than seventy years old – much younger than the great hotels of Scarborough, Brighton or Blackpool are today – it pre-dated the tumultuous years of the French Revolution and the Napoleonic Wars and was referred to, by the elderly especially, with the kind of fondness that many reserve for the scenes of their youth.

But even from its earliest days Dessein's had been recognised as a place of quite uncommon attractions. Doubtless there were travellers who, having endured a long and discomforting – or worse – crossing of the Channel, were so relieved to be once again on terra firma and in the dry that they somewhat over-egged the pudding of praise, awarding a metaphorical five stars when four would have done. There is perhaps a hint of this in the account of Marguerite Gardiner, the beautiful Countess of Blessington, who having undergone a dreadful voyage, 'The horrors of crossing the Styx may be imagined, but the realities of a crowded packet exceed all the powers of imagination,' found Dessein's,

'a most comfortable exchange from the packet, and our rooms opened into a beautiful garden, breathing perfumes – most gratifying to the senses after the noxious air we had lately been inhaling.'[1]

The travel writer Marianne Baillie was similarly grateful to arrive at Dessein's. Her passage, in the summer of 1818, had been, 'dreadful, the usual miseries attended us ...I will not make my readers ill by recalling the disgusting scenes which we there encountered,' but the hotel, 'is excellent and the attendants remarkably civil and active. The style of furniture is superior to that of the best English hotels.' She had recovered sufficiently to enjoy, 'a dinner and dessert of the most superior quality,' for which, 'we did not pay more than we should have done at an ordinary inn in our own country for very common fare.'[2]

As we have seen, Fanny Allen, the aunt of Emma Darwin, must have been even more grateful to arrive at Dessein's having, after a dreadful voyage, spent three days in the Quarantine Station because of cholera in England. 'I must admit,' she wrote to her brother-in-law Sir James Mackintosh, 'we enjoyed Dessin's Inn very much when we were let out of Quarantine'. The beds were excellent and, 'the eating not bad'.[3]

Much fairer sailing had been enjoyed on 17 September 1775 when Mr and Mrs Thrale, their daughter Queeney, and friends Samuel Johnson and Giuseppe Baretti made what was to be the Doctor's only trip to the Continent. Alas, Johnson's record of the early days of the excursion has not survived but Hester Thrale's account is typically lively and full of striking detail. The party had sailed from Dover at nine in the morning which was,

> Queeney's Birthday. She is now eleven Years old, God preserve & continue her Life till mine is spent: on this day we weighed Anchor in a very neat Sloop – Captn Baxter, an old school fellow of Mr Thrale's. The weather was lovely – the Ship all our own, the sea smooth & all our Society well but Queeney, whose sickness oppressed her beyond Conception. Sam and Molly [the servants] too were cruel sick, but Queeney worst of all or I thought her so.[4]

Although she was not impressed by the population of the French town ('the Soldiers with Whiskers and the Women mostly so ugly and deform'd') Hester thought the inn, 'kept by one Dessein is the most magnificent I ever saw – the Mount at Marlborough is nothing to it'. They had an 'excellent' dinner and that night, 'slept in Ease & even Splendour'.[5] This was high praise from a woman whose husband, a wealthy London brewer, had recently improved their house at Streatham where the library was hung with thirteen portraits of Thrale's friends by one of their number – Sir Joshua Reynolds.[6]

Of the earliest British visitors to the Hôtel d'Angleterre, Sterne, who was writing a novel rather than his travels, had nothing to say in praise of his accommodation although, as we have seen, he did recommend the hotel to his wife whilst, at the same time, telling her to be wary of Dessein – 'a Turk in grain'.[7] Later in the same year, however, Horace Walpole's friend, the antiquarian and rector of Bletchley, William Cole, returning home after three very rewarding months in Paris, was happy with his stay at Dessein's. On the outward journey of, 'the 2 great Inns at Calais, the *Lion d'Argent* or Silver Lion & the *Hôtel d'Angleterre*, or the English Inn', he chose to stay at the former, 'as I have been there several times before'.[8] On his return, however, having a chaise assigned to Dessein, 'I remained at his Inn'. He found that it was, 'new built, & was a fine large Quadrangle, with most sumptuous Apartments & elegantly furnished, which was preferable to all'. What is more, he discovered the Master of it to be, 'a very civil & obliging Man'.[9]

The Hôtel d'Angleterre quickly became the preferred hostelry of most English travellers. The young barrister Harry Peckham stayed there in 1769 at the end of a tour of the Low Countries and northern France. He was not over impressed by the town. 'I confess my surprise to see a place which has been so often mentioned in history, which withstood the army of Edward III for near twelve months and which made so considerable a figure in the treaty of Chateau Cambresis in 1559, so contemptible as it at present appears.'[10] Peckham's account of his tour is a guide as much as a travelogue and he is careful to make a note of the inns – including Dessein's – at which English travellers would be advised to stay.[11]

George Selwyn, wit, politician and another friend of Walpole, had a particular motive for compiling a list of Continental hotels. In 1777 he found himself obliged to return his adopted daughter, the six year-old Maria Emily Fagnani, daughter of the Marchesa Fagnani, to Italy. He was deeply attached to the little girl – known as 'Mie-Mie' – and, in the words of the editor of his letters:

Among innumerable other evidences of Selwyn's anxious solicitude to secure her comfort and safety during the journey, it appears... that he had carefully made himself master of the merits of the resting-places and inns of which he considered it expedient that she [with her escort] should pass each night on her route from London to Milan.[12]

The list included, *'à Calais, chez Dessein, Hôtel d'Angleterre'*. The exterior appearance and structure of the hotel can be easily envisaged from this description which appeared in *The Scots Magazine* for January 1803:

It is an extensive suite of buildings, forming two neat squares, of which the one serves as an entrance to the other. Both are lined with vines pinned against the walls, and the inner one, where we lodge, includes a very nice garden. One side of this square consists of a theatre, billiard rooms and other places of entertainment.[13]

To this list of public rooms a German publication of 1834 adds a coffee room and reading room[14] and a French guide-book of the following years refers to *'des bains publics'*.[15] Johanna Schopenhauer, the mother of the philosopher, was almost certainly right to describe it as, 'one of the largest inns in the world,'[16] but an article in the *Gentleman's Magazine* may have verged on hyperbole in asserting that it, 'is indeed itself a town: it contains squares, alleys, gardens ...and innumerable offices'.[17]

The garden was, according to an English naval officer, 'about 50 yards square'.[18] A more florid description is provided by Robert Bell Calton:

> The garden and shrubbery, as well as the courtyard of the hotel, ornamented by beautiful acacias, geraniums fully nine feet in height, and every other exotic, are excessively tasty in their arrangements; whilst the house itself clad with the vine, the climbing rose and jasmine, resembles more the ancient chateaux of the Courcis or Montmorencis than an inn; so quaint, yet imposing, are its extensive fronts and aristocratic features.[19]

Like most hotels Dessein's must have gone through cycles of refurbishment and redecoration. Thus *The Courier* of 28 June 1824 carried the following notice:

> Quillacq's Hotel, Calais – A. Quillacq (son of the late Proprietor and Occupier of Dessin's Hotel in this town) begs to inform his friends and the Public in general, that he has completed his intended alterations and entirely new furnished his hotel, in a manner which he feels confident will ensure the comfort and convenience of all persons who may favour him with their support and has great satisfaction in being enabled to appeal to the Nobility and Families who have already honoured him with their approbation. The largest Families may be accommodated with single sitting rooms. Most commodious Hot and Cold Baths are provided in the House.

Of course, those who visited at the end of such a cycle would be less impressed than those who arrived soon afterwards. Arthur Young, who made a number of visits to

France in the years immediately prior to the Revolution, always seems to have stayed at Dessein's. In 1784 he and his son had taken a journey, 'for farming intelligence,' through the south-eastern counties of England and, 'being at Dover, we went over to Calais just to enable us to say that we had been in France ...We lived three or four days at Dessein's celebrated inn,'[20]   Four years later, on a tour through western France, however, he came across what he believed to be a superior establishment. It was the inn at Nantes:

> I am in doubt whether the Hotel de Henri IV is not the finest inn in Europe. Dessein's at Calais is larger, but neither built, fitted up, not furnished like this, which is new ...It contains 60 beds for masters, and 25 stalls for horses ...It is without comparison, the first inn I have seen in France, and very cheap.[21]

A visitor to the hotel in the same year as Arthur Young was the French travel writer François Marlin who appears to have been far more impressed. He speaks of a hotel, '*unique par le grandeur, le beauté, l'ordre*'.[22] Despite the fact that he was given by no means the best room in the hotel but, '*une des plus médiocres,*' he describes it as both pretty and commodious. The floor was carpeted and polished, there was a good chintz-covered bed and chairs, arm-chairs, tables, a writing desk and, something which he had apparently not come across before, a supply of ink, paper and pens.[23]

During the Revolution and the Revolutionary Wars which followed, movement across the Channel shrank to a trickle (some neutrals, such as Americans, still managed to make the crossing). When Henry Swinburne was in Calais in November 1796, on a mission to negotiate the exchange of prisoners, he found the hotel closed and not due to reopen until the following spring.[24] Nevertheless, when peace negotiations were taking place in 1801 Dessein's was still in business and doubtless anxious to welcome the resumption of cross-Channel trade and as soon as it was thought safe to do so there was a flood of English keen to witness the consequences of what had happened during and since the Revolution. Among them was a young Irishwoman whose colourful, sometimes breathless but always entertaining account of a tour of France and Italy supplies us with one of the better descriptions we have of the interior of the hotel at that time: she was Katherine Wilmot.[25]

Katherine, in her late 'twenties, was a single woman who together with two friends, Lord and Lady Mount Cashell, their two daughters, Helena and Jane, and four servants, had initially been intent upon a tour of England but, with the Peace all but official, they had decided to extend their tour onto the Continent.

The party's experience on board the *Countess of Elgin*, Captain Sampson, was a good deal less happy than that of Dr Johnson and his companions. They had to endure, 'a desperately rough passage of five hours,' followed by, 'a cruel delay before we were permitted to land'. Katherine, who was to prove a sturdy traveller, was soon sufficiently recovered to enjoy, 'the contemplation of novelty …Every man in a cock'd hat, three colour'd cockade and gold ear-rings, savage black whiskers and frequently a muff on his arm. Indeed this was the costume of every ragged poltroon,' she records in the journal she wrote for her brother Robert back in County Cork.[26] They were served, 'a most splendid repast,' at Dessein's before retiring to their rooms but then, as she reveals in her Journal for 30 November 1801:

On waking at a very early hour with the confusion incident to that state, you will laugh at me when I confess to you the flash of transport I experienced on saying to myself 'I absolutely then am in France,' and in drawing aside the curtain of my bed to prove it to myself, by contemplating the painted ceiling, the white marble tables, the looking glass panels, the polish'd oak floor, and all the little circumstances of difference in the apartment. Without exception I never remember in all my life a moment of such unfeign'd extacy! Instinctively I fancied some metamorphoses was taking place in me, and putting up my hand, to try if my nightcap at least was not turning into a 'cap of liberty' (still leaning out of bed) I lost my balance and down I slump'd upon the floor, to the utter destruction of all my glorious visions and abhorring those prodigious looking glasses, which multiplied my downfall without mercy, in every direction and wherever I turned my eyes.[27]

Thus Miss Wilmot with typical Irish sparkle, humour and energy gives us a glimpse of Dessein's splendour.

Although the peace of Amiens was eventually ratified it did not last and it would be another twelve years before the British would appear again in the courtyard of the Hôtel d'Angleterre. Between 1803-1805 Napoleon's Army of England was concentrated at the Channel ports, in anticipation of the order to invade and, as was reported in the *Hull Packet:*

The beautiful Hotel d'Angleterre at Calais, formerly kept by Dessein, is now entirely filled with French soldiers, the principal apartments are kept as mess rooms for the officers.[28]

On the 9 December 1804 the peace of the whole town was shattered. The officers of the garrison had put on a ball for the ladies of Calais at Dessein's hotel. As it drew to an end, at about three in the morning, a terrible noise was heard accompanied by a powerful shaking which upset the card tables. The officers, in silk stockings and dress breeches, rushed to their barracks believing an attack had been launched by the enemy. In fact a British expedition, under the command of Captain Sir Home Popham, had attempted to blow up the Fort Rouge which protected the entrance to the harbour. The attack was only partially successful but it did result in almost all the windows of the town being broken.[29]

The threat of invasion had diminished even before Nelson's crushing defeat of the French and Spanish fleets at Trafalgar and by 1806 the Royal Navy was blockading the French ports so that when, in 1807, the American Lieutenant-Colonel Ninian Pinkney travelled from Calais to take up the post of resident US minister in London, he discovered that,

There was no shipping in the harbour, and even the stock in the shops had every appearance of having remained long, and having to remain longer in its fixed repose.[30]

Despite this economic stagnation, 'Dessein's ...still maintains its reputation and its name.' Having travelled through much of France, Pinkney had no hesitation in pronouncing it to be, 'the only inn which could enter into any reasonable comparison with any of the respectable taverns of England or America.' For, 'A clean and housewife-like bed,' was so rarely met with once the traveller had gone, 'but a few miles from Calais,' that he regarded a pair of sheets and a counterpane as, 'necessary a part of his luggage as a change of shirts.'[31]

Among the many who rushed to the Continent following Napoleon's first fall, was Katherine Wilmot's fellow country-man, the 23 year-old John Mayne who, 'after a tedious passage,' lasting some twelve hours, arrived at Calais on the morning of 24 August 1814 together with his travelling companions; his eldest brother, the Revd Charles Mayne and Charles's wife Susan. There they stayed, 'At the Hôtel d'Angleterre, formerly Desseins, now kept by Quillacy [Quillac] and Duplessis, considered the greatest establish-ment in Europe'.[32]

Mayne tells us that the hotel accommodated between seventy and eighty beds and fifty more for servants. The bedrooms he says are 'large and airy' and the beds, although they themselves lacked curtains, were placed in curtained-off recesses. These were large enough to, 'admit of walking room round the bed, and form a little apartment quite necessary when ladies and gentlemen are expected to sleep indifferently in the same room as Charles, Susan and I did here'. He goes on to contrast the elegance of the marble tables, handsome chairs and, 'great looking-glasses in every direction,' with the rudeness of the large fireplaces lacking grates and adapted to wood fires in which, 'strangely misshapen tongs were the only fire-iron,' and the doors on which in the place of locks there is simply, 'an iron bolt a foot long, moved by a coarse iron handle'.[33]

An anonymous English traveller who arrived at Calais within two months of Waterloo, began his account, serialised in *The New Monthly Magazine* – as did Katherine Wilmot, as he woke up to find himself in Dessein's Hotel '(now Quillac's)' –

....when I awoke in the morning at Calais I had no recollection of the journey I had undertaken and was astonished when I looked to the top of the lofty curtains hanging from the very high ceiling in form of a throne; but soon, coming to my recollection, I said to myself, I am in France.[34]

After remarking on his surprise that, 'so great a difference should exist between two shores in sight of each other,' he continues his account with a description of his immediate surroundings:

The English traveller is surprised at almost everything that surrounds him – the lofty ceilings of the bedrooms; the bed curtains fixed to the wainscot, almost at the height of the ceilings, terminating in a covering like the canopy of a throne; stone floors even in the upper stories; immense chimneys yawning at him in an almost circular form, adorned, or rather deformed by heavy marble scrolls of a sombre colour, having still in them the cinders of last winter, between two iron bars to support the wood, which are faced brass ornaments that appear not to have been scoured since they were made; ponderous frames with bad wavy glass in the lofty windows; antique chests of drawers or Chinese cabinets out of repair; shallow wash hand basons without soap; stone stairs with iron balustrades. These, however, provide an excellent security against the spreading of fire...

The modern ornaments in these large rooms consist principally of fine gilt clocks, large pier glasses, paper hangings with landscapes, buildings and pictures of which nymphs and cupids generally form the subject.[35]

In 1820 Dorothy Wordsworth, together with her brother William, the poet, and his wife Mary, returned to France, en route for the Rhineland, Switzerland and Milan, for the first time since 1802. Dorothy wrote in her Journal:

What shall I say of Calais? I looked about for what I

remembered, and looked for new things, and in both quests was gratified... On my bedroom door is inscribed, *'Sterne's Room'*, and a print of him hangs over the fireplace. The walls painted in panels, handsome carpets, chimney-piece marble-coloured, hearth red, bed-curtains white, sheets coarse, coverlet a mixture of cotton and woollen, beautifully white; but how clumsy all contrivances of braziers and smiths! The bell hangs on the outside of the wall, and gives a single, loud, dull stroke when pulled by the string, so that you must stand and pull four or five times, as if you were calling the people to prayers.[36]

By the time Augustus Bozzi Granville arrived at Dessein's en route for St Petersburgh in 1827, he was already very well-travelled. Born in Milan in 1783, the son of the postmaster-general, he had studied medicine at Pavia, and practised in Turkey and Spain before settling in London where he was to have a distinguished career as an obstetrician. In 1814, his warning to the British government of Napoleon's impending escape from Elba had been ignored. His Anglophilia perhaps colours this comparison between Dessein's and the inns of Dover:

When you enter Dessin's at Calais the magnitude of the establishment, the size and height, and number of the apartments, with their trumeaux [pier-glasses], ormolus and damask curtains, strike you with astonishment; for you have just left the York or the Ship, with their four-feet square parlours, and a narrow passage leading to them, instead of an extensive courtyard and garden. But, *per contra*; at Dessins, the apartments are uncarpeted, some of the floors are of the colour of boiled lobsters, and the hearth black and slovenly, emits more smoke than warmth, from the tindery faggots, that disappear, like the vanities of this world, in a minute, and the green billets that hiss and drop tears and now and then shoot a small fiery rocket into your coat... whereas, at the Ship, or at the York, the Wilton and the Brussels are equally spread under your feet; and a heap of blazing Wallsend within the bars of a bright grate, give out a cheerful and permanent warmth.[37]

Perhaps the 'handsome carpets' which had pleased Dorothy Wordsworth had worn thin and been discarded or maybe 'Sterne's Room' was designed especially to appeal to English travellers.

The complaint about the fireplaces was not confined to visitors from the British Isles. In November 1825 an American journalist, Nathaniel Hazeltine Carter arrived at Dessein's and whilst he found it, 'above the ordinary standard of French inns ...handsomely finished and furnished,' he too made an exception of the floor and fireplaces,

> both of which are uncomfortable in cold weather. Count Rumford's philosophy does not appear to have reached the firesides of France. There is a want of system and economy in the mode of constructing chimneys and warming houses, a fact the more remarkable, since fuel, consisting almost entirely of wood, is scarce and extravagantly high. In winter it costs a family more to supply the hearth than the table.[38]

The Rumford fireplace, introduced in the 1790s, was tall and shallow, with a streamlined throat designed so as to efficiently carry away smoke whilst minimising loss of heat.

Not all English visitors, however, found the French system of heating a room inefficient. When the Revd Burroughes Norgate arrived at Dessein's in May 1816, he wrote of how,

> One is greatly struck on first coming to France at finding no grates; but the fuel is laid directly on the hearth, there are two iron bars raised about two or three inches from the hearth; where the billets are first laid; and in this manner a most excellent fire is kept up.[39]

The freshness of the hotel's bed linen was frequently commented upon. The English novelist William Makepeace Thackeray, a Dessein devotee, looking back on his first visit in the late 1820s, recalled, 'the red-calico canopy under which I slept, the tiled floor, and the fresh smell of the sheets.'[40] But perhaps the most closely observed description of the hotel's apartments comes from late in its history. The

detail with which the writer treats his subject is remarkable
because he was not a young person in the first flush of
Continental enthusiasm but a middle-aged, widely-travelled
man on his way to Egypt who might be expected to be
impatient to reach the banks of the Nile. He was the fifty
year-old surveyor and civil engineer Thomas Sopwith,
grandfather of the aviation pioneer. His companions were
the fellow north-easterner and great railway engineer
Robert Stephenson and the landscape painter and Royal
Academician Frederick Robert Lee.

Sopwith's biographer, Stafford M. Linsley, quotes one of
the engineer's friends who described him as, 'the very soul
of order and exactitude,' qualities which are in ample
evidence in his *Notes of a Visit to Egypt*, printed for private
circulation in 1857. Linsley adds that he was, 'obsessive about
punctuality,' so it is no surprise to read that, armed with a
copy of Murray's *Handbook on Egypt*,

We arrived [at Dover] three hours before the time appointed
for the mail packet to leave for Calais. This afforded leisure for a
comfortable dinner at the Lord Warden Hotel; and at half past
seven in the evening we left in the mail steam packet, crossed the
Straits of Dover and at ten o'clock were comfortably located in
Dessin's hotel at Calais.[42]

Sopwith goes on to use Dessein's (he calls it Dessin's) to
give the reader, 'a fair idea of the style of decoration and
comfort usually to be found in good European hotels':

No observant eye can fail to admire that delicately-tinted paper,
with its neat and unobtrusive flower-like pattern, scarcely one
shade removed from the nearly white tint on which it is placed.
This extreme simplicity of form and chasteness of colour is relieved
by a deeply-tinted crimson border, five or six inches in width.
Almost every room contains one or more richly-gilt mirrors, and
an ornamental clock of bronze or or-molu, mounted on a marble
stand. On either side are vases of painted porcelain, or not
unfrequently bronze statuettes, derived from classical or
historical subjects, and covered with large and costly glass shades.
The untravelled stranger steps cautiously over polished and

slippery floors, but in Dessin's, as in most of the large hotels
frequented by the English, the best rooms are provided in winter
with carpets, in which richness of colour and good taste in
ornamental design are conspicuous…. An abundance of marble,
in mantel-pieces, window seats, and dressing tables, is another
general feature… and almost every bedroom contains a neat
writing desk.[43]

If Dessein's was typical then the bedroom heating
arrangements had been improved by the middle of the
century:

The open hearth has wooden billets resting on two slightly
raised pieces of iron, or, more frequently, stoves of iron or
porcelain are substitutes for the fireside of which Englishmen are
so proud; but which, if more cheerful, is much less economical
than the continental modes of warming rooms.[44]

Sopwith was not the complaining sort and although
he had some reservations about Continental bedding
arrangements, which appear to have changed since
Katherine Wilmot's day, he was always prepared to make the
best of what he found:

Much has been pleasantly said and written on the so-called
short, narrow and open beds of French and German hotels,
and no doubt they present a considerable contrast to the
gloomy grandeur and ample area of an English four-post bed,
with its extensive and rigid-curtained walls. But although some
inconvenience may at first be found in such a transition as the
traveller finds in this respect, limited to a narrow and thinly
covered space, and warmed for a time by an eiderdown pillow of
balloon-like size and lightness, which soon falls off; yet, with due
precaution, and the addition of a plaid or dressing-gown, these
inconveniences are easily surmounted and I have rarely, if ever,
been otherwise than perfectly comfortable in these foreign beds.[45]

Many of the wealthier class of British traveller will no
doubt have been even more attracted to Dessein's once it
became known as *l'auberge des rois*. The first crowned head to

have rested there was that of the young Christian VII of
Denmark who stayed there en route for England in 1788.
The French king, Louis XVI, ordered the Commandant of
Picardy, the Prince de Croy, to provide a brilliant reception
as a consequence of which Pierre Dessein presented the
town of Calais with a bill of *692 livres 10 sols and 6 deniers*
[approximately 28 English guineas] for a single banquet, a
sum which threatened to upset the municipal finances. If
his *Memoires* are to be believed the Prince himself was obliged
to disburse a further 7000 livres from his own, admittedly far
deeper, pockets.[46]

Napoleon stayed at Dessein's in 1803, when planning
the invasion of Britain, whilst Louis XVIII spent his first night
back on French soil there – 24 April 1814. It may be no
coincidence that shortly after the Restoration the then
owner, Louis Quillacq, was the citizen on whom the largest
amount of tax was levied. Louis-Philippe, Leopold I of the
Belgians and Napoleon III lent further lustre to the
guest-book.[47]

Whether British travellers would have been attracted to
Dessein's following George IV's brief sojourn in 1821 is
doubtful for he was a highly unpopular monarch. Following
his magnificently expensive coronation, he visited his domin-
ions in Ireland, Hanover and Scotland. Within a fortnight of
enduring atrocious weather in returning from Ireland, he
set off to visit his German possessions. The royal yacht sailed
not from Dover, which the year before had received his
estranged queen, Caroline, with rapture, but from Ramsgate;
George not being one to leave a grudge undisturbed. Once
more the crossing was rough. The yacht could not get into
Calais harbour and the King, showing a good deal of
courage, was tranferred to a French fishing boat which
promptly became stuck on the bar. By the time he was
eventually put ashore the boat was half-full of water. There
he was welcomed, on behalf of the French king, by the Duc
d'Angoulême with whom he apparently walked across the
Places d'Armes to the Rue Royale and Dessein's hotel where
a 'sumptuous' dinner was provided.[48] The diners, in addition

to the King and the Duc, included the courtiers Sir William
Knighton and Sir Benjamin Bloomfield and the Steward of
the Royal Household – and husband of George's mistress –
Lord Conyngham. Knighton, the newly-appointed Keeper
of the Privy Purse, who had come a long way since being a
Plymouth doctor, wrote home to his family from, 'Dessin's,
Calais, Tuesday, after midnight':

Here we are safe at Calais, thank God, all well, – a rough
passage towards the close. Our reception at the embarkation this
morning at Ramsgate was magnificent and the same at this place.
I am working hard – much writing and little rest. But nothing can
equal the affection and kindness of the King towards me. You knew
what I determine to do, I do well: this, I hope will be the case in
this instance.

The King has been at the theatre to- night. The music was very
agreeable, and I was much amused and gratified. I believe you
would hardly know me in my new costume; the whole of it is so
comical, that I can scarcely believe my own history. It is more like
a romance than anything else.

Tomorrow night we prepare to sleep at Lisle, and the next to
reach Brussels, from which place I hope to write to you again. You
must not expect long letters; but when I return, I hope to give you
the happiness of telling you everything. The dear King leaves me
not a moment. You cannot understand it unless you were present.

Ever yours etc.
W.K.
Wednesday morning; six o'clock
I have just been with the king, and am putting everything in
motion for our departure, which is no joke. Adieu.[49]

Because of his relatively humble origins, Knighton's
influence with the King was much resented by the prime
minister, Lord Liverpool and his circle.[50] He was, however,
immensely loyal, hardworking and, in the words of his
biographers, 'greedy neither of money nor of honours'.[51] Yet
George's visit to Dessein's is best known for the man, greedy
of both and now a resident of Calais, that he spurned that
day – his former friend Beau Brummell. More of him anon.

5

SOME FELLOW GUESTS

Hotels are places of social intercourse and Dessein's was certainly no exception. Whilst today people will probably encounter their fellow guests in the lift, in the eighteenth century it would be at the *table d'hôte* that strangers were most likely to become acquainted, although at a well-appointed hotel such as Dessein's, the meeting place might equally well have been the theatre, the garden or, as was the case with Yorick and the Lady, at the door of the *remise*.

The high church Anglican clergyman William Jones – 'Jones of Nayland' – had long promised himself a trip to France and when it eventually took place, in August 1776, regretted that he had not been before. It is consequently rather surprising that one of the highlights, possibly *the* highlight of the journey, was a meeting with a fellow countryman which took place on his return to Dessein's hotel. This gentleman's aim for some time had been to, 'spend the whole course of the year, as nearly as may be, under one equal temperature of the air, as the bird of passage does.'[1] With this in view, he spent the summer in England, the autumn in Paris and the winter in Italy. Jones was a staunch defender of the traditions of the Church of England who tended to, 'cultivate a practical spirituality based on good works'[2] so it is unsurprising that he approved of this story told by his Calais acquaintance:

He reflected with a degree of compassion, which shewed great superioty of mind, on the unnecessary trouble men give themselves in avenging petty worthless injuries. We are all dreadfully afraid, said he, of being imposed upon, and give ourselves ten times as much uneasiness as a matter is worth, to avoid the appearance of it. The vanity of this humour is one of the greatest plagues of human life. I remember, added he, a remarkable instance of it in myself. I was upon the road near one of the towns in *Italy* , and the master of the post-house, which stood about a mile from the town, was determined to force a number of horses unjustly upon my equipage, and made such a noise about it, that a concourse of people were gathered together to see the issue of the dispute. I argued with the man; but it signified nothing: I grew impatient, and declared I would walk on foot to the governor of the town to complain: but still he was inflexible. I actually set out as I had threatened; but when I had walked part of the way, I began to ask myself what I was about? I was going to complain of one rogue to another who might be a greater; and, if I should succeed, how much would be saved by it? Two shillings. These reflections soon turned me back again. As I drew near to the inn, where the mob was still assembled, it happened that a priest was riding by upon a mule: he looked very sickly, and with his sickness had all the appearance of poverty. I enquired where he was going? He told me he was on his journey to the mineral waters of a place at some distance: that the journey was more than he could afford, but there was no other hope of his recovery. I was touched with his case, and gave him a piece of gold. The poor man, in the overflowings of his gratitude, descended from his lean beast, and fell upon his knees to thank me; protesting he would pray for me to the last hour of his life. The people, seeing what had passed, cried out, *Bravo, Signor Inglese!* and the master of the post-house, being now convinced that money had not been the object of my dispute with him, harnessed four horses instead of six, and mounted himself on one of the foremost to drive me as a postilion. Thus did this affair end as it should do; and I had more satisfaction in giving up the point, than I could possibly have found by succeeding in it. I have seen so much, added he, of that vain disturbance which the mind suffers from its own pride in, and save me the trouble: and, in the course of my life, I never yet found, but that somebody or other, in due time, revenged my quarrel, far and that he felt himself happy in the effect, whatever was the cause of it.[3]

Whether this paragon of philosophic virtue ever crossed the threshold of Dessein's Inn or was, as is more likely, a device created by Jones during a two day wait for favourable winds, we shall probably never be sure. Of an altogether less philosophic disposition was Edward Kelly of the 1st Foot Guards who was the subject of a conversation held at Dessein's (by then Quillacq's) some forty years later. An Irishman, born at Portarlington, in what is now County Laois, in 1771, he had fought in the Peninsula before distinguishing himself at Waterloo. His exploits that day included the killing of the colonel of the 1st regiment of French cuirassiers from whose uniform he had stripped the epaulettes as a trophy which he presented to his own commander, Lord Uxbridge.[4] Kelly went on to serve in the 23rd Light Dragoons in India where he rose to the rank of Lieutenant-Colonel and died at Mallye, a small garrison town about a hundred miles north of Patna, on 6 August 1828. His fellow Irishman Andrew O'Reilly tells this tale linking Kelly's death on the edge of the Gangetic Plain to the shores of the English Channel:

Immediately before intelligence of his [Kelly's] death reached Europe, I happened to meet, at the Hotel Quillac in Calais, a number of Indian officers who had just arrived there on their return home. On my way I inquired of them for 'Ned Kelly', they said that he was pretty well but much grieved in consequence of his bereavement [news of his son's death having reached him]. A gentleman at another table asked:
    'Is he in low spirits?'
    'Very!'
    'Then,' said the gentleman, an old soldier, 'I am sorry to say he is "ordered to join". I lament this, for he was a noble fellow. I have

served seven-and-twenty years in India, myself, and have never known a desponding invalid recover, nor a man mentally depressed to live long in that country.'

This prediction was verified. The next mail brought an account of the death of Edward Kelly – 'Waterloo Kelly'.[5]

Whether this is the exact truth we must also doubt – the 'next mail' seems remarkably pat. After Wellington himself, Kelly was probably the best-known Irishman present at Waterloo and O'Reilly may well have been tempted to add a touch of authenticity to his tale by setting it at a location which many would have known. It was there, however, that a Gentleman of York' had encountered the Conquering Hero himself.

The Duke of Wellington had announced his intention to sleep at Quillacq's on Friday night [31 July 1818], and was expected at half past eleven. I sat up considering whether I should go to bed (which I felt much inclined to do), or wait the arrival of the conqueror of France. Whilst I was laid on a large sofa, debating the matter, *considering that I might sleep any night*, but could not see so great a man *any night*; on the other hand, what better should I be for having seen him? Besides, he might not come, or might be behind his time &c? I found my sitting up was not agreeable to the waiter, who every now and then made errands into the room to see if I was wanting to retire. At length, at eleven o'clock, he came into the room, blew out the two candles on the table; and on my calling out for him to leave one candle, he replied, 'Tout le monde va se coucher'. This being the case, I was obliged to retire; for as all the world was going to bed, it was not for John Bull to introduce his bad customs of turning night into day. I could not, however, but suspect that my desire to see the Duke, and my having so repeatedly inquired about his arrival, might determine the waiter to baulk me; as the Duke is no mighty favourite with Frenchmen. The next morning, at seven, I went down to the pier, and saw the Duke's carriage embarked aboard the Lord Duncan packet. He was to sail at high water (between ten and eleven). The wind at

W.N.W. was directly against him, and his passage would probably occupy seven or eight hours at least. The sailors were disputing about the number of tacks to be made, and the course to be steered, in order to get him soonest over. The Duke slept on the ground floor of our hotel, in a room looking into the garden; his sitting room was adjoining his bedroom. He got up between eight and nine, and at nine breakfasted with four of five officers; but the curtains were so much closed, that as we walked in the garden we could distinguish nothing. We determined not to leave Calais till we had seen him. About half past nine the master of the packet came to summon him. The Duke soon after came to the door, and looked up at the sky for a minute; he returned to his room, and in about five minutes set off to walk to the pier, in company with the officers. He said to Colonel Campbell[6] who was near him, 'Is that your carriage, Campbell?' pointing to one in the Court. The Duke is about 5 feet 7 inches high; has an enormous nose; is a cheerful smiling man, and without the gravity which the portraits of him represent; he is about 50[7]; he was dressed in a blue frock coat, white trowsers, and short boots. He appears stiff, as if he wore stays; the French say he has armour under his clothes, which I don't believe; but although not an ostentatious man, he seems a little of the dandy in his dress.[8] ...After we had seen the Duke, we set off for St Omer....[9]

Whatever the attractions which so bewitched Sterne's sentimental hero, they are unlikely to have been as alluring as those of the great beauty and authoress, Marguerite Gardiner, the Countess of Blessington. The American travel writer and poet Nathaniel Parker Willis described her as, 'one of the most lovely and fascinating women I have ever seen'.[10] Her beauty can still be admired in her highly seductive portrait by Sir Thomas Lawrence in the Wallace Collection, London. Just a few months before that portrait was painted, on 14 September 1821, she was about to continue her journey to the Netherlands when:

...we met in the courtyard at Dessein's hotel, the mourners returning from paying the last sad duty to our late unhappy Queen. The party consisted of Lord and Lady Hood, Lady Anne Hamilton, Dr and Mrs Lushington and several gentlemen.[11] I was presented to Lord Hood, and by him introduced to Lady Hood, who appears to be the most worthy, honest, warm-hearted woman; she related many circumstances connected with the last hours of her unfortunate mistress, of whose perfect innocence she expressed her belief in language which strongly marked the warmth and sincerity by which it was dictated. She declared her conviction that the Queen died of a broken heart, and added, that so great was the mental anguish which she endured that all who truly loved her, must rejoice at her being freed from a life of persecution and suffering.[12]

This was the conclusion of a dramatic if unedifying story. Caroline of Brunswick had been separated from her husband, now George IV, for more than twenty years. She had endured the loss of her only child, Princess Charlotte, the humiliation of her (abandoned) trial and her exclusion from the coronation. The story that she died of a broken heart, although it found its way into the first edition of the *Dictionary of National Biography*, has today been replaced by a more credible, if less romantic, explanation; she was taken ill at the theatre and died a few days later, on 7 August 1821, of an intestinal illness.[13] Marguerite, whose first husband, a Captain Farmer, was prone to uncontrollable fits of rage, doubtless and understandably, sided with the Queen.

She and Lady Hood were by no means alone. The government had hoped that the funeral cortège – en route for Harwich and, finally, Brunswick – could be got across London with the minimum of public display but the London mob, always sympathetic to Caroline, had other ideas. They had clashed with the Life Guards, who killed two of their number, at Hyde Park Corner and ensured that the procession passed through the heart of the City. As the coffin had left British waters her supporters had placed upon it the inscription, *'Caroline, the injured Queen of England'*.[14] Lord Hood was Henry Hood, the second viscount, son of the naval hero, and his wife was Jane Wheler of Whitley Abbey, Warwickshire. That Jane was still so animated in her defence of the Queen, more than three weeks after the internment and after a long journey, is testament to the strength of opinion which the new King's behaviour had aroused.

Rather as William Jones used a meeting in Calais to forward his ideas on practical religion, so did the radical politician and novelist Edward Bulwer Lytton employ an encounter between an Englishman and a Frenchman to air his views on the contrasting forms of social advancement in the two countries in his unflattering account of the English national character – *England and the English* of 1833. It concerns the author's friend D_____ who, on the ferry to Calais notices a fellow passenger with 'something mysterious, moodful, and majestic' about him. D____ attempts to engage the stranger in conversation by offering him his newspaper but it is refused. Later,

My friend made another attempt at a better acquaintance but about this time the motion of the steam vessel began to affect the stranger –

'And his soul sickened o'er the heaving wave.'

Maladies of this sort are not favourable to the ripening of acquaintance. My friend baffled and disappointed, shrunk into himself; and soon afterwards amid the tumult of landing, he lost sight of his fellow passenger. Following his portmanteau with a jealous eye, as it rolled along in a foreign wheel-barrow, D____ came at last into the courtyard of M. Dessin's hotel, and there sauntering leisurely to and fro, he beheld the mysterious stranger. The day was warm; it was delightful to bask in the open air. D____ took a chair by the kitchen door, and employed himself on the very same newspaper that he had offered to the stranger, and which the cursed sea winds had prevented his reading on the deck at that

ease with which our national sense of comfort tells us that a
newspaper ought to be read. Ever and anon, he took his eyes from
the page and beheld the stranger still sauntering to and fro,
stopping at times to gaze at a green britzka with that paternal look
of fondness which declared it to be an appropriation of his own.
The stranger was visibly impatient: now he pulled out his watch –
now he looked up to the heavens – now he whistled – and now he
muttered 'These d____d Frenchmen'. A gentleman with a mincing
air and a quick gait entered the yard. You saw at once that he was
a Frenchman. The eyes of the two gentleman met: they recognised
each other. You might tell that the Englishman had been waiting
for the newcomer, the '*Bon jour, mon cher*' of the Frenchman, the
'How do you do' of the Englishman, were exchanged; and D____
had the happiness of overhearing the following conversation:-

French Gentleman. 'I am ravished to congratulate you on the
distinguished station you hold in Europe.'
English Gentleman (bowing and blushing) 'Let me rather
congratulate you on your accession to the peerage.'
French Gentleman. 'A bagatelle, sir, a mere bagatelle; a natural
compliment to my influence with the people. By-the-way, you of
course will be a peer in the new batch that *must* be made shortly.'
English Gentleman (with a constrained smile, a little in contempt
and more in mortification) 'No, monsieur, no; *we* don't make peers
quite so easily.'
French Gentleman. 'Easily! why have they not made Sir George
B___ and Mr W____ peers? The one a mere *elegant*, the other a
mere *gentilhomme de province*. You don't compare their claims with
your great power and influence in Europe!'
English Gentleman. 'Hum – hi-hum; they were men of great birth
and landed property.'
French Gentleman (taking snuff) 'Ah! I thought you English were
getting the better of those aristocratic prejudices: *Virtus est sola
nobilitas.*'[15]
English Gentleman. 'Perhaps those prejudices are *respectable*. By-the-
way, to speak frankly, we were a little surprised in England to see
your elevation to the peerage.'

French Gentleman. 'Surprised! – *diable!* – why?'

English Gentleman. 'Hm – really – the editor of a newspaper – ehum! –hem!

French Gentleman. 'Editor of a newspaper! why, who *should* get political rank, but those who yield political power? Your newspaper, for instance, is more formidable to a minister than any duke. Now you know, with us M. de Lalot, M. Thier, De Villele, Chateaubriand,[16] and, in short, nearly all the great men you can name, write for the newspapers.'

English Gentleman. 'Aha! but do they *own* it?'

French Gentleman. 'Own it, to be sure; they are too proud to do so: how else do they get their reputation?'

English Gentleman. 'Why, with us, if a member of parliament sends us an article, it is under a pledge of the strictest secrecy. As for Lord Brougham, the bitterest accusation ever made against him was, that he wrote for a newspaper.'[17]

French Gentleman. 'And *did* Lord Brougham write for that newspaper?'

English Gentleman. 'Sir, that is a delicate question.'

French Gentleman. 'Why so reserved? In France the writers of our journals are as much known as if they add their names to their articles; which, indeed, they very often do.'

English Gentleman. 'But supposing a great man is known to write an article in my paper, all the other papers fall foul on him for demeaning himself: even *I*, while I write every day for it, should be very angry if the coxcombs of the clubs accused me of it to my face.'

French Gentleman (laying his finger to his nose). 'I see, I see, you have not a pride of class with you as we have. The nobleman with us is proud of showing that he has power with those who address the people: the plebeian writer is willing to receive a certain respectability from the assistance of the nobleman: thus each class gives consequence to the other. But you all write under a veil; and such a quantity of blackguards take advantage of the concealment, that the respectable man covets concealment as a screen for himself. This is the reason that you have not, pardon me, monsieur, as high a station as you ought to have; and why you astonish me, by thinking it odd that I, who, vanity apart, can sway the minds of thousands every morning, should receive' (spoken with dignified disdain) 'the trumpery honour of a peerage!'

'*Messieurs*, the dinner is served,' said the *garçon*; and the two gentlemen walked into the *salon*, leaving D___ in a fever of agitation.

'*Garçon, garçon,*' said he, under his breath, and beckoning to the waiter, 'who is that English gentleman?'

'Meestare____, the – vat you call him, le redacteur of – de editor of de_____ paper.'

'Ha! and the French gentleman?'

'Monsieur Bertin de _____ , pair de France, and editor of de *Journal des Debats.* [18]

'Bless me!' said D_____,'what a *rencontre!*' [19]

6

Of all the adventures which were to overtake Laurence Sterne's Sentimental Traveller none took place in crossing the Channel for, 'the packet sailing at nine the next morning – by three I had got sat down to my dinner upon a fricassee'd chicken, so incontestably in France, that had I died that night of an indigestion, the whole world could not have suspended the effects of the Droits d'aubaine....[1] In fact death by indigestion would appear not to have been a fate likely to have overtaken M. Dessein's guests, the great majority of whom – at least insofar as they are represented by the written record – seem to have been satisfied with both the cost and quality of the food he provided. This despite the fact that many English visitors would have arrived with a prejudice against what Parson Woodforde called 'frenchified' food. Indeed among the conservative majority of Woodforde's countrymen a taste for French food was regarded as little short of treason.[2] Hogarth's painting *Calais Gate* – showing a great side of beef being transported to Grandsire's hotel so that English travellers will not be subjected to a diet of frogs' legs and garlic, 'trumpets this vainglorious patriotism in the most blatant way'.[3]

English taste, however, itself varied. Among the nobility, French cuisine was, if not the norm, certainly well known. In the words of the American food historian Barbara Ketcham Wheaton, ' After the restoration no great establishment was complete without a Frenchman presiding over its kitchen. One of the most famous of these emigrant chefs was the Duke of Newcastle's chef Clouet. The Earl of Chesterfield, he of the famous *Letters to His Son*, arranged for that young man to dine at the duke's as a part of his education.'[4] In less

aristocratic households, however, French food was regarded
with the greatest suspicion.

The naval officer and playwright George Collier was one
of the minority who was less than impressed when he stayed
at Dessein's in April 1773:

> The auberge of Mons. Dessein is well known to most of the
> English who travel this road; but we found the accommodations
> did not answer our expectations by any means, our dinner being
> indifferently dressed and served in a bed chamber; such being the
> elegant custom in most of the inns of the polite kingdom of
> France.[5]

Collier's biographer says that he died 'embittered' having
received insufficient recognition for his distinguished service
in the American War of Independence (although he became
a knight and Vice-Admiral of the Blue).[6] But it may be that
his jaundiced view of the world pre-dated the American War.
He could not believe that the loss of Calais had broken
Queen Mary's heart – 'At present we esteem the loss of all
our possessions in France as one of the most fortunate events
that could have happened'.[7] Nor was he charmed by the
inevitable begging monk:

> We were just drinking our coffee when the door opened, and
> in entered, *sans cérémonie*, an impudent mendicant friar. It was not
> the venerable and modest *religieux* whom Sterne so strikingly
> describes: it was the figure of a glutton, making his demands upon
> our purses with the same sort of civility as a highwayman when he
> stops you upon the road; only instead of a pistol he flourished an
> empty bag, into which he seemed to demand us to put something
> "for the honour of the blessed Virgin". As I thought the Virgin
> could hardly commit her honour to the charge of such a guardian,
> I gave him nothing; but my worthy companion,[8] having more
> charity, or at least more compliance, dropped a livre into the
> Virgin's bag, with which the mendicant departed without either
> thanks or ceremony.[9]

He also writes of M. Dessein's 'dissatisfaction' and
'rapacity'. By contrast both the kitchen and the cellar chez

Dessein usually met with the approval of British guests. Such was the case as far as the banker Sir John Dean Paul was concerned. En route for Paris in the summer of 1802 he and his 'party of pleasure' attended the theatre and then,

....returned to an elegant, if light, dinner served with such good taste as is unknown in England: we were served Champagne, Côte-Rotie and Chablis; the first two at six, the other at four livres a bottle; we were given an elegant desert with cheese as well, a thing quite unknown to us.[10]

Similarly, two years after Collier's visit Mrs Thrale, in the company of her husband, the brewer, together with Dr Johnson, arrived at the hotel, the impression she received could hardly have been more different:

We had an excellent Dinner which a Capuchin Fryar enlivened by his Company. When it was over we were entertained with a Sight of his Convent, Cells, Chapel & Refectory: the library was locked, & I was not sorry, for Mr Johnson would never have come out of it. The Fryer was a handsome Man....[11]

Collier complained of being obliged to eat in a bedroom but by 1782 when his fellow playwright Frederick Reynolds was at Dessein's, there was certainly a *table d'hôte* and in 1802 Dawson Warren, a British Chaplain accompanying the diplomatic mission negotiating the Treaty of Amiens, writes of how he 'walked up the great staircase of the auberge amidst a profusion of waxlight, and entered a salle à manger'.[12]

Even after Reynolds' visit, however, it appears that the table d'hôte was not a permanent feature. The Frenchman François Marlin, who stayed at the Hotel d'Angleterre in 1788 seems to have regarded the absence of a common eating place as something of a virtue:

There is no table d'hôte Chez Desaint [sic]; each traveller is served in his room at the price he wishes to pay. For my son and myself I ordered the common bill of fare at three francs; I expected soup and boiled beef, nothing more; I was served with two chickens, a tart and dessert; true, one pays for wine separately.[13]

By the nineteenth century in addition to the salle à manger it appears that there were also private dining rooms. When the Quaker businessman Joseph Fry and his party were in Calais in October 1814 a potentially awkward dispute arose with the Duchess of Richmond's maids as to who was to eat where in the hotel which was now run by Messrs Quillac and Duplessis. His digestion, perhaps assisted by the happy resolution of the 'dispute', Fry went on to enjoy his dinner:

Our dinner was excellent. Potage au vermiceil, fricandeau à l'oreille, Beefstake and un volaille roti were the chief, & some excellent champagne. I tasted the vin ordinaire blanc & found it very pleasant as a summer beverage, but it would be too tart for weak stomachs.[14]

This verdict on the quality of the cuisine was shared by at least one of the Duchess's party. Spencer Madan, her sons' tutor, betraying the fact that this was his first visit to France, wrote home to his father in Leicestershire, 'At Mr Quillac's at Calais I was surprised by a most excellent and superb dinner à la mode française (I don't know whether that is right) but on explanation it proved that we paid 3 francs or 2s. 6d a head'.[15] Madan doubtless thought this expensive but nevertheless concluded 'Quillac's hotel is an excellent one'.[16]

It may be that the wily Dessein and his successors made some concessions to British tastes. In 1777, the lawyer John Mitford, a future Speaker of the House of Commons, arrived at Calais after the town gates had been shut for the night, he stayed at an inn in the lower town kept by Dessein's brother where 'the good lady of the house... has been taught to boil bacon and poach eggs à l'angloise'.[17]
Something similar is certainly suggested by John Mayne who, like Fry, was among the flood of Britons visiting France

in 1814. Whilst his only comment about eating Chez Dessein concerned the breakfast knives – 'something between a worn-out English one and a penknife' – by the time he reached Amiens he found that his dinner was 'wholly French... (with the exception of a small bit of roast veal) all swimming in oil'. Nevertheless, he, 'set off with a resolution to eat without mercy all kinds of sauces, fricacies, oils, bad butter etc.'[18]

However, when Katharine Wilmot, together with Lord and Lady Mount Cashel, arrived at Dessein's during the brief interruption to hostilities in 1801, she had noted in her Journal that:

we sat down to a most splendid repast, not a single dish of which I had ever seen before and during the dinner (the successive courses of which I thought would never end) we were symphoniz'd by Republican tunes, play'd outside the window on the organ and tambourines, and a hundred compliments passed on *Mi Lor Anglois*. [19]

As Barbara Ketcham Wheaton has pointed out, the table d'hôte provided a solution to many of the problems of eating and, especially in the case of newly-arrived foreigners, was regarded as a good place to practice speaking French.[20] In his autobiography the playwright Frederick Reynolds writes amusingly of the difficulties into which French pronunciation could lead a young Englishman, ambitious to practise the language. As a seventeen year-old travelling alone he had arrived at Dessein's in August 1782 and deciding to take a walk had asked the waiter, 'who spoke English very tolerably' the French for 'pier'. 'He, thinking as *Milord Anglais,* I could mean nothing but *peer,* or lord, replied *paire'.*[21] This led to difficulties when young Reynolds returned from his walk and decided to take his place at the table d'hôte where,

...the commandant of the troops of the town sat next me; and among other officers and gentlemen at the table were the President of the Council at Ratisbon, a Russian count, and several

Prussians; in all amounting to about twenty, not one of whom (as it appeared to me) spoke a word of English, except a remarkably pretty Irish woman.

I thought I would never please a Frenchman so much as by praising his town; "Monsieur," I said condescendingly to the commandant, "J'ai vu votre paire"; meaning I have seen your *pier,* but which he naturally misunderstood, I have seen your *père,* father. This address from a perfect stranger surprised him: "Il est beau et grand, Monsieur," I continued. The commandant examined me from head to foot with astonishment that imparted to me an almost equal share. I saw there was a mistake and I attempted to explain by pronouncing very articulately,

"Oui, Monsieur, j'ai vu votre *paire* – votre *paire* sur le havre."

"Eh, bien, Monsieur," replied the commandant, "et que disait-il?"

I was astounded; and looking round the room for the keeper of the supposed madman, I discovered that the eyes of the whole company were upon me. "Monsieur", I cried, again attempting to explain, with as much deliberation and precision, and in as good French as could command, "Monsieur, est-il possible que vous *residez* ici, et vous ne *connoissez* pas votre *paire,* votre *paire* si – si long?"

This speech naturally only increased the incomprehensibility of the whole conversation; and the commandant beginning, in rather *haut en bas* terms, to demand an explanation, like all cowards, when driven into a corner I became desparate.

"Messieurs," I cried, somewhat boisterously, "il faut que vous connaissez votre paire! Le *paire* de votre ville qui est fait de pierre, et à la tête de bois – et à ce moment on travaille a lui racommander sa fin, a laquelle le vent a fait du mal!"

This was the *coup de grâce* to all decorum; every Frenchman abandoned himself to his laughter, till the room fairly shook with their shouts; and even the astonished commandant himself could not help joining them.

"Allow me, Sir," said a gentleman, sitting by the side of the Irish lady, and whom I had not previously observed.

"My dear, Sir," interrupted I, "you are an Englishman, pray, pray explain."

"Sir," he replied, "you have just told this gentleman," pointing to the commandant, "that his father is the father of the whole town, that he is made of stone, but has a wooden head and at this moment the workmen are engaged in mending his end, that the wind has damaged."

I was paralyzed. "Tell me," I cried, as if my life had depended on his answer, "what is the French for *pier*?"

"*Jetée*, or according to the common people, *pont*," he replied.

I had scarcely sense enough left, to assist the Englishman in his good-natured attempt, to unravel the error. He succeeded, however, and then commenced, in French, an explanation to the officers. At this moment, the waiter informed me that the St Omer Diligence was about to depart. I rushed from the scene of my disgrace, and stepped into the vehicle, just as the Englishman's recital exploded an additional *éclat de rire* at my expense.[22]

By the time Reynolds came to write his *Life and Times* he had a successful career as a comic playwright behind him; a skill which he no doubt brought to the telling of this surely at least partially imaginary, or at least creatively embroidered, tale. Nevertheless, many of his readers who had travelled to France would certainly have sympathised with young Reynolds' predicament. Even for those accustomed to the manners of the French table d'hôte such dining might prove a good deal less than satisfactory. Towards the end of the eighteenth century Louis-Sébastien Mercier wrote of his distaste at dining,

in the midst of a dozen strangers... The centre of the table (toward what are called the *pièces de résistance*) is occupied by the regular customers who monopolize these important places... Armed with tireless jaws, they eat up greedily as soon as the signal is given.... Unhappy the man who is slow to chew up his share. Seated between these greedy, agile cormorants, he will fast during the meal. In vain will he ask the servant for sustenance; the table will be cleared before he is able to get served.[23]

Although loosely the equivalent of the ordinary – the meal served at a fixed time and price at a common table – in English inns, the difference in French manners and language difficulties could cause embarrassment. The solitary female, for example, could be the victim of the unwanted attentions of her fellow diners. When Reynolds was next in Calais, in 1792, he was in the company of his

mistress, the actress Mary – known as 'Becky' – Wells who was
taking a 'Calais holiday' to avoid her creditors. They were
freshly arrived at the Lion d'Argent when they discovered
that,

dinner [was] just served at the table d'hôte [and] we joined the
party, which consisted chiefly of officers, at least, of people in
uniform. As the 'petites tourtes' were placed on the table, I was
called from the room, owing to the customary custom-house
confusion, and there, compelled to attend the arrangement of
some disputed points, during a few minutes. When I returned, all
impatience to rejoin my fair fellow traveller, my eye searched the
room for her in vain – she was gone. Applying to the waiter for
information, he told me that the lady had retired to her own
private apartment, and expressed the most anxious desire to see
me. Thither, therefore, I repaired; and found her both deep in
rage and grief; to use her own expression, "she had been insulted".
"The moment you quitted the room," she continued, "these sons
of equality and commonalty, conceiving, I suppose, Sir, that I was
also common property, one and all rushed towards me, and I only
escaped their insolent gallantries by taking refuge here."[24]

Not being, 'exactly the person to call a whole revolutionary table d'hôte to account', Reynolds and his mistress were
obliged to suffer their humiliation.

Mercier's distaste for the table d'hôte was shared by that
irascible sportsman Colonel Peter Hawker. Arriving at Calais
on his way home from Paris on 22 December 1814,

…we found Calais a perfect scene of confusion; the hotels were
all crowded, and in preference to starvation and sitting in the yard,
we joined the table d'hôte, which I could compare to nothing but
an ill-regulated kennel of foxhounds. The imposition, the misery,
and the aping of the English was at this place laughable.[25]

Whichever hotel this was it would appear not to have
been Dessein's which Hawker visited in May 1819 (having
crossed the Channel with, 'a mass of vomiting cockneys')
and found to be, 'first-rate, clean, and superbly furnished'.[26]

Dining hours were later in the nineteenth century than they had been a century earlier. The English were accustomed to the idea of taking a second breakfast especially when travelling. Typically, a light breakfast would be taken prior to departure and then something more substantial would be eaten upon stopping later in the morning. The French equivalent was the *déjeuner à la tasse,* usually coffee, taken on rising, and the *déjeuner à la fourchette,* a meal in which meat and more solid food, requiring the use of a fork, was eaten between ten o'clock and noon. In 1789 the American politician Gouverneur Morris ate a 'very good' breakfast of broiled partridge prior to setting off across the Channel.[27]

In the year after Waterloo the Revd Burroughes T. Norgate, whilst he thought little of Calais ("a nasty little town"), was full of praise for Dessein's Hotel where he partook of,

> .....an excellent *"dejeuner à la fourchette"* alias "a good knife and fork breakfast", mutton cutlets, eggs, rolls and butter, and *café au lait.*[28]

By the 1830s the *déjeuner à la fourchette* had become a fashionable social occasion in Britain, satirised in the *New Monthly Magazine* in 1834 in verses which include the following stanza:

> I've ordered the people to water the road
> All the way from the town to my rural abode;
> 'Till three, I suppose, not a soul will arrive –
> Bless me! there's a chaise at the end of the drive!
> 'Tis old Mrs Smith! What can bring her so soon?
> She thinks herself late too – a breakfast at noon!
> And dressed, I protest in her best tabinet, -
> What a blot on my "Dejeuner à la Fourchette"![29]

Dinner was of course the main meal of the day and English visitors were generally impressed by what they received at Dessein's. Towards the end of 1801, for example, John Gustavus Lemaistre an Englishman with French relatives who had obtained His Majesty's licence to visit France 'in order to ascertain my claims to a legacy left me at Paris', had arrived in a country which had long been the enemy.[30] Having been entertained by, 'the great moustaches of the grenadiers, the wooden shoes of the peasants, and the close caps of the grisettes' – he then at six o'clock, 'sat down to an excellent dinner, at the celebrated hotel, formerly kept by Dessein, who is now succeeded by his nephew Quillacq, a very respectable man'. In the following year the banker-poet Samuel Rogers wrote to his sister Maria Sharpe, with whom he had travelled to the Continent eleven years previous. After a 'delightful' three hour crossing he wrote – "I need not describe Calais to you. The people are just as we saw them; the military cocked hats are enormous; the womens' heads are as large as ever; and six little children, not bigger than Sutton [his young nephew] or little bigger, were dancing together a *cotillion* in the street just now, the boys with *long tails,* to a passing tambourine'.[31] He then sat down to, 'a grand entertainment of soup, cutlets, fish, fowl, partridges &c.' before going to the theatre.

As we have seen, Joseph Fry pronounced his dinner, 'excellent' in 1814 and in 1821 Rowland Hill, writing to his mother at Hawkstone in Shopshire, declared that, 'we have just eaten a remarkably good dinner for six franks at Dessin's Hotel'.[32] In the same year a 'Man of Fashion' wrote, 'My stay at Calais was only one day, merely to taste Quillac's excellent wines and cuisine Francaise'.[33] Thirty years earlier, however, another young man had written to his mother in a rather different, rather over-excited, tone. This was Edward Daniel Clarke, a future professor of mineralogy at Cambridge, who wrote from Calais on 18 October 1791:

Here we are! Even I in France. Would you believe it? I have found my father's name written with a pen upon the frame of an old looking-glass. The date is almost worn out, but a rude guess makes it to be, December 1772. I am half dead with sea sickness – twenty four hours passage from Dover. Just now I sent for Monsieur Dessein, and asked him if he remembered Sterne. He speaks broken English, and I worse French, so you may suppose what an edifying tête à tête we had. When I arrived I was half-starved and, seeing a number of waiters crowding round me with 'Que voulez-vous, Monsieur?' I dispatched them all for something to eat. They all came back again, 'Et pardonnez-moi Monsieur, que voulez-vous?' 'Beef! and be hanged to you!!' said I, out of all patience, and away they flew saying, 'Mon dieu! en verité, mi lor Anglois!' Presently in comes a troop of them with Dessein at their head, bringing in tea but no beef, and an old overgrown hen, by way of cold chicken. 'Allons!' say I, 'portez le beff!' Monsieur Dessein made a low bow, 'Non pas beef, Monsieur! La Voila, un petit pullet!' 'Un petit Turkey cock!' said I; Monsieur Dessein bowed again. I laughed and got over the style. You will think me mad or drunk, so I'll wind to a close. I am in such spirits I cannot write sense.[34]

After a few days spent in Calais, Clarke and his companion returned to Hothfield in Kent. Another letter-writer, a 'Gentleman of York', whose letters were published in the *Gentleman's Magazine,* supplied more detail in the summer of 1818:

As a specimen of French dinners, I will tell you what we had at Quillacq's; premising that the table was a deal board, set upon cross-sticks – soup, soles, mutton Maintenon, veal fricandeau, potatoes, chicken and artichoke, pastry, cheese, cherries, gooseberries and plums; this was a dinner for two; the table d'hôte was on a larger scale.[35]

This was very similar to the dinner served to the Wordsworths (the poet, his wife and sister) when they were at the same establishment at the beginning of their tour of the Continent two years later. Dorothy recorded it, 'as being our first meal in France'. It consisted of soup, turbot, boiled chickens, veal chops, potatoes, cauliflowers, spinach. Dessert – almonds, biscuits, currants and cherries.[36]

Writing under the name of 'Peter Pry', the picaresque hero of a popular farce, in 1826, a contributor to the *Literary Gazette* wrote of his 'Travels' that:

To show I knew something of ordering from a French *carte*, I commanded our repast for five [at Quillac's] – *Soup à la Julienne, cotelettes de mouton, salmi de perdreaux, rognons au vin de Champagne, à pullet au jus*. Second service – *un canard sauvage, une sarcelle, macaroni des epinards, beignets de pommes and une omelette souflée*. The dessert was good according to the season; and for all the charge was four francs – 3s 4d per head. *Vive* M. Quillac![37]

Whether this dinner was ever actually ordered or whether it simply served to demonstrate the author's command of the French menu card it is impossible to say but it does seem to match tolerably well with meals we know were consumed.

One of the acknowledged British authorities on French cuisine was the epicure and writer William Kitchiner (1778-1827). He was undoubtedly a man of considerable talent – an expert on optics who was elected to the Royal Society – but there was also something decidedly dodgy, almost Dickensian, about this son of a wealthy London coal-merchant.[38] He claimed that he had been educated at Eton and had taken a medical degree at Glasgow University, so that he was usually known as Dr Kitchiner. In fact he had attended neither of these places of education. His book *The Traveller's Oracle*, published in the year of his death, a vade mecum for travellers, was written by a man who had never set foot outside the country.

The Traveller's Oracle was launched on the back of an earlier success – *The Cook's Oracle* of 1817. This was certainly an aid to kitchen practice and was acknowledged as an inspiration by Mrs Beeton. Of course the fact that he had never been in France was not an insurmountable obstacle in the way of having considerable knowledge of French food. Following the Revolution, London had no shortage of French chefs who had followed their *émigré* masters into exile. He succeeded in providing an endorsement of French soups which many travellers must have found reassuring saying that, 'a French potage is worth a whole English dinner'. [39] The *soup à la Julienne* to which 'Peter Pry' refers would have been a clear vegetable *consommé* in which the shredded vegetables had been slowly cooked in butter. It would, no doubt, have been especially welcome to those not quite recovered from a rough passage.

One of the dishes mentioned by the Gentleman from York – *mouton Maintenon* – would quite likely have rung a bell with readers familiar with the bawdy sequel to *A Sentimental Journey* which was published as *Yorick's Sentimental Journey Continued* by Eugenius in 1769 and which was once thought to have been the work of Sterne's friend John Hall-Stevenson. In that book Yorick, on his return journey re-visits Amiens where at the inn,

> I asked my host what he could speedily provide.
> *"Tout ce que vous-voulez."*
> "Everything you please."
> A very comprehensive bill of fare.
> "But what have you got in the house?"
> *"Tout ce que vous-voulez."*
> "Have you any partridges?"
> *"Non."*
> "Any woodcocks?"
> *"Non."*
> "Any pullets?"
> *Non, Monsieur, qui sont propres à manger."*
> "No, Sir, not that are fit for eating."
> "Then you may as well not have them for a man who is riding post."
> "Any fish?"
> *"Point de tout, aujourd'hui."*
> "None today."
> "What the p-x then does everything consist of?"
> *"Des coutelets de mouton à la Maintenon."*
> "Mutton chops with Maintenon sauce."[40]
> "In the name of Famine, let's have them, good Mr Boniface!"

Dessin's cellar appears to have been as renowned as his kitchen. In the early days drink seems to have been confined to wine and, perhaps, cider. The American Quaker Jabez Fisher complained that, 'They have no Ale here. We drank an ordinary wine instead.' By 1837, however, Victor Hugo writing of his walking tour along the coast from Ostend to

Boulogne, wrote, 'If I am asked, "Did you drink good beer during your trip to Belgium?", I reply, "Yes, in France. I drank excellent beer at Dessin's hotel in Calais."[41]

The cellar was replenished with wine from Champagne, Chablis, the Rhône (Côte Rôtie is frequently mentioned by travellers), Burgundy and Bordeaux. Sometimes it appears to have been drunk in great quantities. For some a holiday spent at Dessin's was the forerunner of the modern 'booze cruise'. Charles James Apperley, the sportsman who wrote under the pen-name 'Nimrod', described an evening spent with Charles and Francis Sheridan, grandsons of the playwright and politician, Richard Brinsley Sheridan who drank himself to death:

> I found them to be chips of the old block, in the true acceptance of the term; and Nature appears to have been as lavish of her favours on their persons as on their minds.
>
> "These are two fine young men," said Charles the head-waiter at Dessin's in Calais (and who does not know Charles at Dessin's?) to me the day after I had dined with them at eight and left them singing at three the next morning – "how well they sing but how long do they mean to live?" "Live!" replied I, "why as long as other people; they are young and stout, Charles;" "They are that," resumed Charles, "but I can only say they have been here three days (this last sentence was accompanied by a significant wonk), and they would very soon kill a Frenchman."[42]

It can well be imagined that the hotel's owners did extremely well out of the more splendid parties for which they catered. Not always, however, as well as they might. On the occasion of the coronation of Charles X as King of France in May 1825, George IV was represented by the Duke of Northumberland who, in the role of Envoy-Extraordinary, was to invest Charles with the Order of the Garter. The Duke's arrival was heralded with a salute from the guns of the escorting frigate and the town's batteries. He then made his way to Dessein's where he entertained at dinner the British Consul, the English naval officers, the Mayor of Calais and other local officials before spending the night at the

hotel. According to James Planché who was also travelling to
Rheims for the coronation although, in his case, to make
drawings of the dresses and decorations for an exhibition at
Covent Garden, "the bill was enormous" despite which,

> ...it would have been paid without a murmur if the proprietor
> had not been so short-sighted as to charge a couple of francs for a
> broken wine-glass! This piece of stupidity [he opined]– for the few
> sous could scarcely have been a matter of calculation in such an
> account – so disgusted Mr Hunter, the King's messenger, who had
> the entire travel arrangements of the mission under his control,
> that he took the Duke to Boulogne on the way back and sailed
> from that port to Dover, avoiding Calais, and thereby depriving
> Mons. Dessein of more francs than would have purchased a
> waggon-load of wine-glasses.[43]

Some English visitors found Dessein's much more to
their taste, so much so that they got no further. As the wife
of one of Napoleon's generals, Laure Junot, the Duchess
d'Abrantès, whose *Memoirs* are as sarcastic as they are
slanderous, could not be expected to think highly of the
English but there is no doubt an element of truth in her
description of that hotel:

> Dessein's establishment is truly astonishing; this house which
> has had European renown for so long is perfectly managed to
> attract the English, containing, as it does, within its walls all that
> money is able to buy immediately. We found it in a state of deepest
> sorrow as a result of the breaking of the Treaty of Amiens on the
> strength of which they had gone to great expense in order to make
> their house worthy of the 'special attention' of the English, such
> lovers of the wines of Champagne and Bordeaux, who come to
> Calais and take up residence for a fortnight Chez Dessein, having
> no other occupation than to drink, eat and to command, on
> waking from a drunken stupor, the next dinner menu. Thus for
> some English go by the days, often the weeks, that they have set
> aside for a journey across France; and then, after settling their bills,
> they realise they no longer have sufficient money to continue their
> trip, they embark on the first packet and return to their counties
> to boast of having made the tour of France. Such cases were not
> rare during the late peace.[44]

Even when Dessein's had passed the acme of fashion, the kitchen and cellar continued to be the subject of admiration. Charles Hervey, for example, having visited Dessein's for a *diner improvisé*, whilst he awaited a train in 1849, discovered that,

...though the *liste de voyageurs* seldom receives a new entry, though Sterne's Room – in which many years ago I passed my first night in France – is usually tenantless, M. Dessin's *cuisine* and cellar are still irreproachable as in more palmy days; and such creature comforts as a tender *côtelette* and a glass of sound Bordeaux being, after all, the most appreciated by a bird of passage such as myself, I performed my omnibus transit in the very best of humours.[45]

7

MUCH HANDSOMER WHEN YOU APPROACH IT
FROM THE WATER

The Victorians, who had more of a taste for the medieval, perhaps appreciated the townscapes of Calais more than did the classically-inclined Georgians. In the mid-nineteenth century John Ruskin, Percy Fitzgerald and Thomas Sopwith all expressed an attraction for the place whereas the lawyer Harry Peckham, writing on his return from Paris in 1772, summarizes it as follows:

> The town is small, the streets are narrow and the fortifications trifling. There is indeed a fossé which can be filled either with salt or fresh water and a citadel advantageously situated to annoy the enemy from every quarter. I was not allowed to enter it but it seemed incapable of making any material defence.[1]

Ruskin, by contrast, saw the same scene quite differently:

> Poor little Calais had indeed nothing to be proud of, but it had a quaint look of contentment with itself on those very terms; some dignity in its strong ramparts and drawbridge gates; and, better than dignity, real power and service in the half mile of pier, reaching to the low tide beaches across the field of sand.[2]

Similarly with the inhabitants of the town. Whilst Mrs Thrale, three years after Peckham, was,

> ...vastly surprized when I landed at Calais to see the Soldiers with Whiskers and the Women mostly so ugly and deform'd. They however seemed desirous to hide their frighfulness, for all wore long Cloaks of Camlet that came down to their heels.[3]

It was not the French inhabitants of Calais that appalled Philip Thicknesse in November of the following year (1776) on returning after a trip to Spain, but his compatriots.

I found in this town, the very sink of France, and the asylum of whores and rogues from England, a group of English men and women, than which nothing can be more extraordinary. At the head presides L——Y B——L, the Yorkshire fellow, called King Collins, Messrs Dry—er, and L——ES, a Canterbury alderman, a fellow who ran away with the paupers' money from Bristol, and twenty other geniuses,

> *Whose necks are protected from the stretch of a halter,*
> *By twenty one miles of Gallic sea water.*[4]

We shall meet more of their like later.

Dorothy Wordsworth, perhaps more charitably inclined than Mrs Thrale, visiting the town for a second time, in 1820, although observing that, 'Everyone is struck with the excessive ugliness (if I may apply that word to any *human* creatures) of the fish-women of Calais', nevertheless felt that 'the clean, tight dress of these females prevents all disgust in looking at *them*; however you may dislike the smell from their slovenly baskets.'[5]

Dorothy was travelling with her brother, the poet, and his wife Mary and Mary's cousin. Tom Monkhouse and *his* wife who were on honeymoon. From Mary's journal it is clear that not all Calais shopkeepers were bilingual;

Went into Shops, I wished much for *Doro* to help me with her French. Wanted a hair pencil, which after much difficulty T.M. & I procured, we entered a shop at random - The Master and Madame with great importance in their manner, sent for a little Girl who understood English - the little Bustler came, & though a plain Lass she looked so good-humoured, & so happy to turn her "few words of English speech" to account, that I could have kissed her –paid 6d & brought away two pencils.[6]

Mary was much impressed by Calais, 'a finer town than we had expected to see', and by its inhabitants:

These French are certainly attractive creatures, nothing surly about them, whatever happens; & it is pleasant to observe their honesty, we have had an amusing reckoning with the Laundress, – for with all Dorothy's French we were at last obliged to hold out the money & suffer the good woman to pay herself.[7]

The town which was home to these attractive individuals consisted of an oblong appoximately 1200m (600 toises) by 500m (250 toises); the longest axis running from ENE to WSW. The long, landward side was fortified with bastions flanked with demi-lunes and a moat (the fossé) 30-50m wide which, as Peckham observed, could be filled with either sea or fresh water.[8] The short, western side was protected by the walls of the Citadel in the middle of which there was, until the Revolution, a bronze bust of Cardinal Richelieu, on whose orders it had been built in the 1630s. The fortifications were pierced by two gates: on the landward side, the Porte Royale, and on the seaward side, the Porte du Havre, across the inner harbour from which was Fort Risban. The two gates were joined by the line of the Rue Royale, the western side of the Place d'Armes and the Rue de la Mer. In 1820 the gates were closed in summer between 9 p.m. and 2 a.m. and in winter between 5 p.m. and 5 a.m.[9] The former was demolished in 1843, the latter in 1882. In the north eastern corner of the town, between the fossé and the outer harbour, was the fishermens' quarter of Courgain, whilst beyond the southern wall, was the lace-making district of St Pierre.

Harry Peckham's opinion of the town may have been better had he, like the majority of British travellers, approached it from across the Channel. In fact his tour of the Low Countries and northern France had begun at Hellevoitsluis in Zeeland and ended in Calais, so he entered the town from Boulogne through the Porte Royale. A fellow Oxonian, William Jones (of Nayland) thought that,

Calais makes a more handsome appearance when you approach it upon the water than the town of Dover; and its towers began to become visible when we had reached the middle of the Strait.[10]

This was not the universally held view. The American, Nathaniel Carter, writing some fifty years later (in 1825), found,

> the harbour....small and inconvenient, being entirely artificial; and the town, owing to its sunken position, does not appear to any advantage from the water, although it is not wanting in a due portion of churches, steeples, monuments and other architectural ornaments.[11]

The same churches, steeples and monuments, together with the Pier and the picturesque sight afforded of the shipping in the harbour, certainly meant that the appearance of the town, as seen from a short distance off-shore, was a great favourite with landscape artists who, no doubt, aimed to appeal to the likes of Thomas Sopwith who, on the morning after his arrival,

> sauntered through some of the streets of the town and along the quays of the harbour, to see shop-window novelties, to buy a few local engravings, which, however small, or inferior in execution, often prove agreeable reminiscences of travelling.[12]

That Sopwith was not alone is suggested by the following commentary which, in 1821, accompanied some drawings of French scenery made by Captain Batty of the Grenadier Guards and engraved by Edward John Roberts:

> English travellers often remark that Calais is one of the most striking towns in France. The impression can, to a certain extent, be attributed to the novelty of the scene in general and of each thing in particular in contrast with England. Calais is, however, also worthy of attention by virtue of the intimate connection with our own history.[13]

Certainly, of the prominent buildings that would have been seen by the traveller approaching from across the Channel, several would have dated back to the period of

English occupation which had ended as long ago as 1558 with its capture, or liberation, by the Duc de Guise. Of these, in the words of Robert Bell Calton:

> The grand old church of Nôtre Dame, grey and venerable in its marked Anglo-Norman features and erected by the English, or as some antiquaries assert, augmented by them, when we quartered the *Fleur-de-Lis*, is the most striking object of the *coup d'oeil* of Calais.[14]

In his view, whether,

> Beheld from the sea or land, the old pile of Nôtre Dame looms reverently and picturesquely to the eye. The square, massive Norman tower, relieved by its three-arched belfry windows on each face, surmounted by corner turrets, and a conically-shaped tower of octagon proportions, topped again by a short steeple, serve to give the venerable edifice a singularly quaint and impressive mien, as the mariner in the offing sights the well-known landmark, or the wanderer of the plain views it on the horizon.[15]

John Ruskin was similarly impressed:

> I cannot find words to express the intense pleasure I have always felt in first finding myself, after some prolonged stay in England, at the foot of the tower of Calais church. The large neglect, the noble mightiness of it, the record of its years written so vividly, yet without sign of weakness or decay: its stern vastness and gloom, eaten away by the channel winds and overgrown with bitter sea-grass....I cannot tell half the strange pleasure and thought that comes over me at the sight of that old tower.[16]

Although Calton's 'grand old' church dates back to before Edward III and the two hundred years of English occupation, most of it belongs to that late medieval period. As we see it today, it has been substantially rebuilt following inadvertent allied bombing in 1944 but it remains an imposing edifice and, although the plain exterior rarely attracted much comment from British travellers, the interior certainly did. Even Peckham, generally dismissive of the

ill.4'

'I cannot find words to express the intense pleasure I have always felt,' wrote Ruskin, 'in first finding myself, after some prolonged stay in England, at the foot of the tower of Calais church.'

town's attractions, could scarce forbear to cheer:

> The church, dedicated to the Invocation of the Virgin, is built in form of a cross and ornamented with eleven chapels. The grand altar is decorated with two basso relievos in alabaster; the one represents the Manna showered from Heaven: the other, the Lord's Supper. Both of them are well executed.[17]

After the Revolution, John Edmund Eyre, was attracted not so much by the detail of the retable, described by Peckham, as by the High Altar itself:

> This being Sunday, went and heard Mass; as Calais has suffered less from the fury of the democrats than any other town, the interior of the church is yet uninjured. There are several fine tombs and paintings which adorn the aisles, and the mural inscriptions are very numerous. The Maître Autel is richly ornamented, and in each side stand two figures carved in stone, perfect specimens of sculpture.[18]

Although of the opinion that the interior of the church was, 'one of the prettiest in France', Edward Planta, writing in the 1820s, did not consider the ascent of the tower worth the effort:

> The traveller will.... lose his time if he be seduced by the rhetoric of his guide to ascend the tower of the church, to enjoy the superb prospect which will there be presented to his view. When he has painfully wound his way to the top, and given his franc to the specious orator, he will perceive nothing but a dreary expanse of country, relieved indeed by a sea view, yet infinitely inferior to that he has so lately admired in Dover.[19]

British visitors to Nôtre Dame tended to be more interested in the worshippers and the rites of the Catholic church than in the art, the architecture or the view from the tower. Eyre, who attended Mass on a Sunday in the summer of 1802, noted that the congregation was large and sat, 'not as with us in separate pews but upon chairs hired for the purpose,'[20] which James Albany described as, 'high backed with a flat top for the missal to rest upon for the use of which they pay 1 sou'.[21] Nor was there, since the Revolution, the class segregation in the seating of worshippers to which the British were accustomed; as Eyre put it, the seating was, 'without any formal distinction of rank'. He also took notice of the collection boxes *('troncs')* about the church, such as one beneath a wooden image of the virgin, *'pour l'establisse-ment de la chapelle de la Vierge'*, and observed that some had an English translation, not always accurate, as was the case with an appeal for the hospitalised poor: '*For the poor Hospita-bles'.*[22] Calton recorded that the organ had been built at Canterbury, 'probably a century and a half ago', that it had a deep and mellow tone and was 'highly ornamented by figures in relief'.[23]

As for the congregation, Albany found it to be almost entirely female and, 'of the middle and lower classes'; the latter, attired in their dark hooded cloaks which, with their white, uncovered caps, produced, 'a striking effect'.[24]

Dorothy Wordsworth, although unmoved by the church and its rites, 'bad pictures and tawdry images... vocal service... utterly contemptible,' was, typically, interested in and sympathetic towards the worshippers. Visiting the church in mid-week she found,

Old men and women - *young* women and girls kneeling at their silent prayers, and some we espied, in obscure recesses, before a concealed crucifix, image or altar. One grey-haired man I cannot forget, whose countenance bore the impress of wordly cares subdued, and peace in heavenly aspirations.[25]

With the exception of some, 'pleasing chaunting', Dorothy was not impressed by the service, although, despite being, 'gabbled over', all appeared to join in. Her attention was especially drawn to, 'a squalid, ragged woman'.

She sate alone upon some steps at the side of the entrance to the quire: there she sat with a white dog beside her; no one was near, and the dog and she evidently belonged to each other, probably her *only* friend, for never was there a more wretchedly forlorn and miserable-looking human-being: she did not notice us; but her rags, and her melancholy and sickly aspect drew a penny from me, and the change in the woman's skinny, doleful face is not to be imagined: it was brightened by a light and gracious smile… she bowed her body, waved her hand, and with a politeness of gesture unknown in England in any station of life, beckoned that we might enter the church….[26]

Earlier travellers, prior to the Revolution, had often visited the town's monasteries and convents. To the latter, in particular, English Catholic families would sometimes send their daughters. Thus when, in 1775, Mrs Thrale was in Calais with her husband and Dr Johnson, she was taken to the Convent of the Dominican nuns.

Where I chatted at the Grate with a most agreeable English Lady who said she had been immured there for 20 years; she was of course not young, but an elegant Figure & entirely the Manners & Look of a Woman of high Fashion. She asked me about Diversions we had in London now, as she was an English woman and we chatted about Mr Foote & his Controversy with the Duchess of Kingston. She was the Superior of her Convent, & related to Lady Pennyman – her name is Gray.[27]

The party also visited the Capuchin convent to which they were invited by a friar, Father Felix, who, in the manner of Sterne's Monk, had visited them at Dessein's begging for alms. There they were, 'entertained with a Sight of his Convent, Cells, Chapel and Refectory'. The library was locked for which Hester Thrale was, 'not sorry, for Mr Johnson would never have come out of it'.[28] That night, the eve of his sixty-sixth birthday, a prayer printed in his posthumous *Prayers and Meditations* and, 'Composed at Calais in a sleepless night and used before dawn at Notre Dame', suggests that the Doctor was more inspired by his visit to the Convent than seduced by the comforts of the hotel.[29] Sadly, when, nine years later, Hester – by then Mrs Piozzi – again went to see, 'my old Acquaintance the Dominican Nun… she had forgot me'.[30]

During the Revolutionary years the nationalisation and

selling off of Church property meant the end for many of these communities. Dawson Warren, the chaplain attached to the British peace mission in 1802 observed a loss which Dr Johnson would also have regretted:

> Alas poor Sterne! Hadst thou lived to revisit Calais in its present state how would thy feelings have been lacerated on beholding the spot where once stood the Monastery of the Capuchins converted into the gardens of a griping usurer. The spirit of thy gentle friend the monk would have risen to pour his complaints into thy bosom, and to mourn with thee the effects of revolutionary madness. Pigaud bought the site and ruins of the Monastery and has converted them into a very pretty-looking residence.[31]

He makes no reference to the similar confiscations of Church property which had taken place in Britain more than 260 years before, or to those members of the British upper classes whose address was the 'Abbey', 'Priory' or 'Grange'.

The other prominent buildings, as viewed from the packet coming from Dover, were the Tour de Guet and the Hôtel de Ville, both on the southern side of the central Place d'Armes – the market square. The Tour, or watch-tower, had stood since at least the time of the English occupation and, since 1658, when it had been rebuilt following a fire, it had served as a lighthouse. In 1818 six parabolic reflectors and a revolving light had been installed which for thirty years provided mariners with a guide to the harbour entrance until replaced in 1848 by a new, higher lighthouse on the ramparts of Courgain.

Immediately to the west of the watch-tower and between the Place d'Armes and the Rue des Boucheries was the Hôtel de Ville, another building which dated back to the period of English occupation but which had been substantially reconstructed in 1740 when a balcony supported by pillars had been added to the front facing the Place. British opinion of it varied but John Ruskin, certainly the most authoritative architectural critic of his day, was in no doubt, expressing his, 'preference for the Hôtel de Ville at Calais to the Alcazar at Seville'.[32] For him, its chief charm was, 'in being seen from my bedroom window at Dessein's, and putting me to sleep with its chimes'. Sterne's biographer, Percy Fitzgerald was similarly entranced by the music from the belfry:

Not long since, arriving at the old town at mid-night, I walked up along the piers towards the town. Passing through the dark streets, I emerged in the Place, and at that moment the silvery chimes began performing in the picturesque steeple of the Town Hall.[33]

An earlier writer was less enchanted both by 'the principal public edifice of Calais' and by the bells:

The uniformity of the 'Place' is broken (not very agreeably) by... the town hall; a half modern, half antique building which occupies about a third of the south side, and is surmounted at one end by a light spiring belfry, containing a most loquacious ring of bells, which take up a somewhat unreasonable proportion of every quarter of a hour in announcing its arrival; and, in addition, every three hours play "Le petit chaperon rouge" for a longer period than (I should imagine) even French patience and leisure can afford to listen to it.[34]

Ten years later, according to a writer in *Blackwood's Magazine* the tune, which prevented him from getting to sleep, had changed to *'Depuis longtemps j'aimais Annette'*.[35]

As for the belfry iteself, Calton described it as:

...bivaulted by a crypt of exquisite workmanship and proportions... miraculously unmutilated... surmounted by a trebly coroneted turret in open work, surrounded by numerous pinnacles of sharp and curious device, singularly quaint and attractive in its appearance... The several faces of the tower... relieved by numerous rosettes and escutcheons in Caen stone, now mellowed and fretted by the lapse of more than six hundred years.[36]

When Eyre had visited the Town Hall in 1802, although he found the exterior 'noble', thought the interior did not, 'repay the labour of ascending the dirty steps' except for that, 'it was the very spot on which Eustache de St Pierre offered himself as a voluntary sacrifice to avert the threatened destruction of the town, and of his suffering compeers'.[37] A reference to the heroic leader of the burghers of Calais who saved their town from devastation at the hands of the English in 1347.

With the Restoration of the monarchy some further alterations were made so that when Edward Planta was in Calais in 1828 he found, in front of the building busts, of Eustache de St Pierre, the Duc de Guise and that of Cardinal Richelieu which, during the Revolution, had been removed from the Citadel. Inside he found that it,

...contained busts of Charles X and Louis XVIII, as well as a portrait of the latter. Here also was preserved the balloon and car with which M. Blanchard and Dr Jefferies crossed the Channel [in the first Channel crossing by balloon on 7 January 1785]; and over the stairs a portrait of Pierre de Belloy, who wrote the *Siege of Calais*.[38]

By this time the Passport Office had been relocated to what Dr Roberts refers to as, 'a noble room, elegantly papered with crimson paper covered with fleur de lis and imperial arms' whilst in one of the principal rooms he saw a 'fine painting' of, he believed, Louis XV.[39] With the 1740 restoration the upper part of the modern portion of the building had been devoted to what Calton describes as, 'a well-stored and easily accessible library of some 8,000 volumes'.[40]

The Place d'Armes itself tended to excite the interest and often the approval of British visitors. Although some English market squares, those of Norwich and Nottingham for example, are large and surrounded in part at least by imposing buildings, they are the exception. Those of the Continent are often more impressive and Calais was not unusual. An article which appeared in *The Mirror of Literature* in 1827 describes the Place as, 'an entirely open square of about 150 paces by 100', in which 'you can scarcely look upon a more lively and striking scene'.[41] The author perhaps gets a little carried away with himself in characterising the shops around the square as being, 'like nothing so much as so many scenes in a pantomime – so fancifully and variously are they filled, so brightly and fantastically painted'.[42] Furthermore, 'the general strangeness of the effect is completed by the excellence of the pavement, which is of stones like those of our best London carriage-ways, but as white as marble in all weathers, and as regular as the brick-work of a house front'. Writing at about the same time, James Albany described the houses about the Place as being, 'of light yellow brick' with french windows on every floor, the window frames being painted light green, giving, 'a gay appearance.' In contrast with the unflattering portraits often painted of the fish-women, Albany was much taken with the, 'open, sprightly and good humoured' market-women: 'never before did I see such an assemblage of handsome, plebian females'.[43]

Market days were on Wednesdays and Saturday, the latter tending to be especially busy. By the middle of the nineteenth century Calton was full of praise; the market stalls being, 'amply supplied with fish and butcher's meat, all of excellent quality... the delicious John Dory is met here in abundance and perfection.' Prices were, 'comparatively moderate', although 30% up on a decade before.[44]

What protestants from across the Channel tended to disapprove of was the purpose to which the Place was put on a Sunday. Even Charles Apperley, the sporting writer 'Nimrod' – more Regency roué than Victorian sabbatarian – although enjoying much about life in Calais, could not reconcile himself to the sight of a Sunday when,

> while Divine Service was actually in progress, you might see a mountebank in the Grande Place surrounded by a crowd of all descriptions; not only that, but every shop in Calais would be open as on a week-day, the tailors and shoemakers working as usual until it is time to dress and go to the skittle-ground, the dance or the theatre.[45]

James Albany, having been to High Mass on a Sunday

morning in 1829, returned to the Market place where he witnessed the game of *Poule*, a primitive version of roulette, being played:

A round table is printed in compartments of different colours, in which compartments pieces of gingerbread are placed. The player touches an iron rod which immediately moves round the table several times. If it stops opposite to the *locale* of one of these depots of gingerbread, the player wins. This, of course, seldom happens.[46]

Since its construction in 1822, Anglican worshippers wishing to occupy their Sunday in a more traditionally British way, could have made their way to the Chapel of St George in the Rue des Prêtres.

For those who sought blameless exercise a number of possibilities presented themselves. Since they had first been made accessible in 1792, the town's ramparts had been planted with trees affording, 'most pleasing and refreshing walks', known as the Esplanade and the Cours Berthois. As he walked about the walls in 1829, the observant Albany was struck by two notices: one advertising a *Pensionnat* or 'Academy for Young Gentlemen' kept by M. Wille in the Rue des Prêtres; the other in a café, temporarily closed for refurbishment, but with a pretty garden where, 'On trouve tous les jours des Glaces depuis trois heures'.[47]

The most popular place for a walk was undoubtedly the Pier which, in 1822 was extended to a length of 900m. An article in the magazine *The Mirror of Literature* compared it favourably to that high point of British civil engineering Waterloo Bridge which had been opened in 1818.

...the pier is a most striking object, especially at high water, when it runs out, in a straight line, for nearly three quarters of a mile into the open sea. It is true that English engineers – who ruin hundreds of their fellow citizens by spending millions upon a bridge that nobody will take the trouble to pass over, and cutting tunnels under rivers only to let the water into them when they have got all the money they can by the job – would treat this pier with infinite contempt as a thing that merely answers all the purposes for which it was erected!   as if *that* were merit of any but the very lowest degree. "Look at Waterloo Bridge!" they say; "we flatter ourselves *that* was not a thing built (like the pier at Calais) merely for use. Nobody will say that any such thing was wanted! But what a noble monument of British art, and what a fine commemoration of the greatest of modern victories!" True: but it would have been all this if it had been built on Salisbury Plain; and in that case it would have only cost half the money. The pier of Calais is, in fact, every thing that it need be, and what perhaps no other pier is; and yet it is nothing more than a piece of serviceable carpentry, that must have cost about as much, perhaps, as to print the prospectuses of some of the late undertakings, and pay the advertisements and the lawyer's bill.[48]

This rather improbable comparison perhaps came into the author's head when he considered the popularity of Calais Pier on the one hand and the way in which the first Waterloo Bridge, which required the payment of a toll, was very largely ignored by the London public, on the other.

Ruskin, as we have seen, likewise applauded, 'the real power and service in the half mile of pier.'[49] (few English Writers agree as to its length) but the fullest tribute perhaps belongs to Robert Bell Calton:

This unrivalled jetty – a work of much credit to French engineering – extends fully a mile into the sea, and is ever a refreshing, health-inspiring promenade for Calaisians.

Planked with an elastic flooring, perfectly clean in all weathers, and of ready access from the town, this breezy, pleasant resort is alone a vast recommendation of the place; and, to our own fancy, not being able to unite the twain, would not be compensated for through the exchange of the most picturesque bit of inland scenery.

The rolling tide, ever at the extreme end of the pier, green and clear as liquid emerald, crashes and surges, or washes softly through the well-secured beams and timbers of the jetty, as you tread high above the deep water, and inhale the breath of the ocean.[50]

He goes on to paint a seascape which is a kind of prose version of Masefield's *Cargoes*:

A fleet of fishermen are spreading their lug-sails to the summer's gale. The French mail, the *"Faun,"* the *"Biche,"* or the *"Daim,"* are in the offing, and may momentarily be expected with their living freight of tourists at the quayside. The *"Queen of the Belgians,"* the *"Princess Maude,"* or *"Lord Warden,"* are hoisting their ensigns and ringing their bells for departure.

The magnificent cutters, the *"Talisman,"* and *"Stormfinch,"* of the Royal Yacht squadron, with over a thousand yards of canvas in their main-sails, are beating into the harbour.

A Swede and a Norwegian are furling their topsails and lessening their way, as they surge past you to the port.

The blocks rattle in the rigging, and the pauls of the capstan click in lively accompaniment to the hearty voice of the crew.

There is every variety by the sea-side, which your glen or mountain, pasture or silent lake – all lovely as they are – do not possess, and in few spots do the scenes shift more rapidly than on the splendid pier of Calais.[51]

Calais pier was also a favourite subject of British artists and the greatest of these at this, or probably any other, period was J.M.W. Turner. His first trip to the Continent was made during the Amiens Peace in 1802, the year in which he was elected to the Royal Academy where his *Calais Pier* was exhibited the following year. Threatening storm clouds dominate the sky and through them a shaft of sunlight illuminates the sail of a packet from which, in rough seas, passengers are being landed by rowing boat. It almost certainly resembled a scene he himself had experienced: on a sketch for the picture he noted that he was, 'nearly swampt'.[52] Although most of his contemporaries criticized what they believed to be the 'unfinished ' nature of the fore-ground, Henry Fuseli, in comparing the work to that of the Dutch marine artist Willem van de Velde, suggested that, 'although inferior to it in execution' Turner's had, 'more comprehension'.[53] Today it is recognised as one of the greatest of the artist's fine Calais works.

Throughout the 1820s promenaders on the pier would have passed the column erected to mark the place where on 26 April 1814 the restored monarch Louis XVIII, after 22 years in exile in England, once more stepped onto French soil. Of that occasion the correspondent of the London newspaper the *Courier* reported that in the evening, whilst Louis dined at Dessein's:

the town was illuminated……..and though I have seen the illuminations of London, I could still behold with pleasure the illuminations on the grand square, and the Rue Royale which only a few hours before bore the name of Rue Impériale.[54]

The commemorative column carried the words:

LE 24 AVRIL 1814,
S.M. LOUIS XVIII
DÉBARQUA VIS-À-VIS DE CETTE COLONNE,
ET FUT ENFIN RENDUE
A L'AMOUR DES FRANÇAIS.
POUR EN PERPETUER LE SOUVENIR,
LA VILLE DE CALAIS
A ÉLEVÉ CE MONUMENT.[55]

A bronze plaque marked the place where the King had first stepped ashore, as recorded by Tom Moore's Biddy Fudge:

By the by, though, at Calais, Papa had a touch
Of romance on the pier, which affected me much.
At the sight of that spot where our darling DIX-HUIT
Set the first of his own dear legitimate feet; [56]

With the Revolution of 1830 the inscription on the column, together with most other symbols of the Bourbon monarchy, was removed and a tale told by Francis Hervé reflects the change of mood:

Another souvenir also must not be forgotten, namely the print of the foot of Louis XVIII, which is cut in the stone, and a piece of brass let in where he first stepped on shore, and undoubtedly represents a very pretty foot; but when a Frenchman who was no *amateur* of the Bourbon dynasty was asked to admire its symmetry, he observed it was very well but that it would look much better if it was turned t'other way, that is to say, going out of the kingdom instead of coming into it.[57]

Away from the Place d'Armes and the Rue Royale, which had been so gloriously illuminated when Louis had first arrived, many of the streets were less imposing. When in 1802 the Wordsworths took an apartment 'Chez Madame Avril' in the Rue de la Tête d'Or, running from the north-eastern corner of the Place down towards the harbour, they had, 'tolerably decent-sized rooms, but badly furnished and with large store of bad smells and dirt in the yard, and all about'.[58] Half a century later, Calton, who shared with Dorothy Wordsworth the view that there was much to interest the inquiring stranger, was obliged to admit that the apartments themselves were, 'far from good'. In particular he found the staircases treacherous, 'unusually, dark narrow and execrable'. He probably had in mind his friend Jemmy Urquhart who,

lived in alternate perplexity and luxury, as his pension arrived and disappeared: and died from the effects of a fall down his execrable *escalier*, in the Rue des Marechaux in the 73rd year of his age.[59]

The streets themselves provided a range of diversions. The Wordsworths were amused by the two ladies who lived opposite them in the Rue de la Tête d'Or who, 'seemed neither to have work nor books, but were mostly at the window'. Street entertainment might be spontaneous and informal as when Samuel Rogers wrote to his sister of 'six little children, not bigger than Sutton [his nephew], or very little bigger... dancing together a *cotillon* in the street just now, the boys with *long tails*, to a passing tambourine'[60]; or the great religious festivals such as that seen by William Harris in June 1821:

We have just witnessed the procession of the Fête de Dieu [Corpus Christi]. The streets are hung with... carpets and white linen. The pavements thrown with rushes and a few flowers – white flags are suspended from the windows which are filled with well-dressed women. A company of 'Pompiers' or Fire men who wear military costume precede the procession with a band which is followed by priests with a portable canopy… and an amazing number of girls dressed in white. The priests halt at intervals and chaunt opposite temporary altars decked out with pictures, flowers and a great deal of finery. At our Hotel they had a superb one.[61]

Less pleasing, at least to the English ear, were the street cries of the fish-women. Several writers comment upon them, few with greater horror than Calton.

The cry of the women when hawking their fish and shrimps beneath your window, is peculiarly frightful; it unites the several notes of screech and wail, and is quite as distracting to the ear as the sharpening of a saw, or the grinding of a hurdy-gurdy.[62]

Of the many Englishmen and women who visited and wrote of Calais during these hundred years none appear to have treated it with such minute attention as James Albany who showed a genuine fascination for the place so that he was able to conclude his remarks on it by expressing the belief that, 'there is no want of *matériel* in the town and its vicinity to make a *séjour* of a few weeks or even months sufficiently agreeable'.[63] This contrasts markedly with the author of *Murray's Handbook* who, being of the opinion that Calais had, 'little remarkable to show', recommended the traveller to, 'quit it as soon as he has cleared his baggage from the custom-house, and procured the signature of the police to his passport'.[64] Albany was a more relaxed traveller for whom enjoyment was by no means confined to Old Masters and Exclusive Company. After the table d'hôte at Dessein's, he and his *compagnon de voyage* would stroll the streets, visit the shops, have a game of billiards, and take a drink. For these purposes he found much that could be recommended. Nor did he adopt the superior attitude to shopkeepers and other tradesmen assumed by many of his fellow countrymen. Thus he shows a great admiration both for M. Pierre-Antoine Leleux – 'a very civil, intelligent man and a decided Libéral' – and for his book-shop in the Rue Royale with its attached reading-room in which English and French newspapers could be found. Leleux was also the editor of an English language newspaper, *The Pas de Calais*, published twice a week and sent free of postage to all parts of France for twenty francs per quarter.[65]

Albany similarly recommended the 'neat' barber's shop of Charles Follet in the Rue Notre-Dame, decorated with 'well-engraved' portraits of the young Napoleon, Prince Eugène Beauharnais, Count Bertrand and others, thus displaying Follet's Bonapartist sympathies, in defiance of the Royalist secret police in a way which the Englishman appeared to admire. When being shaved, the *perruquier* 'placed a blue china basin under my chin. He lathered my face *with his hands*' and, as he did so, assured his victim that during the Reign of Terror, 'not one person had been guillotined at Calais'.[66]

Albany was also partial to both the bars and their *habitués*:

The Cafés are very numerous and all brilliantly lighted up at night. Each of them contains a billiard-table, the charge for playing at which is in general not more than 2 sous (one penny) per game. In these Cafés eau de vie, liqueurs and coffee are served at a bar similar to those in London spirit shops. The *Café Le Grand* is the choicest, and the company who resort to it most select.[67]

Which did not deter him from visiting the *Café Giuliani*, in the Rue Royale, in which,

The panels of the room are painted so as to represent architectural and rural scenery, which are well executed and very pretty. Benches are placed on each side, on which were seated three or four mechanics, wearing on their heads white cotton caps with the ends hanging down. They were quite silent, and perfectly behaved whilst we played billiards. How different it would have been in an English tap-room![68]

Calais had one further feature which has left an indelible mark in English art and letters – the Sands. They stretched, backed by a line of dunes, from Fort Risban some 8 kms to Cap Blanc Nez and included what later became known, in recognition of Louis Blériot's first cross-Channel flight of 1909, as Blériot-Plage. The summer of 1802 saw the arrival in Calais of two of Britain's great creative geniuses - William Wordsworth, visiting the continent for a third time, and J.M.W. Turner, making his first trip across the Channel. Both left evidence of having walked upon the Sands.

Wordsworth was in Calais, together with his sister Dorothy, to meet his nine year-old daughter Caroline (for the first time) and her mother Annette Vallon. They probably made their way out through the Porte du Havre and across the wooden Long Pont and out onto the Sands. Dorothy records that,

The Weather was very hot. We walked by the sea-shore almost every evening with Annette and Caroline, or Wm and I alone. I had a bad cold, and could not bathe at first, but William did. It was a pretty sight to see, as we walked upon the sands when the tide was low, perhaps a hundred prople bathing at a quarter of a mile distant from us and we had delightful walks after the heat of the day was passed away – seeing far off in the west the coast of England like a cloud crested with Dover castle, which was like the summit of the cloud – the evening star and the glory of the sky.[69]

In a sonnet *'Composed by the Sea-side, near Calais. August 1802'*, William expressed the same thought but with a patriotic twist:

Fair Star of Evening, Splendour of the West,
Star of my country! - on the horizon's brink
Thou hangest, stooping, as might seem, to sink
On England's bosom; yet well pleased to rest,
Meanwhile, and be to her a glorious crest
Conspicuous to the Nations. Thou, I think,
Should'st be my Country's emblem; and should'st wink,
Bright Star! with laughter on her banners, drest
In thy fresh beauty. There! that dusky spot
Beneath thee, it is England; there it lies.
Blessings be on you both! one hope, one lot,

One life, one glory! I with many a fear
For my dear Country, many heartfelt sighs,
Among men who do not love her, linger here.[70]

Dorothy went on to describe, 'The reflections in the water…more beautiful than the sky itself, purple waves brighter than precious stones, for ever melting away upon the sands' and the Fort Rouge:

The fort, a wooden building at the entrance of the harbour at Calais, when the evening twilight was coming on, and we could not see anything of the building but its shape, which was far more distinct than in perfect daylight [which] seemed to be reared upon pillars of ebony, between which pillars the sea was seen in the most beautiful colours that can be conceived. Nothing in romance was ever half so beautiful.[71]

Wordsworth, who had greeted the French Revolution with enthusiasm – 'Oh! pleasant exercise of hope and joy!'[72] – was by now disillusioned; the greeting *'Bonjour, Citoyen'* ringing hollow in his ears, he now looks back across the Channel for hope. By contrast, the radical essayist Wiliam Hazlitt, setting foot on, 'the laughing shores of France' for the first time in the same year, was delighted with Calais and listening to, 'a mariners' hymn sung from the top of an old crazy vessel in the harbour', felt he was, 'breathing the air of humanity in general'.[73]

In another sonnet, written at the same time, William wrote specifically of Caroline:

It is a beauteous evening, calm and free,
The holy time is quiet as a Nun
Breathless with adoration, the broad sun
Is sinking down in its tranquillity,
The gentleness of heaven broods o'er the Sea.
Listen! the mighty Being is awake,
And doth with his eternal motion make
A sound like thunder - everlastingly.
Dear Child! dear Girl! that walkest with me here,
If thou appear untouched by solemn thought,

Thy nature is not therefore less divine:
Thou liest in Abraham's bosom all the year,
And worship'st at the Temple's inner shrine,
God being with thee when we know it not.[74]

As we have seen, it is anything but, 'beauteous evening, calm and free' that is depicted in Turner's 1803 painting *'Calais Pier'* but a later (1830) work, perhaps based on earlier drawings, shows Calais Sands at low water with girls, their skirts tucked up above the knee, gathering bait at sunset. Ruskin thought he must have made the drawings for Calais Pier and had then,

been home to Dessein's, and dined, and went out again in the evening to walk upon the sands, the tide being down. He had never seen such a waste of sand before, and it made an impression on him… the storm had lulled a little and there was a sunset – such a sunset – and the bars of Fort Rouge seen against it, skeleton-wise. He did not paint that directly; thought over it – painted it a long while afterwards.[75]

Fort Rouge, on its 'ebony legs' is much as Dorothy described it. It may have been some of the same girls who a year or two before had come, 'scampering… with mouthful importunity' towards Albany and his friend, 'their shrill voices shouting, *'Des sous, Messieurs, donnez-nous des sous!'*[76]

Almost fifty years after Wordsworth had walked on Calais sands with his young daughter another English poet strode across them imagining that,

A thousand knights have reined their steeds
To watch this line of sand-hills run
Along the never silent Strait
To Calais glittering in the sun;[77]

In *'Calais Sands'* Matthew Arnold describes scanning the horizon in the hope of seeing the steam packet on which his sweetheart, Frances Lucy Wightman, is being carried across the Straits of Dover.[78] The young lady was travelling with her father, Sir William, who, as Arnold had no secure income, had forbidden him to court his daughter but the love-lorn poet hoped at least to catch sight of her and, eventually:

> Thou comest! Yes! The vessel's cloud
> Hangs dark upon the rolling sea.
> Oh, that yon sea-birds wings were mine,
> To win one instant's glimpse of thee![79]

Happily, the following year Arnold secured a post as Inspector of Schools and he and Frances Lucy were able to marry so that when they next travelled to the Continent they did so as man and wife.

*   *   *

In addition to the recreation afforded to travellers by walking about the ramparts, on the pier and over the sands or, like Albany, drinking and playing billiards, another, more sophisticated type of entertainment was also available in Calais. It was an initiative of Pierre Dessein.

8

Un Pièce au Théâtre

It seems very likely that it was the success generated by the popularity of Sterne's novel that persuaded Dessein to add to the attractions of his establishment by building a theatre. What is certain is that in 1772 he proposed to the town council the building of '*une salle de spectacles*' at the end of the hotel garden, in return demanding – and receiving – privileged access to performances. By the following summer the theatre had already been added to the hotel's attractions. According to James Essex,

> ...here is a fine garden neatly kept up and a handsom Theater where Travellers who lodge in the hotel may find entertainment while detained by contrary winds without going out for it.[1]

Whether Essex actually attended the theatre is not clear for the official opening did not take place until 6 January 1774 with the performance of Philippe Destouche's comedy *Le Philosophe marié* and a comic-opera, *Le Cadi dupé*, with music by the locally-born composer Pierre Alexandre Monsigny.[2]

In Thomas Holcroft's novel, *Anna St. Ives*, set just a couple of years after Essex's visit, Anna, on arriving from England and writing to her friend Louisa Clifton, has a more jaundiced view:

> We had determined to go to Dessein's... I am amused with the handbill, stuck up against the walls of this inn, or hotel as it is called; announcing it to be the largest, completest, the most magnificent, with a thousand et ceteras, in the universe; and recounting not only its numerous accommodations, but the multifarious trades which it contained within its own walls; to

which was added a playhouse. A playhouse, it is true, there was, but no players; and, as for trades, there was at least as many as wanted.[3]

More fortunate than the fictitious Anna was the small but by no means imaginary figure of Edward Gibbon. On 7 May 1777, a year after the publication and sensational success of the first volume of *The Decline and Fall of the Roman Empire* he was in Calais en route for Paris, there to enjoy what Peter Quennell calls 'the first fruits of celebrity'.[4] He wrote to his friend John Baker Holroyd (later Lord Sheffield) describing:

A pleasant passage, an excellent house, a good dinner with Lord Coleraine, whom I found here. Easy custom-house officers, fine weather &c. I am detained tonight by the temptation of a French comedy, in a theatre at the end of Dessein's garden; but shall be in motion tomorrow early and hope to dine at Paris Saturday.[5]

An anonymous tourist, passing through Calais late in 1801 describes the hotel ('extremely well-kept by Citizens Quillacq and Duplessis') as follows:

It is an extensive suite of buildings, forming two neat squares, of which the one serves as an entrance to the other. Both are lined with vines pinned against the walls, and the inner one where we lodge includes a very nice garden. One side of this square consists of a theatre, billiard rooms and other places of amusement. All these are well-frequented especially on Sundays.[6]

Although English guests often visited the theatre, it also appears to have been popular with the Calaisiens and an entertaining account of local goings-on at the theatre early in the Revolutionary era comes from the playwright Frederick Reynolds who, together with the actress Becky Wells, visited it in March 1792:

The pieces were Nicodème en lune, an amusing satire on aerostation,[7] and an entertainment never before performed,

ill:5

Madame Saqui performing at Vauxhall, 1820.

founded on a local event of a melancholy nature, which had occurred a few weeks before. A French sailor in gallantly attempting to save from ship-wreck the lives of several other sailors off the Calais coast, lost his own life and his death, being witnessed by his intending bride, (the daughter of a respectable farmer in the neighbourhood) the circumstances made so much noise the manager employed an agent to dramatise it.

Expectations being thus excited the house was crowded, and the curtain to the new piece having risen, the heroine entered to slow music; when, to my astonishment, instead of creating interest, she caused a riot, and from every part of the theatre suddenly arose the cry of 'Directeur, directeur!' This gentleman soon appeared, and apparently in considerable alarm, humbly stated his anxiety to know the cause of their exclamation. Owing, however, to the number and vehemence of the furious orators, who all at once answered this interrogatory, the manager could not for a considerable time understand the subject of the *'tintamarre infernal'*. But when he did he shrugged up his shoulders, exclaiming with a look of horror, as he hastily quitted the stage – *'C'est impossible!'*

As may be supposed my horror was even greater than the manger's when I also understood from an Englishman near me that the revolutionary cannibals, not content with seeing the heroine of the piece represented by the first serious actress in the theatre, actually insisted that the part should be performed by the bride herself! The idea that the poor farmer's daughter, in a state of affliction bordering on despair, should be dragged from her retirement on to the public stage, there to outrage the dearest feelings of her soul, by mimicking her own sorrow, was to me so repellent that at first I could scarcely believe that a desire to execute it was entertained even by these sons of liberty and anarchy. I was soon, however, undeceived; for the riot increasing to a most alarming height, the manager, having no other resource left, was compelled to send for the officers of the municipality. A party of them soon arrived, and the chief (a person, apparently, of at least eighty years of age and decorated with all the insignia of office) taking his seat in the front row of the box next to me, and impatiently demanding silence, half the pit rushed towards him, to the great detriment of the persons and clothes of the more peaceable part, to explain and complain of the arbitrary conduct of the aristocratical manager.

The old gentleman shook his head, and persisting in

preserving the peace, proceeded to harangue them; when they immediately interrupted him a most animated discussion ensued. During a full quarter of an hour I could catch nothing but the words, *'Liberté - égalité – la voix du people – à bas les tyrans – vive la nation – vive la loi – vive les magistrats.'* Suddenly the whole theatre resounded with acclamation and the chief officer, advancing his tremulous hands over the box, the mob in the pit seized them, and gently lowering him they conducted him to the centre of the pit; where, forming a circle they all danced around him, shouting the chorus, while the enthusiastic octogenarian as fantastically danced and wildly joined the revolutionary song of *Ca ira, ça ira.*[8]

On this most unforeseen termination of the affair, the manager had no alternative but to make a second appearance on the stage and, after a most ample apology, with a promise of 'better things' for the future, he most humbly requested them again to receive their money. This petition was granted without much entreaty, with infinite condescension, and there the matter terminated: neither the bride, nor the bride's representative, being ever afterwards troubled on this strange occasion.[9]

When J.G. Lemaistre published his *Travels after the Peace of Amiens, through Parts of France, Switzerland, Italy and Germany* in 1806 he was treated pretty roughly – 'savaged' would not be too strong a word – by the reviewer of that book for The Edinburgh Review:

Mr Lemaistre seems, as far as we can discern, to be of the great multitude of English idlers whom every suspension of hostilities pass over the face of the Channel, and who fortunately return, for the most part with as little inclination as talent, to become writers of travel.[10]

Lemaistre had, in fact, been one of the first English travellers to take advantage of the thaw in Anglo-French relationships and had arrived 'at the celebrated hotel formerly kept by Dessein who is now succeeded by his nephew Quillacq', in November 1801. Despite the fact that he carried with him, 'a passport from M. Talleyrand', he was obliged to stay overnight to exchange it for one endorsed by the Mayor of Calais:

I accordingly passed Tuesday in the town, which gave me an opportunity of visiting the theatre, which is still at Dessein's. To the best of my recollection there is no alteration in the building since the war; and from the darkness of the house I am inclined to think that even the painting has not been changed. The actors are not very good, yet better than the generality of our country performers in England. The house was full, and the company well dressed. In short, this amusement may be considered a very pleasant resource for travellers detained at Calais either by contrary winds or by a delay in the delivery of passports.[11]

Although similarly unimpressed by the condition of the theatre when he visited in August 1802 the banker Sir John Dean Paul had a more agreeable experience than Reynolds:

The theatre is not very clean, I imagine that it has not been touched since the Revolution: during the war the house ceased in effect to be an inn and was transformed into a house of commerce, just a depot for all kinds of merchandise. That at least is what we are told; but I have difficulty in imagining what kinds of merchandise were available at Calais during the war. In the theatre we experienced an example of good manners the like of which, I confess, we are unaccustomed in England. At our entrance, two gentlemen, sitting in a box, seeing that we were in the company of two ladies and that we didn't have seats, left the box and insisted that we took their places. This they did so naturally and were so insistent that it was impossible to refuse. This contrasted so strikingly with what so often happens in similar cases at home that we were given a most favourable impression of French manners.[12]

Despite the grubby nature of the theatre, a feature commented upon by a number of English visitors at this time, Sir John appears to have been well entertained, '...we made our way thence to the theatre and we there had much to amuse us. The performance consisted of a short comic opera and was entirely pleasant; the actors were tolerable and one in particular who was already of a certain age reminded me of our favourite Parsons'.[13]

A similar judgement was pronounced by Edmund John Eyre (like Reynolds, a playwright):

Having taken an admirable cup of coffee [at the *Lion d'Argent*] and ordered our supper, we went to the Play-house, where we were rationally entertained with a musical after-piece. The theatre is not very clean, and badly lighted; the performances, however, were above mediocrity, and gave us a favourable specimen of the French stage – Thirty sous, or fifteen pence English, gained us admittance into the boxes.[14]

Although Dessein's does appear to have acted as a kind of warehouse for some of the time during the war – no doubt to compensate for the lack of visitors from across the Channel – it seems that it continued to operate as an inn at least during the summer half of the year. Henry Swinburne, who travelled to Paris in November 1796 to negotiate an exchange of prisoners, says that it was then closed but that it would re-open in the spring.[15] The theatre, however, appears to have remained open and Swinburne describes it as follows:

…we go there every evening, it providing us with an agreeable distraction, the show rarely finishing later than 8 or 9 o'clock. The auditorium is pleasant and, although not of great size suffices for a fairly numerous public. It is situated behind the well-known hotel of M. Dessin….

The actors are better than mediocre and the price of admission is reasonable, the best places in the boxes not exceeding 25 sous. Some families subscribe and have a box for the season at a slightly greater price; having been presented to several of them we were assured of good company. The military are regular frequenters and tend to occupy the higher part of the pit.[16]

The month after Paul's visit another banker, the poet Samuel Rogers, arrived and wrote to his sister Maria Sharpe describing a visit (after a 'grand entertainment of soup, cutlets, fish, fowl and partridges') to 'the Comedie':

The Municipalité sat under a very handsome canopy in a kind of state box. The drop-scene between the acts was inscribed with the names of Eustache, St. Pierre &c., the six heroes of Calais when besieged by Edward III; and the orchestra consisted of above twenty performers, as close as they could sit, who, together with the actors, made as much noise as they could. The acting was far from bad …In a very handsome retiring room they served you with raspberry vinegar and other refreshments.[17]

The same drop-scene was also commented upon by the anonymous contributor to the *Scots Magazine* who had referred to the popularity of the theatre on Sundays – a scandal to Presbyterian Scotsmen – mentioning a fellow-traveller, 'Poor Edward', who 'was very much shocked when… urged to spend last Sunday evening *à la comédie*':

Yet he went notwithstanding – and he reconciled his conscience to it by this argument, that he could receive no harm from being present at the entertainment, as he could not understand a word that was said.[18]

Interestingly, whilst many English travellers visited the theatre commenting upon the building and the audience, very few refer to the plays themselves suggesting perhaps that Edward's ignorance was not uncommon.

Like Sir John Dean Paul, this Scots traveller did not find the theatre as clean as he would have wished and was unimpressed by the scenery but in other respects found the experience an improvement on the English custom:

The theatre is of wonderful size for the extent of the town, and is always full on Sundays. It is dark and dirty and the scenery is very indifferent. The drop scene represents a monument to the six heroes of Calais – alluding to the celebrated Eustace de St. Pierre and his five friends who nobly devoted themselves for their native city at the end of its memorable siege by Edward III of England. The actors seem to perform their parts with less restraint than you observe at the provincial towns of England. The prompter thrusts up her head through an aperture in the front of the stage, among the lamps, and is concealed from the view of the audience by a screen of wood, in form of a batchellor's oven, or plate warmer. Though this screen is rather an eye-sore to an Englishman, I am not sure but that, on the whole, the French plan is better than our custom of placing the prompter behind the scenes. In France the actors can apply for assistance without quitting their natural station and without their application being observed by the house – but when an English actor is at a loss, he runs to the side of the stage, turning his back perhaps on the person he ought to address while the assistant has to repeat his part before him so loud as to be heard by the whole of the audience. It is as well for the actors that the house is so fully attended, otherwise from the price of admission they would come badly off. You can get into paradise, the lowest place for 35 centimes = three pence halfpenny! A ticket to place distinguee or stage box, which is the dearest cost only three franks = two and sixpence.

An anonymous 'Young Gentleman' who visited the theatre in the following year was provided with two very different kinds of entertainment on succeeding nights and suggests that the price of admission was greater than might be expected:

There was a ball in the [theatre] in the first evening of my arrival, and it was so crowded with fashionable people and charming girls, half English, half French, promiscuously dancing the walse, that whilst I was on the brink of leaving France in despair, I was reconciled to it on this agreeable occasion... The entertainment of the second night were a dramatic piece, prettily acted, and, after that, a display of Mons. Val's ingenious tricks; such as stopping the repeating of a watch, taking away and restoring the life of a bird, and passing a small ring over the much larger circular end of a key. The expense of admission to all these continental theatres is on the same scale as at Paris.[19]

It seems likely that this performance took place early in 1803, prior to the breakdown of the Treaty of Amiens, for by the spring of that year Val was in London performing at Willis's Rooms which, according to a newspaper of the time 'are metamorphosed into the Temple of Fashion, as often as M. Val, surnamed the *Unique,* gives specimens of his most extraordinary art; nor is it surprising that they should become the favourite lounge of polite society, while this wonder-working man, like a magnet, attracts all to that centre.'[20] An appearance at the Calais theatre no doubt provided a suitable rehearsal venue for Continental performers travelling to England.

The anonymous author of, *A Tour in France, 1802,* has some further interesting details regarding the prompting arrangements, which involved a screened-off opening at front centre stage, the *trou du souffleur*:

> The prompter, who is a woman, rises from a trap-door in the centre of the stage, close to the edge, with a screen to hide her head from the audience, though she is very plainly seen from the stage boxes. I was extremely entertained with her industry and value of time, during the songs and recitatives: when her assistance was not wanting, the work of knitting was immediately taken up, and not an instant lost.[21]

The same author also provides information about the cost of attending the theatre – gallery 3d; pit 6d; boxes 1s 3d and two stage boxes ('generally filled with English') 2s 6d.[22] In the light of the fact that, 'when we were there there was not above an hundred persons', in the audience, in a theatre which could accommodate four or five hundred, he could not believe that the box office would pay the expenses.

As we have seen, Frederick Reynolds tells of a riot in the theatre occasioned by an actress playing the part of a local girl; the rioters preferring to see the grief-stricken young woman in person. Ninian Pinkney, the American minister in London, who visited both Dessein's ('which still retains both its reputation and its name') and the theatre after the treaty of Amiens had broken down and war resumed, tells a very different thespian tale. After dinner which, 'according to our orders was composed in the English style',[23] he went to the comedy:

> ...the theatre is within the circuit of the inn. The performers were not intolerable, and the piece, which was what they call a proverb (a fable constructed so as to give a ludicrous verification

or contradiction to an old saying), was amusing. I thought I had some obscure recollection of a face amongst the female performers, and I learned afterwards, that it was one of the maids of the inn; a lively brisk girl, and a volunteer, from her love of the drama. In this period of war between England and France, Calais has not the honour of a dramatic corps to herself, but occasionally participates in one belonging to the district.[24]

With the resumption of hostilities in 1803, theatres throughout France were forbidden to perform anything containing allusions complimentary to the enemy and orders were issued that, in towns such as Calais where troops were assembling for the projected invasion, plays should be, where possible, of an anti-English nature.[25]

Not, of course, that such prejudice was confined to the French side of the Channel. The London *Times* of 4 January had already contained an article complaining of, 'the political ill-consequences of the spread of the French language throughout Europe' and went on to suggest that:

Except as a *first step* and beginning of mischief, all apprehensions from the representation of a French Comedy are ridiculous. It is as the *mali labes,* the first spot and eruption, that we are induced to contend against anything so contemptible as the pic-nickery and nick-nackery – the pert affectation, and subaltern vanity of rehearsing to an audience that cannot understand, in a language one cannot pronounce![26]

With the temporary outbreak of Peace in 1814 there was a further rush to the Continent just as in 1802. One of the tourists was the Hon. Richard Boyle Bernard, MP for the Irish constituency of Bandon Bridge. Detained on his return to Dover by stormy weather, he visited the theatre and, '…was sorry to observe that a sentiment introduced into the performance expressive of satisfaction at the peace between France and England excited much disapprobation from the officers present.' [27] He went on to assert that,

The jealousy which prevails against the English in France is very striking, after the cordiality with which they are received in

Germany. It seems to be the Englishman's purse alone that commands a certain interested assiduity, which they take care shall be amply remunerated.'[28]

Presumably, he would not have been surprised to discover that the transports he had observed in the harbour at Dover on his outward voyage, 'bringing home a large portion of our cavalry', would soon be heading in the opposite direction.[29]

With the end of the Napoleonic Wars and the return of English tourists, a permanent company was re-established at Calais under the directorship of Monsieur Le Metheyer although from 1818 it seems to have been shared with the theatre at Arras.[30]

Whilst English writers often mention visiting the theatre, they rarely mention the titles of the plays they saw, tending to concentrate on those things – the condition of the house, the drop scene, the prompting arrangements – which do not require knowledge of the French language. Visitors to the town in the spring of 1817, however, would have had the rare treat of witnessing Napoleon's favourite tragic actor François-Joseph Talma performing in a number of pieces from the classical repertoire – *Andromaque*, *Hamlet*, *Manlius*, *Iphigénie en Tauride* and *Abufar*.[31] This last play was seen by the Revd Stephen Watson, when en route for the Simplon Pass:

At Calais I thought myself very fortunate since the first object I saw in Quillac's yard, announcing Talma's debut in *Abufar* which gave me the opportunity of walking, after dinner, quietly across the garden of my own hotel into the house, for five francs, to see the first actor of his line in France play a favourite part before true judges of his merit in his own country; when a short time before you were obliged to take pains to intrigue for tickets for a garbled evening of his abilities, for the most part mis-understood and untasted; this, you will say, applies to me, whether at a French play in London or at Calais; with this difference if you please, that if I did not admire French declamation so much as to scream with joy, yet I had the pleasure of seeing all around me in true raptures at the one theatre, and in false paroxysms of applause *à contre tems* at the other. You remember the story of Abufar, in which the dénouement is made by discovering that the sister he is in love with is not his sister. The company in the balcon and in the boxes was very brilliant; Madame Georges, though not on the stage, contributed something to the splendour of the house, which in a distant province is not very great.[32]

A piece of a very different nature from these classical tragedies which must surely have been performed at Calais was a farce entitled *La Route de Paris*, seen by Stephen Weston at the Théâtre de Vaudevilles in Paris in 1814, in which a British Milord is 'good-naturedly burlesqued' to the great amusement of the audience.[33] An English reviewer sets the scene which is decidedly post-Restoration: 'a pretty *Auberge*, or inn, of a post town, which hangs out the sign of the three *fleur de lis*, supposed to be eight or ten miles from the capital'.[34] Various characters are introduced: the landlady, 'a Cauchoise (or Normandy gossip)', a Gascon courier, a Swiss veteran, a French grenadier etc. but,

The most interesting characters, however, were an English *Milord*, who entered the inn with *Milady*. The Lord and Lady are dressed admirably. The Lord was a gouty man about forty-five years of age, and splentic; his Lady a dashing woman of twenty, who had assured him that Paris was the only place to cure his gout. Their bad French was delightful: the Lord entered, talking to his servant without: – '*Allez, doucement, petit William: ne fatiguez pas le cheval; nous nous ARRETIR nous ici, pour le déjeuner.*' The landlady then asked them what they would have for breakfast? The Lady chose *milk*; and the Lord – '*Pour moi le BIFSTICK*'. The Lady complains of the length of the journey, to which the Lord assents – '*Goddem, Yes, Milady: le chemain, il est plain de longueur*'.

All this amused the Parisians excessively; the actors were interrupted with bursts of laughter and the people looked every minute at such English travelers as happened to be present to see how they bore it. Milord said his wife spoke English very well: '*Mais pour moi, Godden, Yes, je ne suis pas fort pour le parlement.*' At last the Lord got into a terrible passion at the Landlady saying – the French gentlemen would be very fond of his wife, and vowed he would only pay *one guinea* for his breakfast. This astounded Madame de la Hostellerie, 'What', said she, 'a guinea, 25 francs!' '*Ah,*' he replied, *'that will teach you to say the French will love my wife: Elle n'aime que moi'*. Exit in a Rage.... The satire of the piece caused abundance of laughter; and equal applause for all the characters, ten, at least, were personated by the same actor, Joly, with admirable address.[35]

Another of Napoleon's favourites appeared at Calais the following year and was seen by a British traveller who, had her act involved speech, would certainly have understood her. He was the British foreign minister, Robert Stewart, Viscount Castlereagh, who, in September 1818 was on his way to take part in the Congress of Aix-la-Chapelle which was to negotiate the terms on which allied troops were to be withdrawn from French territory. According to *The British Neptune, or Naval, Military and Fashionable Advertiser:*

Lord and Lady Castlereagh, and suite, who sailed on Thursday 1st from Dover in the Chichester packet, had a passage of only three hours and in the evening attended the theatre to see Madame Saqui's performances. The following day they passed at Calais and left that place for Lisle on Saturday morning.[36]

Lady Castlereagh too would appear to have been an accomplished French-speaker for when the American Ambassador, Richard Rush, dined at her house, he discovered the dinner-table conversation to be in French and when he, 'glanced at the books which were lying about' he found them all to be, 'In the French language'.[37] Castlereagh had wooed Lady Amelia Hobart by sending her a copy of Stéphanie de Genlis's novel *Adéle et Thèodore*.[38]

The Castlereaghs' fluent French would not, however, have been necessary to appreciate Mme Saqui's act for she was a tightrope dancer – *une danseuse de corde*.[39] Her performance, which involved all manner of feats of acrobatic daring, also included the miming of stories such as, for the Emperor's benefit, the Crossing of the St Bernard, the Battle of Wagram and the Capture of Saragossa. The British minister doubtless witnessed something less imperial but whether he saw any analogy between tightrope-walking and diplomacy we are not told. We do know that from Cambrai a couple of days later he wrote to his brother Charles, who was a member of the British delegation already at Aix, advising him to rent a small house rather than, 'Encumber yourself with a great Hotel,' but this was not, as might be thought, the consequnce of an unfortunate experience at Dessein's but rather stemmed from a desire to ensure that Charles avoided the kind of scandal to which he was notoriously prone.[40]

Something very different from Talma's tragedies and Saqui's feats of agility was performed, following its publication in 1819, namely, *Douvres et Calais, ou Partie et Revanche,* a two act *comédie-vaudeville* by Marie-Emmanuel Théaudon. It included the following air perhaps more popular with the Calaisiens than the visiting English:

Rivage heureux! douce patrie!
France, je te revois enfin!
Je rétrouve, ici la folie,
L'amour, l'honneur et le bon vin.
Dans le tendre et noble délire
Que ce moment heureux m'inspire,
Versez, milord, versez, je vais
Boire à la gloire de Français!
En vain la fortune ennemie
Voulut abattre notre Coeur,
On vit toujours, en ma patrie
Unir le courage au malheur.[41]

In 1825 the Calais municipality purchased the theatre from the hotel for the sum of 70,000 francs.[42] It thereafter became known as the Théâtre de la rue Leveux, the name of the street on which it was situated having been changed from the rue de la Comédie.[43] Le Metheyer was re-employed as the director, receiving a grant of 2500 frs from the municipality. Typically, at that time performances in the winter season ran from 5.45 in the evening until 9 p.m. and consisted of three contrasting pieces.[44]

In January 1826 the British enthusiasm for the stage

encouraged the management of the theatre to launch an English season; the programme allowing Calaisiens without any knowledge of English to understand the action. The critic for the *Journal de Calais*, M. Pigault de Beaupré, praised the performers with the exception of a certain M. Vining who, in a nice reversal of the usual stereotype, would have been perfect had, 'his voice not issued from his nose'! He attributed it to, 'an immoderate use of tobacco'.[45] It seems likely that the actor concerned was Frederick Vining (1790-1871), one of a thespian family who spent most of his career performing in the playhouses of Kent and Sussex.[46]

The year 1827 saw the arrival on the steam packet *Crusader* and, 'without the slightest symptom of marine indisposition,' of James Albany and his friend 'C.W'. They visited the theatre, 'rather smaller than the Lyceum in the Strand,' on three nights in succession.[47] On the first night they took their seats in the Parquet which he describes as, 'the five or six benches in the Pit nearest to the Orchestra… like the Stalls recently established at the Opera in England'. The house was well-filled and the audience well-behaved with 'no hissing and little applause'. The acting was superior to what might be expected in an English provincial theatre. The main offering was Michele Carafa's comic-opera *Masaniello* which had been performed for the first time earlier that year. On the third night the travellers treated themselves to a place in a Stage Box where they witnessed a performance of the farce *Le Beneficiaire* which Albany describes as, 'resembling Sheridan's *The Critic*'. It is a play in which a *'Milord Anglois'* is,

...in a good-natured manner held up to the ridicule of the audience, among whom he excited much laughter. He was attired in ill-made clothes, which hung about him loosely and awkwardly, and wore on his head a large badly-shaped white hat. These peculiarities, together with his slouching and shuffling gait and broken French interlarded with English words pronounced in a drawling tone, particularly, 'Yee-ess', which occurred continually, were irresistibly funny.

One of the best English accounts of the theatre comes from
this period: it appeared in 1828.

The theatre at Calais is not a San Carlos[48] ...It must be a poor
town, indeed, in France that cannot boast its *salle de spectacle*. Calais
has one, which the critical Calicots[49] of Paris, I dare say, turn up
their noses at, when they pass through on their occasional visits to
London. But a very tolerable share of amusement may be extracted
from it nevertheless: for if its artists are not quite competent to give
due effect to the masterpieces of Racine and Molière (which the
classical tastes of their *abonnés* compel them occasionally to
attempt) they can at least get through, with becoming spirit, the
delightful little vaudevilles of MM. Scribe and Desaugiers &c.[50]
with which the French stage so abounds, and which, in fact, play
themselves. They have an actor, however, of the Calais theatre, who
must not go unnamed, in a description which professes to point
out all that is worth particular notice in the place to which it refers.
For dry, easy and unaffected humour of the low kind, there are
very few cities, either Paris or elsewhere, who exceed M. Plante.[51]
His Fronting,[52] and that class of characters, have not the liveliness
and spirited impudence of Potier,[53] or even of Laporte, or, among
ourselves, of James and Wrench;[54] and his Jocrisses[55] are without
the almost affecting simplicity and truth of Brunet.[56] But his
manner in whatever he does, is quite his own; and his quiet,
unpretending, but at the same time, rich and racy drollery, is
infinitely entertaining. Perhaps the way in which the talents of
Plante make his performance stand out from those with which they
are associated, induces one to estimate him rather more highly
than he deserves; but I confess that he has amused me rather more
than any of the Paris actors always excepting the very best; such as
...Joly, Perlet &c.[57]

The efforts of Plante and his colleagues, however, were
insufficient to prevent the theatre from entering into a
period of long decline. In April 1837 it made a loss of
1400.80 francs and similar deficits were being recorded each
month. This despite what a local historian describes
as, 'the best actors and (thanks to the advent of steam
navigation) the wealthiest audiences'. Furthermore the
theatre itself was becoming increasingly antiquated; the

sound was poor, the seating uncomfortable and lighting bad.[58]   Then, with the arrival of the railway, fewer and fewer travellers stayed overnight in Calais and the English presence at the theatre diminished.

Plans for the present fine theatre on the Boulevard Lafayette were first conceived in 1885 when Calais and neighbouring St Pierre were amalgamated into a single municipalité. It was opened in 1905.

9

BREAKDOWN, DETENTION AND 'A LITTLE FINESSE'

William Wordsworth had welcomed the French Revolution, 'Bliss was it in that dawn to be alive' but was quickly disillusioned and by the summer of 1802 he was contemptuous of his fellow countrymen who, like himself, took advantage of the peace to flock to France:

> Is it a Reed that's shaken by the wind,
> Or what is it that ye go forth to see?
> Lords, Lawyers, Statesmen, Squires of low degree,
> Men known, and men unknown, sick, lame and blind,
> Post forward all, like creatures of one kind,
> With first-fruit offerings crowd to bend the knee
> In France, before the new-born Majesty.[1]

In reality, the Britons who during the Peace of Amiens visited the Continent were by no means 'creatures of one kind'. Wordsworth was in Calais to see his daughter, Caroline, and her mother, Annette Vallon with whom he also shared a hatred of Napoleon. Whilst, as Peter Thorold says, there was probably, 'a heavy weighting of Whigs and radicals', who may have had some admiration for Bonaparte, others went in search of long-lost relatives, on long-delayed business, going to see the works of art collected in the Louvre, or out of curiosity to see a country they had known before the Revolution.[2] Lord Whitworth and his fellow negotiators at Amiens, whilst patient and diplomatic, would not have been inclined to 'bend the knee', not least because Napoleon was yet to become Emperor.

By the spring of 1803 the peace talks were stalling. Both sides broke the terms of the truce. In Britain, where the Peace had initially been greeted with enthusiasm – it meant more trade and lower taxes – there was a growing feeling that Napoleon, who continued to extend his empire in Switzerland and Italy, was gaining more from it than was Prime Minister Addington. The first Consul, on the other hand, was irritated that the British were proving reluctant to vacate Egypt and give up the Cape Colony to his clients, the Dutch, and positively refusing to leave Malta.

Aware that the French were rapidly increasing the size of their fleet and making other preparations for the resumption of war, it was the British who moved first. An ultimatum was issued which was never going to be acceded to in Paris, with the consequence that Whitworth was withdrawn. He left France on 13 May and on 17 May before war was officially declared, the Royal Navy arrested all French and Dutch shipping in British waters, taking their crews prisoner. Napoleon countered by arresting all British males between the ages of 18 and 60 who were on French territory. Their detention was justified on the grounds that if they were allowed to return to England they could be recruited into the armed services. As Catriona Kennedy has said of them, however, 'the number of gouty and consumptive invalids seeking the benefits of a southern climate, families hoping to economize and artists, grand tourists and others wishing to see the sights hardly constitued a threat to France'.[3] The British state never introduced reciprocal measures against French citizens not least because many of them from the comte d'Artois (the future Charles X) downwards were themselves refugees from the new régime in France but also, perhaps, because they already had a far greater number of French prisoners-of-war than there were British prisoners in France.

More than a thousand Britons were trapped in France: some would remain there until Napoleon abdicated in 1814. There had already been a mad dash for the Channel ports:

Daily, nay hourly, the postilion's whip resounded in Calais streets, every one hastening to his native land, or waiting at the point of embarkation... The hotels, large as they are, were so filled their owners knew not where to place fresh comers. Many, whose fears overcame every other consideration, hired vessels at any price....[4]

The English action in capturing French shipping, prior to a declaration of war, was seized upon as further proof of Albion's perfidy, and retaliation was swift. Whilst the British community in Calais were in a position to escape across the Channel with relative ease, many were nevertheless caught in Napoleon's net, thanks not least to the efficiency or, as Britons were inclined to say, the vindictiveness, of the commissary general of police in the town, that same M. Mengaud who we met in an earlier chapter. The English packet, the *Prince of Wales*, Captain Sutton, and the cutter *Nancy*, Captain Latimore, were boarded in Calais harbour, their skippers and mates put on parole and the rest of their crews imprisoned. When, some weeks later, Bonaparte himself visited the town, Sutton's petition for release was immediately refused and when the two vessels were pointed out to him in the harbour, he is reported to have said, 'You have plenty of mud there: let them lie and rot.'[5]

According to one British inhabitant of Calais, William Wright, a translator, some who might have escaped across the Channel did not do so because in the last few days before hostilities were resumed M. Mengaud, 'either was, or pretended to be, absent and no passports could be obtained until he returned'.[6] Once war had again broken out, all Englishmen between the ages of 18 and 60 were summoned to the house of the town's commandant, General Brabaçon. There they were required to sign their names, state their age and profession and were informed that they were to be confined to the town. Those who had been in business for twelve months or more, and had paid the requisite fee, were not required to sign. Women and children were free to go to England.[7] Shortly afterwards restrictions became a good deal more onerous. British citizens were summoned to Mengaud's office for passports. They were being sent to Valenciennes, a hundred miles inland.

Those who could afford to do so set off, 'some in the barks by the canals, others in cabriolets, coaches and on horseback'.[8] Others, who could not run to the expense of paying for transport, set off anyway carrying such of their worldly goods as they could manage on their backs. Some remained behind in the hope that the restrictions would be relaxed and they would be allowed to stay. Wright himself was given leave to remain in the town on condition that he acted as interpreter to Brabaçon. His first duty was invidious in the extreme. He was required to draw up lists of those British citizens whom he considered unable to meet the costs of the journey to Valenciennes and those in easier circumstances. Those in the second group were summoned to the general's office, issued with passports and told to leave next day on pain of being committed to prison before being sent inland in the custody of the gendarmerie. Artisans were, in some cases, obliged to sell the tools of their trade, and with them their means of earning a living, in order to meet the requirements of the journey. Some others, remaining in Calais, were the victims of extortion. Wright tells of,

> One poor gentleman, of the name of Mallison, a cripple, who had repaired to Calais for the benefit of sand-baths, and whose removal to the interior would probably shorten his life, petitioned to remain, as having an abscess removable by no other method in the opinion of his surgeons. I was sent to him (not immediately from the general, but through his orders) to return him his petition, and to tell him unless he paid ten guineas into the hands of a person named to him, he would be sent off. I could not make an offer of the kind to him, but pointed out to him the person alluded to; and who, I told him, could obtain him the possession necessary for his health: he settled with him, I believe, for he was not sent off.[9]

In making his preparations for the invasion of Europe, Napoleon himself visited Calais towards the end of May, staying at Dessein's hotel. Upon his departure the position of the remaining British patentees was made more difficult in that they were confined to within six leagues of the coast. However, in one respect at least – if Wright is correct – things improved:

> Happily for the inhabitants of Calais, M. Mengaud is stripped of a great part of his power, and will most probably lose the remainder; it is now vested in the mayor and corporation. It was a change long seriously wished for, as all persons, whether French or English, were insulted by his language, beat with his hands, cane, or whip, sometimes in his office, in the street, or at the theatre, and afterwards put in prison at his pleasure without reason or remedy.[10]

Wright goes on to explain how he himself managed to escape from the town. After aborting a plan to get away in a boat that was being used to carry stone for the repair of the pier, he hit upon the idea of escaping, with the help of a friend, hidden in a trunk that had been carried on board a neutral ship bound for Dover. It is a story straight out of Captain Marryat:

> As the Danish brig, the *St. Anna*, was to sail the next day, I went with a friend to all the dealers in trunks, to find one to my purpose, and curious to relate, was shewn a trunk in which a man had escaped from England; at length my friend bought one as for himself and, on trial it answered very well; holes were made to admit air, and having losely put my cloaths &c. in, it was sent to the custom-house with other baggage, and being examined was conveyed on board. Meantime I went down on the port dressed as a sailor, and within ten yards overtook the commissary of police, who in war time, attended by the town sergeants and a guard, takes all the passports. Well knowing if he went on board, it would be impossible for me to effect my purpose, I asked him if he was going on board? He replied in the affirmative. I told him it was too soon, as we had not got all the baggage from the custom-house, and none of the passengers were yet come down; he returned, imagining probably I belonged to the vessel, and I passed the sentinel placed at the side, and descended into the cabin. I then ordered my trunk down there, saying it was a gentleman's who desired I would see it placed there; they on board believing I was authorised to do so, instantly lowered it down. The captain being a man I could not trust, it was necessary to have him out of the way; this also was accomplished

by a little finesse, when my friend entered and held the cabin door, while I tumbled everything out of the trunk into a bag I had ready for the purpose, then stripping off my jacket and waistcoat, I leaped in.

Agitated and hurried, not having a moment's time, I could not compress myself sufficiently to allow the trunk to be locked at first or second trial, and my friend, being terrified was on the point of quitting me, saying our lives were forfeited. At that moment, determination enabled me to compress myself as much as possible, and I begged him to jump on the lid, which forced it down, and I was locked up. He had scarcely done so when the custom-house officers came on board, also the commissary; when the vessel having undergone the search, joyfully did I hear the order to cast off, and still more happy to feel the vessel under way.

The heat of a very warm day was so increased from my confined situation, as to be scarcely bearable, and the cramp seized my legs in about ten minutes after I was locked in. Great as was the pain, I dared not breathe hard, fearful of being heard; the pain at last subsided, and from my knees downwards I lost all sense of feeling, and, even at the moment that I am writing, I feel the effects of that confinement.

Well convinced, if detected, my life would be sacrificed to their vengeance, under the pretence that I was carrying over intelligence to the English, but in reality as an example to others, and to gratify the avarice of individuals in power, I had made up my mind to succeed or perish in the attempt. My spirits being so harassed by anxiety that death would have been far preferable to a state like mine, separated as I was from those dear to me, for whom and for my country I would again hazard my life, or bleed in defending.

On gaining the Roads, an anchor was let go, to wait for the turn of the tide, which runs to the eastward about three hours after high water, and the wind being westerly would have taken us out of the course for Dover. The key to my trunk had been given to a gentleman on board, who fearful I should be suffocated, came down into the cabin, and finding by the mark which was the right, opened it in presence of the captain, when I, naturally thinking all was safe, lifted up my head. The captain was terrified beyond expression, as the pilot-boat had not quitted the vessel. However, I got out of my confinement; and though at first not able to stand, put on another dress.

Scarcely had I so done when the pilots came down into the cabin for their money, one of them the greatest villain in Calais. Another person also came down with them, who knew me at Calais and whether I am to attribute to his good offices the pilot's not giving information respecting me or whether it was owing to the pilot's being employed in taking out the passengers of the mail-packet, Captain Dell, which came into the Roads just at this time, I am at a loss to determine. Be it which it may Providence favoured me and after suffering the most uneasy sensations for two or three hours, the passengers urged the captain to get under weigh; when, as were at the point of getting the anchor up, a boat came out of Calais harbour and made directly for us. It was to me a subject of alarm; but seeing only three persons, I remained tolerably easy, until we ascertained it was not for me. The boat came aboard just as we were under sail, and there jumped upon deck another unfortunate prisoner, of the name of Estill, now in London. He had walked down to the pier, when two young men, who had been waiting for him seized the opportunity, when no one was observing, of placing their boat so as to receive him: he sprung into it, and was saved. The young man who had performed this friendly office, on his return was denounced; and to escape from the death that awaited him, was under the necessity of flying to Dover to save his life. Being an alien, he of course was there stopped, but application being made for his liberation, I have reason to believe he is come to London. His name is Lutz.[11]

Whilst many felt an obligation to honour their parole and some feared the consequences of being caught, some did escape from the citadel of Valenciennes in which the *détenus* were confined. Conditions were far better than in the penal depots such as Bitche in Lorraine but neverthess left much to be desired. A young Midshipman, Edwards Boys, who daringly escaped, wrote of the majority of prisoners that they were,

...by endless, grinding ennui… reduced to such a state of apathy that they were worn down into mere brute existence: while those who had still any energy left magnified the most trifling occurrences into an important event.[12]

In 1807 some of the detainees at Valenciennes were moved still further inland to Verdun after it was rumoured that they were contemplating a break-out.

Such were the conditions which many endured until 1814. More than most, those who had been detained at Calais must have looked back over the long years with the tantalising knowledge of having been 'so near and yet so far'.

10

"A STATE OF GREAT DESTITUTION"

When, in 1829, James Albany ventured beyond the Porte Royale to visit the Basse-Ville, or 'Bazile' – describing it, rather strangely, as being to Calais what the village of Barnwell was to Cambridge – he noted there a 'petty Cabaret' called the 'Robin Hood and Little John' which offered, 'Neat Wines – Good Dinner for One Shilling – Coaches Daily – English Ale – Fine Purl'.[1] He offered no explanation either for the characteristically English sign or the, equally characteristic, English Bill of Fare. He also took, unexplained, note of the 'Britannia Inn and Coffee House' and the 'English Brewery'.

Despite having a fine appreciation of what in more recent times might have been described as the sociological, he seems not to have made the connection between the presence of the 'Robin Hood' and the frequency with which he observed, 'in almost every street' a 'Fabrique de Tulle' or lace works. Those heroes of English legend Robin Hood and Little John being, of course, denizens of Sherwood Forest in Nottinghamshire, the county most strongly associated with British lace-making.

Lace-making had long been established in France – Tulle itself being a town in the Limousin – but it was in Nottinghamshire that, evolving from the indigenous hosiery industry, the manufacture of cheap, machine-made lace had been developing for the past forty years. There a series of innovations – of the point-net frame in 1778, of John Heathcoat's warp-loom in 1807 and of John Leaver's bobbin and carriage machine in 1813 – combined with the ready availability of capital from Smith's Bank in Nottingham, eventually gave rise to the rapid growth of the industry in that city.[2]

The post-war industrial depression, together with an initial, Luddite, resistance to innovation, led to a quite different kind of ingenuity. It was illegal under English law to export machinery which might disadvantage British manufacturers by permitting competition from abroad and the lace-makers of Nottingham were especially jealous of the developments in their industry. Nevertheless, faced with the downturn in the industry, four of Heathcoat's workers hit upon the idea of smuggling a loom across the Channel which they set up at Douai in February 1816 and at the end of the same year another Nottingham engineer, Robert Webster, transported to Calais the disassembled parts of a lace-making frame as 'old iron'. The Douai enterprise quickly failed but Webster was a good deal more successful. He set up a factory on the corner of the Rue Lengaigne (now Rue de Vic) and the Quai du Commerce in St. Pierre, otherwise the Basse-Ville. Working with Webster was another Englishman, Robert West, and shortly afterwards they were joined by two others, James Clark and a man called Bonington. Within a couple of years these latter two were each working on their own account and Webster had moved his premises to 11 Rue Lafayette.[3]

Children born in the Parish of St. Pierre lès Calais, 1823-32 with 'English' surnames.									
1823	1824	1825	1826	1827	1828	1829	1830	1831	1832
10	16	22	22	20	24	24	31	36	20

(Calais - Etat Civil de Saint-Pierre-lès-Calais:Tables Décennales, 1823-1832; archivesenligne.pasdecalais.)

For a time the English kept the secrets of their trade to themselves; Webster, for example, always taking care to lock up his workshop himself each evening.[4] In 1822, however, an Englishman, called Austin went into business with a French industrialist Jean-Nöel Dubout and from then on Anglo-French co-operation became the norm. Nevertheless, English workers, both men and women, experienced in working with the mechanised looms, continued to be employed and the English population of the district rapidly increased.

By the time the 1841 census was conducted there were 149 Britons living on the Rue Lafayette alone. Some of the smaller streets in St Pierre were dominated by the English. Of the 39 inhabitants of Rue St Eustache, 28 were English, as were all 15 who lived in the little Rue Pont-Neuf.[5] In addition to English lacemakers, mechanics and designers, there were a number of English retailers (grocers, coffee-shop owners, a bookshop owner) several doctors and a lawyer.[6]

ill.6

Sarah Bromhead, born to an English family in St Pierre in 1846.

Her family were among the many who emigrated to Australia in 1848.

Gillian Kelly describes the kind of homes in which many of the English lived in St. Pierre;

Most of the houses were single storied and fairly solidly built, usually with a tiny attic under the eaves. They were whitewashed each year, and sometimes a little yellow colouring was added to this. The footings were treated with tar, giving a nice contrast, and often woodwork was painted with bright colours.

The ground floor often lacked a hall, and the entrance was straight into a room paved with red tiles. This was both kitchen and living room. Sometimes, if the house had a hall, there would be a small, very narrow room at the front. This made a kind of sitting room, used only on special occasions. A coal fire would be lit in the 'prusienne' – a fire with an open hearth, but with a grille that could be lowered to prevent cinders flying out or a child falling in![7]

The development of the industry was by no means without its problems. The production of high quality lace was dependent upon the use of suitable cotton thread from England the importation of which was prohibited under protectionist legislation designed to encourage the nascent French cotton textile industry. Its availability was dependent upon smuggling so that the supply could not be guaranteed. By contrast with this brake upon the progress of the industry was the adaptation in 1833 by an English engineer called Fergusson of the Jacquard system to the production of lace, permitting the production of 'Chantilly' lace in Calais.[8] Productivity was increased by the gradual introduction of steam power after 1835; this, however, was a development which increased the likelihood of over-production.

The English lace manufacturers were, of course, conscious of being foreigners but the disturbances of 1830 which overthrew the Restoration régime of Charles X gave them an opportunity to pull off a diplomatic coup. As the old Bourbon white flag and fleur-de-lys disappeared, they seized the opportunity of presenting the town with a magnificent tricolour, re-installed, together with the 'Marseillaise' by the victorious Louis-Philippe.[9]

It was when régime change was next in the air, in 1848, that disaster struck the English industrial workers of Calais and St. Pierre. An economic crisis had been gathering in France since the mid-1840s. A succession of bad harvests gave rise to an increase in the price of food and a consequent slump in industrial demand. Bankruptcies were common and the rate of unemployment rapidly increased. Luxury industries, such as lace-making, were especially hard hit. Nationally matters came to a head with the 'June Days' in Paris when some 1,500 revolutionaries were cut down by troops under General Cavaignac.

Prior to that in Calais, as the position of the workers became increasingly desperate with some 12,000 men and women in St Pierre unemployed, spasmodic rioting broke out and, as is not uncommon in such circumstances, it was the foreigners – the English – who were the butt of the anger of locals. The *Times* accused them of ingratitude.[10] English workers, many of them often in a state of, 'most deplorable destitution' began to return across the Channel. On 24 March the following letter, addressed to the Lord Mayor of London by the British Consul in Calais appeared in *The Standard*:

My Lord, I have the honour to report, for your Lordship's information, that I am sending over tonight to London (where they may expect to arrive at about 2 p.m. by the General Steam Navigation Company's packet *Menai*) 81 distressed British subjects, including children. They consist of lace-makes and flax-dressers who, owing to the closing of the factories, leave this country and are in a state of great destitution. I fear a still larger number will follow. The state of ruin to which the flourishing factories in this vicinity are reduced by the stagnation, or rather entire stoppage of all trade, consequent upon the recent occurrences in Paris, is lamentable. It only remains for me to recommend to your Lordship's protection these unfortunate persons thus compelled to quit a country where they earned an honest livelihood by their industry. They will present themselves to you on their arrival with a certificate from me.

I have the honour to be my Lord,
Your most obedient humble servant
Edward Walter Benham[11]

The Lord Mayor himself announced that he had received a sum of £61.19s from French citizens of London for the relief of the distressed workers.

Benham was correct in his prediction that the *Menai's* returning workers would not be the last. According to the *Journal de Calais* between the end of April and the beginning of June 622 Britons returned across the Channel.[12] But by no means all of them were bound for Nottinghamshire. Knowing that the economic situation in the UK was little better than that in France, a meeting of English laceworkers, held in St. Pierre and supported by the Consul, petitioned the Colonial Secretary, Lord Grey, requesting that they be sent to the colonies. The Colonial Office acted with speed, money was raised in both London and Nottingham and on 30 April the *Fairlie*, with 56 lacemakers from Calais on board, left Deptford bound for Sydney. On 6 June another ship, the 669-ton barque *Agincourt*, Captain Thomas Scott, left Gravesend for the same destination with 262 emigrants on board.

In between times, the 571-ton *Harpley* had, on 12 May left Deptford for Adelaide also with passengers from Calais. One of those on board left the following account of the voyage:

> The poop of the ship was transformed into a habidasher's shop from which everything necessary was gratuitously and unsparingly supplied to those who were in need. Only two deaths occurred on the voyage out, those of an older man and a delicate infant. As a result 256 healthy people arrived on Saturday 2nd September 1848, on board a remarkably clean and well commanded ship.[13]

Smaller groups followed in further vessels.

Embarkation would not have meant an end to anxiety. Whilst the lacemakers would doubtless have been happy to wave goodbye to the 'hated' Calais as they left it to port as they sailed through the Straits of Dover, they must have had concerns about the four month voyage and about their futures in a strange land best known as a dumping ground for criminals.[14] Within six weeks of the departure of the *Agincourt*, Calais-born youngsters Mary Shaw, Robert Woodford and Emma Johnson had all died and been committed to the deep in what must have been a particularly heart-breaking ceremony for their poor parents.

There was no textile industry in Australia at this time and the migrants were compelled to seek such employment as they could find. The experience of the Bromhead family is probably not untypical. The family consisted of Joseph Bromhead and his wife Sarah Greensmith, their daughter Sarah, their son John who had been born in East Leake,

Nottinghamshire, in 1820 and his wife Jane Swift born in Loughborough in the same year, and their granddaughter Sarah-Ann who had been born on 22 July 1846 in the Rue du Jardin des Plantes, Saint Pierre. Left behind in Calais were Sarah-Ann's younger twin brothers who had both died in February 1848 within a few weeks of their birth.

The *Agincourt* arrived in Sydney harbour on 6 October but few of the migrants were permitted to land. One group were directed onto river steamers and were taken up the Parratta River to the town of that name from where they walked 110 miles over the Blue Mountains to Bathurst. The remaining group, which included the Bromheads, were put onto another steamer which sailed up the coast to Newcastle at the mouth of the Hunter River up which they then sailed to the small village of Morpeth. From there the party, including the heavily pregnant Jane, walked the three miles to a migrant hostel at East Maitland. Within a few weeks the family had moved the short distance to West Maitland where John established a barber's shop. The eldest Bromheads both died there, she in 1865 and he in 1882. Sarah Ann's own mother known to later generations as the 'French grandmother' died in 1893 and her father in 1903. She herself, who must have been one of the last of the Calais-born Australians, died at the age of 81 in 1927 at Chatswood a suburb of north Sydney.[15]

Many of the descendants of those who left Calais in 1848 are today members of the Australian Society of the Lacemakers of Calais.

Despite the mass exodus of that year by no means all of the English lacemakers left the Calais area. The 1851 Census indicates that there were 332 English living in Calais and 1046 in St. Pierre.[16] With the restoration of stable government under Louis-Napoleon, who seized power at the end of that year, the industry re-established itself despite always being prone to economic fluctuations – production fell again during the Crimean War between 1854-56, for example – and to variations in fashion.

Gradually the English population became assimilated

as their children attended French schools and inter-marriage with the local population occurred. Nevertheless, the patois, especially of St. Pierre, remained strongly impregnated with English expressions. Families with English antecedents tended to remain protestant, attending either the Anglican Chapel of St George which had been established in the Rue des Prêtres in 1822, or the Wesleyan chapel founded in the Rue du Temple in 1830.[17] By the time Nelly Mulard published her book on Calais in the Age of Lace in 1964 she was still able to list a considerable number of Calaisien families descended from the lacemaking pioneers – 'Brown, Stubbs, Jones, Walker, Smith, Williams, Barton, Barker, West, Hiram, Stevenson, Austin &c.'[18] Lacemaking in Calais still flourishes, long outlasting the Nottingham industry.

11

'No better than a sort of Alsatia'

Until the second half of the nineteenth century Calais was normally beyond the reach of the English legal system. According to an article in *Blackwood's Magazine* – 'If you believe in maligners, Calais is not better than a sort of Alsatia to England, a kind of extension of the rules of King's Bench'.[1] Alsatia was a cant name for the Whitefriars district of London, a maze of courts and alleys to the south of Fleet Street, which had a reputation as a sanctuary for debtors and other law-breakers. The Rules of King's Bench applied to the area around the King's Bench prison in Southwark within which debtors were immune from prosecution. Even as late as 1852, a young American writing home from Calais, where 'We put up at Quillacq's', found, 'the place generally has three or four thousand English, many of whom are refugees on account of debt.'[2] Many was the man who naturally having, 'the earliest information of what was impending, arranged to read at Dessein's at Calais the intelligence of his own eclipse.'[3]

In addition to debtors, who were rarely allowed to long outlive their welcome at Dessein's, runaway lovers would there hope to find what was to be, in fact if not in name, their honeymoon suite. The opening scene of Samuel Foote's comedy *A Trip to Calais,* set in the Hotel d'Angleterre, pictures just such a romantic situation.[4] Kit Cable, Dick Drugget and Jenny Minnikin enter:

CABLE: Harkee, messmates! Look about! You had better bring to in this creek: here you will find the best moorings. The Hotel d' Angleterre they calls it in French; but you'll find the names of things plaguily transmogrified all along this coast.

DICK: They be civil people, no doubt.

CABLE: Civil? ay, ay, if you will bring a good cargo of cash, you are welcome to anchor here as long as you list: But you will find the duties high at out-clearance; therefore take care, d'ye see, and don't run aground. I must take t'other trip to the port for your stowage. [Exit]

DICK: I hope by this time your sea-sickness is pretty well gone?

JENNY: Much mended, dear Dicky, I thank you.

DICK: Well, my dear Jenny, here we are, safely landed in the French country, however. And now, what's next to be done? Consider, my love, we have not a moment to lose; your father will not be long behind us, I am sure.

JENNY: No question of that; therefore our best way will be to get out of his power as soon as we can.

DICK: By what means?

JENNY: By the means that we came hither in search of; by being married, you know.

DICK: True: but how the deuse shall we procure a parson? Perhaps the man of the house may assist us: But plague on't! I can't parley Francee; tho' I understand a few words here and there.

JENNY: But I can, Dicky, you know. .What, do you think I was five years at Madam Vanslopping's, the Swiss French boarding-school at Edmonton, for nothing at all?

DICK: True, true; I had forgot – But I don't think it any mark of their manners, to let us wait here so long without asking us in. Here, house, house!

JENNY: peace, Dicky! How is it possible they should know what you want? – Maison! Seignior de Terre!

Dick: Who? What?

JENNY: Seignior de Terre is as much as to say Landlord in English.
DICK: True, true. Oh! here the man comes.

Monsieur Tromfort, the swindling landlord of the hotel, enters. Some biographical details suggest that he is closely based upon Dessein, and he declares to the young couple:

Yes; I alvays have great penchant, great partiality for dose of your country. Vy dere vas some time ago, ven my house and my good vas burn down by de fire, I never vas taking nodding at all from de French.

DICK: No.

TROMFORT: Pas une sous; but suffer my lors Anglois to build-a my hotel up again to dere own taste, vid out de least interruption.

DICK: How kind to give that preference to us!

Before long, Jenny's parents and her fiancé arrive and a game of cat-and-mouse ensues whilst Tromfort rubs his hands and contemplates a prosperous future:

In ver few year, I shut up my hotel, set up my coach, my carosse, and call myself le marquis de Guinea, in compliment to Messieurs l'Anglois....

In the real world the arrival of angry parents at Dessein's in pursuit of their errant daughters seems to have been by no means an infrequent occurrence. One of the most famous occasions of the kind involves the poet Shelley – a married man – and the future mother of *Frankenstein*, Mary Wollstonecraft Godwin. Shelley, whose ability to believe in the righteousness of his behaviour, however outrageous, was matched only by his precocious sixteen year-old lover's credulity, was living, as he would continue to do, a life of jaw-dropping complexity, the intellectual foundations of which, he claimed were the works of Mary's parents. Mary's mother – the radical feminist, Mary Wollstonecraft – had died only a few days after Mary's birth and Mary had been brought up by her father, whom she adored, and step-mother, Mary Jane Clairmont, whose jealousy of her mother's bravery and brilliance young Mary despised.[5]

Percy Bysshe Shelley had no reason to disapprove of elopement. The very considerable Shelley fortune had been founded on his grandfather's clandestine marriages to two heiresses both of whom died young. At the age of nineteen he had himself already eloped with a sixteen year-old, Harriet Westbrook. Like many other radically-minded young men he sought out Mary's father William – the author of *Political Justice* – and in the spring of 1814 was a frequent visitor to the Godwin's home-cum-publishing house in Skinner Street, Holborn. As well as being besieged by idealistic young admirers, Godwin was, less agreeably, beset by creditors from whom Shelley offered to release him. In need of money himself, Shelley arranged a hugely expensive post-obit loan part of which would go to Godwin. When it became apparent to the older man that Shelley had designs upon his daughter Godwin did everything in his power to persuade Mary to renounce him; everything except refuse Shelley's loan. It was probably this lack of moral courage which undermined the father's efforts to sever the liaison between his daughter and a married man and on 29 July 1814 Mary, together with her step-sister Jane Clairmont, ran away with Shelley to France.

On landing they made for Dessein's hotel where they were given, thanks perhaps to Jane's French, what they were told was the best room in the house – Sterne's. Like him they began to write a Journal. 'Mary was there', wrote Shelley, 'Shelley was also with me' added Mary.[6]

The next evening the desperate Mrs Godwin – Mary's step-mother, Jane's mother – arrived. Mary Shelley's biographer Miranda Seymour describes Mrs Godwin's frantic efforts to detach her daughter from the lovers:

Travelling all night and crossing the Channel by day, an exhausted Mrs Godwin reached France on the evening after the runaways. Shelley and his companions, resting in the best rooms in Dessein's celebrated hotel at Calais could offer, were informed

that a fat lady had arrived and was calling for her daughter. Jane
spent that night in her mother's room and probably swore that she
had been abducted against her will. This was how Mrs Godwin
would tell the story. By the morning, Jane was ready to go home.
Its says much for Shelley's powers of persuasion that it took only
one brief discussion to change her mind. Strolling along the
harbour front later that day, Shelley had the satisfaction of seeing
their persecutor making her way heavily down to the Dover boat.
Tyranny had been vanquished![7]

By contrast with this tale of young love, marital discord
and indebtedness were combined in the case of
Lord Mornington's son William Pole-Tylney-Long-Wellesley,
a notorious rake, and his wife Helena whom he had met,
'while in Europe avoiding his creditors'. All had begun
romantically enough when in 1823 Long-Wellesley, himself
married, had eloped with Helena Paterson Bligh, the wife of
a Coldstream Guardsman. Two years later William's wife died
and he married Helena but spent much of his time and a
great deal of money trying to gain control over his first wife's
children on whom her considerable fortune had devolved.
By 1833 William and Helena were both living in Calais –

...but no reconciliation has been effected, or according
to present appearances is likely to take place. The lady
remains at Dessein's, but complains of want of funds, and
even of an approach to destitution. Mr Wellesley seems as
full of spirits as ever; he appears on the sands in a coat with
a collar of water-coloured silk, a new fashion of his own
invention, and has been displaying his affability by joining
several boarding-house parties, with a Captain T., a military
gentleman, resident at the same place. He is supposed to be
living at the rate of £40,000 per annum.[8]

Only the support of his uncle, the Duke of Wellington,
kept Long-Wellesley from absolute penury and when he died
in 1857 his obituary in the *Morning Chronicle* claimed that,
'he was redeemed by no single virtue, adorned by no single
grace.'[9]

In 1822 Auguste Quillac, the son of Louis, had taken over the running of the Lion d'Argent in the rue Neuve which from that date onwards was often known, as the Hôtel d'Angleterre had been, as Quillac's. This was to witness the climax of a notorious piece of villainy – the Case of the Shrigley Abduction.

In the 1820s Shrigley Hall was the newly-built home, at Pott Shrigley near Macclesfield, Cheshire, of a prosperous calico-printer, William Turner. By 1826 the Turners' only child, Ellen, was attending a boarding school in Liverpool and on 7 March of that year a man arrived at the school with a letter purporting to be from Mrs Turner's doctor, stating that she had been, 'seized with a sudden and dangerous attack of paralysis' and that Ellen was to return home immediately with the bearer of the message.[10] In this way Ellen was released into the care of a servant not of her father but of a 30 year-old fortune-hunter, Edward Gibbon Wakefield. At Manchester Ellen was introduced to Wakefield who claimed to be a business associate of her father. He admitted that the story of her mother's illness was a ruse to get Ellen away from Liverpool without arousing suspicions as to the true reason – her father's financial difficulties. Ellen was then taken not to Shrigley Hall but to a rendezvous with her father who could not go home for fear of being served with further writs. She was taken first to Huddersfield, then Kendal and then Carlisle. Her father, Ellen was told, had received a loan of £60,000 from Wakefield's uncle who thus had the power to evict the family from Shrigley. Only by marrying Wakefield could that dire eventuality be averted. Next stop was across the border at Gretna Green, where Ellen was married to Wakefield.[11]

This was not Edward Wakefield's first marriage. Nor his first clandestine marriage. Ten years before he had married another heiress, Eliza Pattle, with whom he had run away and married at Edinburgh. En route to Scotland the couple had posted a letter to Eliza's mother; designed to mislead any pursuers, it was addressed, but not of course sent, from Calais – 'My Dearest Mother… I hasten to inform you of my

safety, also 'ere this reaches you I shall be a wife'.[12] Wishing
to avoid scandal, Eliza's mother had accepted the *fait
accompli*. The marriage was happy but short: in the summer
of 1820, soon after giving birth to their second child, Eliza
had died.

After the ceremony Ellen and Wakefield returned to
England, the latter still pretending that they would meet
Mr Turner, initially at Leeds and then in London. By this
time Edward's brother had been dispatched to Shrigley to
apprise Ellen's parents of the shocking truth. It quickly
became apparent they were not going to be as complacent
as Mrs Pattle had been. No sooner had the couple reached
London than Wakefield received a letter from his father
warning him, 'to remain in London not a single hour' or
he would be arrested. Now he really did determine to
seek refuge in Calais, persuading Ellen that they were still
following her father as he fled from his creditors.

At Calais they stayed at the Lion d'Argent. Wakefield
knew Auguste Quillac from previous visits and introduced
Ellen to him, referring to her as 'Madame Wakefield'. They
occupied a salon with two connecting bedrooms – 'the mode
of accommodation regularly occupied by married couples'.
Although Wakefield found Calais, 'a wretched place', his
young wife, he declared, found it 'full of novelty and amusement'.[13]

Still hopeful that he could persuade Turner to recognise
the marriage, Wakefield wrote a letter to Shrigley Hall, 'full
of expressions of penitence as well as of tenderness towards
Ellen'.[14]

Each morning they went down to the jetty to await the
arrival of the packets from Dover; Ellen hoping to meet her
father, Wakefield to avoid him. On the fourth day of their
stay Ellen's uncle arrived together with her father's solicitor
and a Bow Street Runner. They carried with them a letter
from the foreign Secretary, George Canning, asking that
Wakefield be placed under arrest and returned to England.
After much argumentation, some of it in the courtyard of
Quillac's hotel, Wakefield eventually handed Ellen over to

her uncle and, aware that Canning's warrant carried no threat, he made his own way to Paris.

After some weeks, always confident of his powers of persuasion, Wakefield eventually returned to England where he was promptly arrested and, together with his accomplices he was committed to stand trial at Lancaster Spring Assizes in 1827.

The trial aroused huge interest. Wakefield's counsel went to great lengths to prove that the marriage was legal and called a host of witnesses to attest to Ellen's apparent happiness whilst she was in Wakefield's company. Among these was none other than Auguste Quillac who, talking through an interpreter, confirmed that he had known Wakefield for some years. Such international support did little for the culprit who, together with his brother, was sentenced to three years imprisonment. Wakefield was insistent that the marriage had never been consummated and it was annulled by Act of Parliament on 14 June 1827.

On emerging from prison Wakefield became a prison reformer and an effective advocate of colonial settlement. Ellen married a wealthy neighbour, Thomas Legh, but died in childbirth at the age of 19.[15]

Calais was a natural first step for English people involved in the many species of marital irregularity. Typical is the tale related in his memoirs by Frederick Leveson Gower (1819-1907) who archly illustrates the point by telling of twice meeting a fellow barrister, William Ballantine, on the Dover-Calais ferry. On each occasion Ballantine was accompanied by a pretty – but different – young woman who he introduced as 'my niece'.[16] Victorian respectability often stopped at the Channel.

Perhaps the case which attracted most notoriety, however, had been that of the bigamist, Elizabeth, Duchess of Kingston. Elizabeth Chudleigh was the daughter of an army officer who had lost his fortune with the collapse of the South Sea Bubble and who had died when she was only six so that she spent her childhood in severely straitened circumstances. It was perhaps her wish to escape these penny-pinching times that led Elizabeth to lead a far from conventional sex life. As a young woman she was a great beauty, to be compared to Emma Hamilton or Marguerite Gardiner, and she continued to make the most of her charms well into middle-age and succeeded in attracting the attention of a succession of wealthy admirers including George II, Frederick the Great of Prussia and even Pope Clement XIV.

In 1744 she married a young naval lieutenant, the Hon. Augustus John Hervey, a grandson of the Earl of Bristol. After six tumultuous years of marriage and a great deal of provocation, Hervey cut off all relations with her. Elizabeth rapidly became involved with Evelyn Pierrepont, the second Duke of Kingston, whose mistress she became. By 1759, however, Hervey's grandfather, the earl, was dead and his elder brother was in poor health so that Elizabeth could see the prospect of becoming the Countess of Bristol. Alarmed about the legitimacy of her marriage to Hervey, she rushed down to the Hampshire village where the private ceremony had taken place and had a page recording the event inserted into the parish register. By the late 1760s, however, with the brother still alive and both Hervey and Elizabeth wishing separately to re-marry, they colluded to persuade a consistory court that the marriage had not taken place. Shortly after the decision Elizabeth married Kingston.

All then went well until, in 1773, the Duke died leaving Elizabeth a great fortune. The will was disputed by Kingston's nephew and heir who, on the evidence of a servant who claimed that the marriage to Hervey had been lawful, had her indicted for bigamy.

Prior to the trial the Duchess received a good deal of damaging publicity in the form of Foote's comedy, *A Trip to Calais* (see above) in which the character of Lady Kitty Crocodile was as thinly disguised as Elizabeth had been when, twenty years before, she had appeared before George II in, 'a covering of the flimsiest flesh-coloured gauze'.[17] Although the play was denied a performance licence, 'On its publication, the town purchased with avidity, and Lady Kitty was universally allowed to be a palpable hit.'[18] The character's name was a reference to the extravagant displays of grief the Duchess had been known to exhibit after the Duke's death.

By the time the case reached court Hervey's brother had at last died so that he became the third Earl of Bristol. Elizabeth could thus claim to be a peer – either as Dowager Duchess of Kingston or Countess of Bristol – and exerted her right to be tried by her peers at Westminster.

The trial before the House of Lords attracted huge interest. As the courtier Mary Delany wrote – 'All the world, great and small, are gone to Westminster hall': the 'great' included Queen Charlotte, the Duke of Newcastle, the Prince of Wales and the Princess Royal.[19] Elizabeth's early twentieth century biographer Charles Pearce imagined the spectacle:

It would be difficult to find a parallel to the scene. The peers in their gorgeous robes; the ladies attired in the very latest mode (their towering complications of hair must alone have been a sight worth seeing, for it was the time when fantastic dressing of hair had reached its height in more senses than one); the picturesque costumes of the men, the varied colours of their long-skirted coats and flap waistcoats, their wigs, their ruffles and lace cuffs; the stately hall and its noble roof, – all combined to form a picture which must have dwelt in the memories of those present for many a long year. Perhaps they were only dimly conscious, at first, of their surroundings, for every eye could not fail to be fixed on the sombre patch of black in the very centre of the hall, the prisoner, who for seven years had been known as the Duchess of Kingston.[20]

The *Lady's Magazine* was able to elaborate upon, 'the patch of black'. The Duchess's mourning dress comprised, 'a black polinesse with a black gauze cape'.[21]

The correspondent of the *London Chronicle* did not need to imagine the scene but was of the opinion that:

Imagination can hardly picture a more solemn, august, and at the same time brilliant, appearance than the Court of Westminster Hall cut yesterday as soon as the High Steward and Lords had taken their places. It was computed that no fewer than 4,000 persons were present, that out of that number 2,500 were ladies.[22]

Solemn it certainly should have been because under the Statute of Bigamy of James I the punishment was death, whipping or branding in the hand. Despite this awful possibility the Duchess managed to remain, 'dignified without arrogance, collected without audacity, and humble without any of those sycophantic arts which characterise the vulgar.' Nevertheless, despite the earlier decision of the consistory court and the case which she presented to their lordships from the bar of the House, at the end of the trial she was unanimously pronounced guilty. Their lordships, however, had no stomach for any of the grislier punishments and, although the former solicitor-general John Dunning for the prosecution asked for branding, he did not over-exert himself and Elizabeth escaped with a warning.

This was a good deal less than her enemies had hoped for especially as she remained in control of her wealth inherited from the Duke. They consequently sought to ensure that she remained within the jurisdiction of the British courts and applied for a writ of *ne exeat regno*. Hearing of this, Elizabeth succeeded in giving the impression that she was continuing to reside in London – having her coach driven about the city and sending out invitations to a party at Kingston House – whilst she made a hasty departure for Dover and her yacht, the *Minerva*.[23]

Upon landing Elizabeth headed straight for her usual hotel – Dessein's. News of the trial and her conviction had, however, preceded her and Dessein, assuming that loss of title meant loss of fortune, received her,

...with cold politeness, he shrugged his shoulders, and by various distortions of face and limbs, expressed his condolences for the misfortune of his guest, but – it distressed him to be compelled to make the confession – he was unable to accommodate his visitor with a suite of rooms; his whole house was occupied and it was with the utmost difficulty he will procure her a single chamber.[24]

Tired, she took it.

By the following morning Dessein had discovered that the title but not the great fortune had been lost so that he suddenly felt able, in the politest manner, to inform Elizabeth that, 'The company who had occupied apartments suitable in every respect pour Madame la Duchesse, were gone to Paris, and consequently they were devoted to her use, if she should so please.'[25] According to the Baroness d'Oberkirch, Elizabeth responded with, 'Ah, Mr Dessein, you have changed your tune. I am "your grace" today and I was only "my lady" last night. Well it is not worth throwing you into despair. I will go down to your fine room; and I am sure that you will be as proud and happy as ever to receive the Duchess of Kingston.' To which Dessein replied, 'Madame la Duchesse, all my hotel is at your Grace's disposal'. Dessein, the Baroness decided, 'was only an epitome of the world'.[26] It is true that History has tended to follow Dessein in restoring Elizabeth's former title. Biographies of the Duchess of Kingston tend to support Sterne's verdict on Dessein – 'a Turk in Grain'. According to Pearce, 'She was completely won over by the tactful Dessein, and remained at his hotel long enough to lend him a £1000. The man was utterly unworthy of her generosity for no sooner was the money in his pocket than, knowing her helplessness in France and how impossible it was for her to return to England, he changed his tone and made her stay at his hotel so uncomfortable that she was compelled to go to another hotel'.[27] She, a well-travelled lady who never seems to have been rendered helpless, in fact appears rapidly to have moved to a property of her own that became known as the Hôtel Kingston. Dessein, according to Pearce, repaid her only in firewood.

A more recent biographer, Elizabeth Mavor, has another example of Dessein's villainy. In the year after the trial she travelled first to St Petersburg, to visit the court of her friend the Czarina Catherine, and then after briefly returning to Calais she set off for Rome from where she wrote to her

London jeweller Mr Cox – the parenthesis is Mavor's: 'M. Dessein (that foxy proprietor of the Hôtel Angleterre) has given me bills of exchange on Bankers who had none of his Money, and I believe I shall lose Eight Hundred Pounds'.[28]

Elizabeth spent the remainder of a restless life travelling, wooing and being wooed and, especially, acquiring property – including a vodka distillery in Russia and a 350-room chateau near Fontainebleau. Huge as was her expenditure her income was even greater and when she died in 1788 her vast estate was squabbled over for years by the heirs of Hervey and Kingston.

In view of the time she spent in the courts of Europe it is perhaps surprising that Calais so captured her affections that in her very lengthy and much disputed will she made numerous bequests to the town's advantage. She left her, 'dwelling house and garden… to be made use of for the residence of the Commandant of the said town of Calais'. She had already donated 3,750 livres to maintain the boys' and girls' schools[29] and in her will gave an annuity of, '100 louis d'or per annum for ever for the benefit of the two schools'. Her executors were also, 'to lay out so much as will be sufficient in building a prison for prisoners of war and debtors in order to keep them separate from the criminals'. If enough money remained it was to be used, 'in erecting a water mill for the use and benefit of the public'.[30]

Elizabeth has tended to receive a poor press in Britain. The author of the ODNB article on her even suggests that the length of her very detailed will, which might be thought a testament to her thoughtfulness and generosity, merely, 'reveals how obsessed she was with possessions'.[31] In Calais she is regarded in a very different light and, despite the fact that the town has something of an inclination to change the names of its streets at frequent intervals, there is still a Rue de la Duchesse de Kingston.

Better known today than the Duchess of Kingston is Lord Nelson's mistress Emma Hamilton. One of England's greatest beauties, Emma had been the young wife of

Sir William Hamilton, the British ambassador to Naples as well as being Nelson's lover, the ravishing subject of portraits by George Romney and Elizabeth Vigée le Brun and the belle of many a London ball.

On 21 October 1806 hours before the first shots were fired in the glorious but ill-fated engagement off Cape Trafalgar, Nelson had added a codicil to his Will:

I leave Emma, Lady Hamilton, ...a Legacy to my King and Country, that they will give her an ample provision to maintain her rank in life. I also leave to the beneficence of my Country my adopted daughter Horatia Nelson Thompson and I desire that she will use in future the name of Nelson only. These are the only favours I wish of my King and Country at the moment when I am going to fight their battle.[32]

Horatia was, of course, the daughter he had by Emma in 1801.

The battle began shortly before mid-day and at 1.15 as the *Victory* closed with the French warship *Redoubtable*, a musket ball fired from the Frenchman's rigging struck the Admiral's shoulder and lodged in his spine. As he lay dying he begged Captain Thomas Hardy to, 'take care of my dear Lady Hamilton'.[33]

Emma was devastated by the news of Nelson's death but once she had overcome her immediate grief she found consolation in spending huge sums on the house which she had shared with her hero – Merton Place. When the period of mourning was over, confident that Nelson's request would be granted, she resumed the extravagant life-style to which she had become accustomed, maintaining a large household and throwing parties fit for the royal dukes – of Clarence and Sussex – who were invariably among her guests. But the pension never materialised and despite the assistance she received from numerous, but progressively fewer, gentlemen friends and the £800 annuity left her by her husband Sir William Hamilton, she could never make ends meet – or even approach one another. By 1809 she was more than £15,000 in debt and two years later she was forced to move within the Rules of the King's Bench, the area surrounding the debtors' prison in Southwark, which provided residents with some protection from arrest.

When in 1811 the Prince of Wales became Regent her hopes of a pension were once more raised but her petitions again came to nothing. Emma's expectations were finally extinguished in April 1814 with the publication of the *Letters of Lord Nelson to Lady Hamilton*. She could probably have solved all her financial worries if she had sold the letters to a publisher herself but her devotion to Nelson's memory forbade any such mercenary move whilst the chaotic way in which she organized her life and her household had made it all too easy for a servant to secretly transcribe the correspondence.

Until this time Emma had enjoyed a considerable degree of popularity but, with the publication of Nelson's love letters, all sympathy evaporated. How could they have been published without her consent? Her reputation was destroyed and with it any chance of future favours from the Prince Regent or the Government. In the words of Robert Bell Calton – 'The codicil proved waste paper'.[34]

Assuming that she was benefitting from the enormous sales which the *Letters* enjoyed, Emma's creditors applied fresh force. Her only hope appeared to lie in the newly declared peace – Napoleon was in exile on Elba and France was once more open to the English. There she could escape her creditors, the Law and the vituperation to which she was exposed in London. Anxious to avoid identification, on 1 July 1814 she and Horatia boarded a small, privately-hired vessel at London Bridge and, after enduring three days of sea sickness, they reached Calais and the comforts of Dessein's hotel.

Even at this point she had not abandoned all hope of receiving some financial assistance from the Government. She wrote to George Rose, who as Navy Treasurer had done much to prosecute her cause:

Hôtel Dessin, Calais, July 4th
We arrived here, my dear sir, after three days sickness, as for

precaution we embarked at the Tower ...and I managed so well with Horatia alone, that I was at Calais before any new writs could be issued out against me. I feel so much better for a change of climate, food, air, large rooms, and *liberty* that there is a chance I may live to see my dear Horatia brought up. I am looking out for a lodging. I have an excellent French woman, who is very good at everything; for Horatia and myself, and my old dame who is coming, will be my establishment. Near me is an English lady, who has resided here for twenty-five years; who has a day school but not eating or sleeping. At eight in the morning I take Horatia; fetch her at one; at three we dine; she goes till five, and then in the evening we walk. She learns everything: piano, harp, languages grammatically. She knows French and Italian well, but she will still improve. Not any girls but those of the first families go there. Last evening we walked two miles to a *fête champêtre pour les bourgeois.* Everybody is pleased with Horatia. The General and his good Wife are very good to us; but our little world of happiness is ourselves. If, my dear sir, Lord Sidmouth could do something for my dear Horatia, so that I can be enabled to give her an education, and also for her dress, it would ease me, and make me very happy. Surely he owes this to Nelson. For God's sake do try for me, for you do not know how limited I am. I have left everything to be sold for the creditors, who do not deserve anything: for I have been the victim of artful, mercenary wretches and my too great liberality and open heart has been the dupe of villains. To you, sir, I trust for my dearest Horatia, to exert yourself for her, and that will be a very passport for me.[35]

Rose had little love for the Home Secretary, Henry Addington, Viscount Sidmouth, and it is doubtful if he had much influence with him. Addington seems to have been in Robert Bell Calton's mind when he summarised the Government's failure to respond to Nelson's last wishes in the following terms:

Upon the ear of no government in the world, save our own, could such words at such a moment from such a man have fallen still-born, as the town register of Calais records them to have fallen upon the adder-deaf minister, to whom they were conveyed by the gallant officer entrusted with them.[36]

Emma appears to have remained at Dessein's for some weeks, living in a style which suggested to the transient British passing through Calais that she was not short of money; a view which they took back across the Channel. Eventually she – or perhaps the management – decided that she needed to seek cheaper accommodation and Emma and her small household moved to a farmhouse at St Pierre, then a separate village. Even this reduction in expenditure proved insufficient to match her meagre means and in November she moved back into town to a small apartment belonging to a Monsieur Damy (or Damas). Robert Calton Bell draws a grimly melodramatic picture of the house in which, 'poor Lady Hamilton breathed her last'. It was situated at 27 rue Française, a street which ran parallel to the town's southern rampart.

From its aspect being due north, the house in question is as cheerless and dreary as can well be imagined; not a ray of sunshine ever gladdens the side of the street in which it is situated, or plays for an instant even in summer on the ever-shaded, cold-looking casements.[37]

By this time Emma, who had been in poor health for some years and was now in real pain, was finding relief only in laudanum and alcohol. Henry Cadogan, the British consul, helped her as much as he could and was given a lock of Nelson's hair in return.

The end came on 15 January 1815. Cadogan arranged the funeral. Calton Bell perhaps captured something of the threadbare spirit if not the literal truth of the occasion:

From the portal of this dismal abode, or rather refuge, in the month of January, with a black silk petticoat stitched on a white curtain thrown over her coffin for a pall, and a half-pay Irish dragoon to act as chaplain over the grave in the timber-yard, were the remains of Nelson's most adored friend removed to their final resting place, with the escort of a sergent de ville.[38]

Things may not have been quite so bleak. According to

the *Gentleman's Magazine,* 'all the English Gentlemen in Calais' accompanied Emma to her grave and her most recent biographer, Kate Williams, finds that the, 'modest funeral' cost £28: hardly a pauper burial but modest indeed by comparison with that of the love of life.[39]

The story of George Bryan 'Beau' Brummell is likewise a classic tale of riches to rags or, more precisely, from the acme of dandified Carlton House fashion to the indignities of a French asylum, tertiary syphilis and dementia.

During the first decade of the nineteenth century Brummell, a wealthy, but not fabulously rich, ex-officer of the Light Dragoons, became the arbiter of fashion among London's *Haut Ton.* From his perch in the window of White's club – the so-called 'Beau Window' – he and his friends approved or, more frequently, wittily condemned, the dress, equipage, style and deportment of those who rode, strolled or were driven along St James's Street.[40]

By 1816, however, Brummell, having alienated the support of his former friend the Prince of Wales, had accumulated huge gambling debts which he had no means of re-paying. All lines of credit among the more reputable money-lenders having been exhausted – his fellow roué Lord Alvanley had told a London dinner party that he needed to discover the Lost Tribe of Israel, he and Brummell had, 'exhausted the other two' – the beau had resorted to sharks of the worst type.[41]

Eventually, inevitably, the true nature of Brummell's circumstances having been exposed at White's by a man to whom he owed money, Brummell was forced to seek sanctuary from his creditors. On the evening of 16 May, having, by way of diverting the bailiffs, appeared at Covent Garden, he hired a carriage to take him to Clapham Common where he was met by his own coach which quickly conveyed him to Dover from where he took a hired boat to Calais. Lacking a passport to travel further he was to stay in the town for the next fourteen years.

On the day of his arrival Brummell sat down in the salon at Dessein's to write the first of many letters home. It was to

the brothers Robert and Charles Manners, with whom he
shared a joint debt but who had the good fortune to be
related to someone who was fabulously rich, their father, the
Duke of Rutland. Brummell's letter is characterised by a
combination of self-pity ('I abandon my country a beggar')
excuses ('The responsibility would still have existed the same
on your parts had I forfeited myself to a gaol') and the
Micawberish ('I still feel anxious in the wish to realise the
promised power of future remuneration').[42]

Within a week the contents of Brummell's Mayfair apartment, described as, 'The genuine Property of A MAN OF
FASHION Gone to the Continent', were being sold off to
meet the needs of creditors. The sale raised £1100, the prices
inflated by bidders anxious to associate themselves with
celebrity, but Brummell himself was dependent upon such
funds as he had been able to escape with and gifts from
friends passing through Calais, who like Harriet Wilson,
visited him as if he were, 'a lion at a zoo'.[43] Prince Esterhazy
and Lord Glenbervie called on him shortly after his arrival
and his early biographer Captain Jesse lists among his Calais
visitors the Dukes of Wellington, Richmond, Beaufort and
Bedford and Lords Yarmouth, Sefton, Jersey, Willoughby
d'Eresby and Stuart de Rothesay.[44]

The Beau had raised some additional cash by selling his
carriage to Louis Quillac at Dessein's but within weeks he
had moved from the hotel to an apartment owned by one
Leleux, a book-seller on the rue Royale. At first he was able
to set himself up in reasonable comfort; in what Robert
Calton Bell referred to as, 'comparative, if precarious,
'feather'.[45] His rooms were, 'elegantly if not fastidiously
furnished in the style of Louis Quatorze'[46] and his dinner
came, as it would continue to do, from Dessein's. Nor,
according to Calton, did he neglect his appearance which
was, 'as faultless as in his palmy days; the impression he made
upon the 'Place' [d'Armes] ...being yet remembered by its
present loungers'.[47]

In August 1820, however, Brummell's most dependable
source of funds and his last connection to the royal family,

Frederica, Duchess of York, died. The Duchess had been not only his most generous benefactor but, by contrast, seems to have stood between him and the one means he had of repaying his debts and returning to England.

In his early years in Calais he was often to be seen sitting in the summerhouse in the garden at Dessin's apparently writing his memoirs. The revelations, especially insofar as they concerned the Prince Regent and his brothers, were likely to prove as damning as the reading public would find them fascinating. By 1818 rumours were rife in London that publication was imminent. According to John Wilson Croker:

Beau Brummell is going, or says he is going, to publish an English Journal at Calais, which alarms some great folks, and it is said the French police have been requested to look at it. I hardly think he can make such an attempt – he only wants to be bought off, but surely no one will buy him off....[48]

In fact it appears as if some time before the duchess's death Brummell had promised her that he would not publish anything during the lifetime of either the Prince or the royal dukes and, he told Thomas Raikes, 'I would rather go to gaol than forfeit my word'.[49] In requesting the suppression of the memoirs the Duchess was almost certainly acting upon the prompting of another of her good friends, the Prince Regent himself. By the time that Frederica died her father-in-law George III had himself died so that the former Prince Regent was now George IV and in September of the following year he travelled, via Calais, to visit his subjects in Hanover.

Brummell was probably not one of that class of men, 'whom you had known in seven guinea waistcoats at White's and Watier's, and found in seven shilling overcoats on the Calais pier'[50] begging from disembarking acquaintances, he preferred to write letters to wealthy friends in England seeking remittances, often by exaggerating the extent of his hardship. Those who had received such appeals, with their references to beds of straw and bran bread, if they subsequently visited him in exile were often surprised to discover that, 'he had a good barrel of Dorchester ale in his lodgings, his usual glass of maraschino and his bottle of claret after dinner' and that, 'although living on charity, could afford to buy new snuff boxes to add to his collection and new knick-knacks to adorn his room'.[51] Such was the success, at least in the early days, of his cash-raising technique.

The news of the King's imminent arrival must have given rise to a surge of hope in Brummell's now middle-aged breast. His former friend was the one person who, by securing for him some Crown appointment could provide both an income and the restoration of a degree of respectability.

The King was by no means uncharitable during the visit. According to Brummell's biographer Captain Jesse,

When the king landed, the pier was crowded with spectators, and as he stepped ashore from the barge his hat fell from his hand: this accident a quick-witted urchin immediately took advantage of, and, rushing forward, restored it to His Majesty, who put his hand into his pocket and drew forth enough of the precious metals to provide the impromptu page with peg-tops and brioches for years to come.[52]

The correspondent of *Jackson's Oxford Journal* caught the spirit, although not always the precise detail, of the occasion: according to an extract from a letter from Dover, dated 26 September,

We have this moment landed, after really a delightful trip. We got into Calais last night about seven, and found the King at dinner chez Dessein with the house illuminated and a guard of honour at the gate. He had come in his yacht from Ramsgate and landed in a boat from which he walked to the Inn. The Duc de la Chartre and Count Jumilliac, the Governor of the Department were sent to meet him at the waterside. They sat down thirteen to dinner including the commanding officer of the region, whom he invited. The whole guard dined at His Majesty's expense and six hundred bottles of wine were drunk. After dinner he went to the play, where we saw him looking particularly well and pleased. He was received with great applause, and his affability and good French delighted all around him.

The idea of the grossly overweight monarch walking from the pier to Dessein's seems rather improbable and it is more likely that, as *The Examiner* had it, he, 'proceeded slowly in his carriage' to the hotel where, in the words of the *Glasgow Herald*, 'the military and corps de Pompiers struck up *God Save the King!*'

The story surrounding Brummell's activities on that day also assume that the King arrived at Dessein's by carriage. According to Jesse, Brummell didn't go to the pier to greet his old friend but was in the crowded street opposite his apartment when the royal carriage drove by en route for the hotel. Jesse quotes Brummell's landlord, the bookseller M. Leleux:

I was standing at my shop door and saw Mr Brummell trying to make his way across the street to my house, but the crowd was so great he could not succeed and he was therefore obliged to remain on the opposite side. Of course, all hats were taken off as the carriage approached and when it was close to the door, I heard the King say in a loud voice 'Good God! Brummell!' The latter who was uncovered at the time, now crossed over, as pale as death, entered the house by a private door and retired to his room without addressing me.[53]

This account varies in almost every particular from that of Charles Macfarlane, according to whose *Reminiscences*, Brummell accompanied the mayor to the pier where, 'many of the English purposely made room for him but the King, who almost touched him as he passed up the pier, must have seen him' but, 'turned his Royal head away, and Brummell turned as pale as a ghost'.[54] A number of other stories about the King's visit involve Brummell. It is said that the Beau loaned his valet, Sélègue, to the hotel during the royal stay on account of his familiarity with the English custom of making punch and that the servant took with him some of the cherry-flavoured liqueur maraschino which Brummell remembered the Prince having liked. After the dinner – which most accounts describe as 'sumptuous' – the king is said to have run out of snuff and one of the local dignitaries sent to Brummell to provide some. The King is then said to have recognised Brummell's distinctive mix but, on being told that his former friend was indeed the source, took the matter no further.

The following day, in what was surely a cry for recognition, Brummell wrote his name in the hotel visitor's book but, although urged by a number of the King's party to request an audience, pride appears to have stood in his way. Later in the day as George and his retinue left for Cassel and as he seated himself in his carriage in Dessein's courtyard, he is said to have remarked, 'I leave Calais and have not seen Brummell'.[55]

Jesse concludes this part of his biography by referring to an occasion some years later when he himself was in Calais and remarked to a female tobacconist that the hotels seemed to have fallen off since he was last in the town. She replied,

Go and see Dessin's before you condemn them; your King slept there once ...and, do you know, a friend of his lived here many years – we used to call him the *Roi de Calais*.

Alas for Brummell, he would not see the King again – on his return he made directly for the royal yacht. Whilst his fortunes varied throughout his remaining years in Calais, the general pattern was of decline. Charles Greville's diary provides a glimpse of him, still recognisable but distinctly threadbare, in 1830:

I found him in his old lodging, dressing; some pretty pieces of old furniture in the room, an entire toilet of silver, and a large green macau perched on the back of a tattered silk chair with faded gilding; full of gaiety, impudence and misery.[56]

Three months after Greville's visit George IV died. The new king, the former Duke of Clarence, was prevailed upon, via the good offices of Greville and the Duke of Wellington, to appoint Brummell to the consulship at Caen. He left behind at Calais his dog Vick, buried in the garden at Dessein's, but took with him a great volume of accumulated debt, including a bill of 11,504 francs owed to the Calais banker Jacques Leveux. Of this no less than 3,488 f. was for dinners eaten on account at Dessein's.[57]

Within two years of taking up the post, however, it had been abolished. Brummell was once more reduced to beggary but now in a town less frequently visited by old friends. Depression, aggravated by the symptoms of syphilis, undermined a less than robust constitution and, although he survived for a further eight years, much of that time was spent either in the prison to which his debts eventually drove him, or in the asylum of Bon Sauveur in which he died on 30 March 1840.

Beau Brummell, Emma Hamilton and the Duchess of Kingston are only the most celebrated of the many hundreds of British citizens who sought sanctuary from the Law in Calais. With the passage of the Extradition Act through the Westminster Parliament in 1870 and the subsequent signing of an extradition treaty with France in 1876, the disreputable Cross-Channel flow of criminals and debtors rapidly dried up.[58]

Plate:1 Hogarth's *Calais Gate* shows a great side of beef being delivered to the English Inn. Note the undernourished soldiers and the Scotsman exiled after the '45 Rebellion.

Plate:2 (below)
An Inn Yard in Calais, very like that of Dessein. The innkeeper invites guests to examine the carriages.

INN YARD AT CALAIS.

Plate:3

Passport issued by the
French Consul General
in London,
4 May 1825,
to William Bulwer,
signed at Calais
by the mayor,
Antoine Bénard.

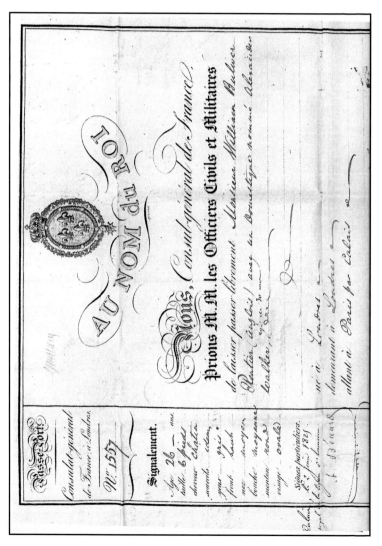

To Calais

Plate:4

      Seasickness – Edward Gibbon called it a 'cursed thing'
to live on an island.

Plate:5 (below)

      William Jones of Nayland thought Calais,
'much handsomer when you approach it from the water.'

Plate: 6
      J.M.W. Turner's *Calais Pier.*   Turner was the most distinguished
           of the many British artists attracted to Calais

Plate:7 (below)
    Landing at low tide. A lady's soaking dress is being carried ashore.

Plate:8

Mrs Thrale with her daughter Queeney.
She thought Desseins's Inn, 'the most magnificent I ever saw.'

Plate:9 (below)

The Passport Office, Calais.

Office of Passports, Calais

176

Routes de
Calais à Paris
provided by the
'Hotel Dessin'.

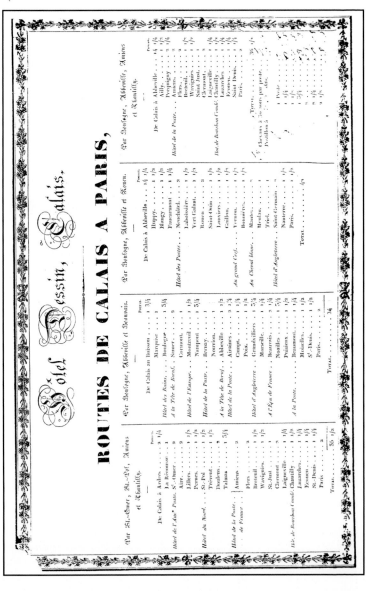

Plate:11

The Duchess of Kingston at her trial for bigamy before the bar of the House of Lords.

Plate:12

Charles James Apperley – 'Nimrod' – enjoyed a long sojourn in Calais:

'Food was not particularly cheap... the savings were in taxes, rent and wine.'

178

Plate:13

An illustration from
The Sentimental Journey
showing the *désobligeant* –
'We were wondering,' said
one who I found was an
Inquisitive Traveller,
what could occasion
its motion.'

Plate:14 (below)
An Englishman's bill for his stay at Dessein's.

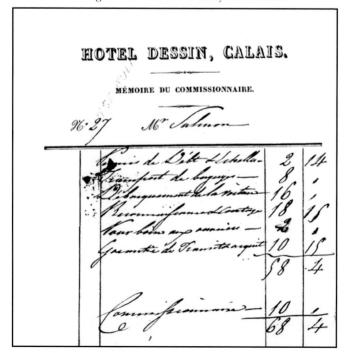

Margaret,
Countess
of Blessington –
'Old Neptune seemed
in a passion at the
thought of us leaving
his favourite isle.'

Plate:16 (right)

Robert Webster,
one of the first
English entrepreneurs to
introduce lace-making
to Calais.

Plate:17 (below)

A sample of lace manufactured at Webster's factory.

Plate:18 (above)
An English party – unprepossessing and inelegantly dressed –
leaves Calais for Paris.

Plate:19 (below)
A grossly overweight Englishman returns to England after a holiday
gourmandising in Calais.

12

'THE MOUSTACHE' AND 'NIMROD'

If anybody in Regency England was more notorious than Beau Brummell it must have been Harriette Wilson. Since the age of 15, Harriette, whose real name was Dubouchet, had worked her way steadily through Debrett, having been the mistress of a succession of lovers, including Lords Craven, Ponsonby and Brougham, the Marquesses of Lorne, Hertford and Worcester and very many others, possibly including the Prince of Wales himself. Not a conventional beauty, she was nonetheless able to exert a powerful sexual magnetism. Sir Walter Scott's biographer, J.G. Lockhart described her as, 'far from beautiful, but a smart, saucy girl, with good eyes and dark hair, and the manners of a wild schoolboy'.[1]

By the mid-1820s, fearing perhaps that her days as a *grande horizontale* were nearing their end Harriette decided to do something which Brummell threatened to do but never did – publish her memoirs.[2] Before doing so she blackmailed her ex-lovers by offering to exclude them from her narrative for a monetary consideration. The Duke of Wellington famously told her publisher, John Joseph Stockdale, to, 'print and be damned'. Others were more cautious.

In 1822, prior to the writing of the memoirs, she encountered in London, 'one of the most manly, interesting and lovable beings I have ever met with in my life'.[3] The 'being's' charms included a striking black moustache, a facial feature which caused William Henry Rochfort to be known as 'The Moustache'. She was thirty-five and he twenty-eight and a prisoner for debt in the Fleet.

Strictly speaking, Rochfort was not imprisoned for he was

a 'ruler', meaning that, on making regular payments to the Warden, he could live within the 'Rules of the Fleet' – the area around the prison, comparable to those of the King's Bench, within which, for a time, Emma Hamilton had been obliged to live. Harriette and William underwent a clandestine 'Fleet marriage' following which she released him from his debts and prison.[4]

Rochfort was an Irish soldier, who described himself as a 'Colonel of Artillery in the service of H.M.F.M. Donna Maria II of Portugal', having earlier served with the British in India. He was a man of imagination and considerable technological ability who might have done very much better in life had he not been obsessed by a desire to prove that he was being defrauded, by his own mother, of the title and estates of the second Earl of Belvedere. He was a man who exerted much fascination – attractive to women and, despite a notable failure to achieve worldly success, admired by men.

Harriette's Memoirs were published in 1825 and, whilst their revelations were by no means explicit, they did name (uninsured) names and achieved a very considerable *succès de scandale.* They were widely talked of, widely deplored but, even more widely, read, being quickly translated into French and German. Within three years 50,000 copies (excluding pirated editions) had been sold, and Harriette was said to have earned £10,000; a sum which ought to have given her financial security for the remainder of her life.[5]

Her love life, however, was not to end in happiness. In 1829, ostensibly so that the rift between Rochfort and his mother, who not only separated him from his inheritance but was appalled by the relationship with Harriette, might be healed, the two decided to live at separate London addresses. Two years later he fell for a younger woman – Mrs Elizabeth Wyatt. The attraction was mutual and it ensured that he and his new lover would spend part of the next decade in Calais. Their tale, with its mixture of pride, desperation and Micawberism, provides a case-study of the kind of straits into which the impoverished British gentry might find themselves, as well as of the problems confronting the British legal system when trying to enforce its decisions in France.

Elizabeth was the wife of Mr Thomas Wyatt of the Bengal Civil Service and most of what we know about her and Rochfort comes from law reports of cases brought against them by him. She had lived with her husband in India but, taken ill, had returned to England with their young son, Henry Hubert, and her sister-in-law in 1825. In a case for divorce brought by Wyatt before the House of Lords in 1841, a Mr Christopher Idle gave evidence that he had met Elizabeth in London at two addresses in 1830 and in Calais, 'in 1833 or 1834' when she and Rochfort were living, 'as man and wife', firstly in the Rue du Havre and later in the Rue des Thermes.[6] Asked whether he ever saw her when she was, 'in the family way', Idle replied, 'Yes, frequently' and when asked if he recalled, 'the fact of the birth', he said that he did because the child had an unsual name, 'Rajphoot Runjheet or something of that sort'.[7]

Another witness, Joseph Spencer Judge, had been prevailed upon to travel to Calais and examine and make a copy of the register of births which had been authenticated by the deputy mayor, M. Legros Devot. A translation of the entry reads:

1835   12 October   4.30 in the afternoon
William Henry Rochfort, aged 40, Lt. Colonel of artillery in the service of the Queen of Portugal living at Calais – declared that on the tenth of this month at mid-day was born a boy child at 200 Rue des Boucheries to whom was given the names Rajphoot Runjheet. He is the father of the child. Mother – Elizabeth Gertrude de Grey, 30 years.
Witnesses: Antoine Leleux, aged 53, printer & bookseller
              Arnaud Castaing, 39, wine merchant
[Copied 17 March 1841][8]

Leleux was almost certainly the same M. Leleux, bookseller, who some years previous had been Beau Brummell's landlord.[9] Castaing was the couple's latest landlord, in the Rue des Boucheries. When this entry was transcribed into the *Tables décennale de naissance de la Ville de Calais* for the decade beginning 1 January 1833 the child's name appeared, incorrectly but perhaps understandably, as 'Rochefort, Raphael'.[10] The 1836 census showed the family as consisting of William Henry Rochefort [40]; Elizabeth Degrey femme Rochefort [31]; Henri Rochefort [13], this was, in fact, Wyatt's son; Rajphood Rungheat Rochefort [7 months] and a servant, Jeanette Sta [38].

Thanks to Judge, we also know something of Mrs Wyatt's appearance as he applied to Mr Marshall, the British Consul in Calais, to discover whether she had been recently issued with a passport. It appears that in July of 1836 she had applied for one under the name of Rochfort to visit Paris. Marshall, knowing that was not her correct name, refused to issue one but granted one to 'Mrs Elizabeth Grey Wyatt'. The Register of Passports describes her characteristics. Her hair was brown and eyes blue, her forehead high, her chin round and complexion *'coloré'*. She was 1m 73 (5' 8½') in height and her nose and mouth 'average'.[11] This, perhaps, does less than justice to the woman who attracted 'The Moustache' away from the amorous gaze of Harriette Wilson.

Rochfort was by no means the kind of feckless scrounger often characterised as typical of the British residents of Calais (see Appendix 3). He appears to have been constantly busy, not least in writing letters to the eminent lawyer Henry Brougham, to whom he was probably introduced by Harriette. Although Brougham must have found Rochfort a nuisance, he doesn't seem to have attempted to shake him off, suggesting that he may have had some genuine admiration for the man. In 1834 Brougham had sent Rochfort to Brussels on what was apparently a secret mission relating to the Duke of Wellington's embarrassingly dreadful relation William Long Wellesley. Alas, Wellesley and he came close to fighting a duel and may well have done so had Rochfort not considered his opponent to be unworthy of him. He was, he wrote to Wellesley, nevertheless determined to communicate with him although only, 'through the medium of an ash plant or a double thonged Crowther horse-whip'.[12] Not the language of a diplomat.

In the year 1835 he wrote from Calais to the United Services Gazette suggesting, at considerable length, an improvement to the manufacture of field gun-carriages. Typically, his idea had been treated with scant respect by the War Department but had been taken up by the French who, however, failed to acknowledge his contribution to the innovation. The following year he published *A Treatise upon Archanography* a system of secret writing which, unfortunately for its ingenious inventor, had been declared 'inscrutable' by the Foreign Office.[13] By 1847 he was trying to interest Brougham in a wind-guage which he hoped – forlornly – would be taken up by the Admiralty.

It is clear that in the mid-1830s he and Elizabeth were living in Calais because of shortage of money. Rochfort was, of course, no longer being subsidised by Harriette and evidence given in the divorce case suggests that Elizabeth was receiving little or nothing from Wyatt. In order to prove that the child could not possibly be that of her husband, Mr Judge, who had been a solicitor in India and an acquaintance of Wyatt, gave evidence that, although a civil and session judge, earning 28,000-30,000 Rupees per year, Wyatt was so much in debt that, 'this was scarcely enough to pay the interest on his debt'. He was in no position to return to Europe.

In the summer of 1836 a writ of *habeas corpus* was obtained on behalf of Wyatt, demanding that Rochfort and Mrs Wyatt, who were, 'living in adultery... at Calais', deliver up Wyatt's son, Henry Hubert, to the Court of King's Bench.[14] The writ was taken over to France and proceedings instituted against the pair in the Court of Boulogne, within the jurisdiction of which Calais lay. A decree was there obtained ordering them to obey the writ. They then moved to Paris, presumably to escape the demands of the Boulogne decree. A further writ was served on them there on 7 December. Rochfort refused to deliver up the boy unless paid for his board for the previous five years, a sum which he estimated, rather outrageously, at £1000! Furthermore, he alleged, Henry

Hubert was earning a guinea a week as a civil engineer, a job he could not give up. But, although this second writ was served in conformity with French law, proceedings could not be taken any further as there was no law authorising an arrest of a British subject in such a case.[15] Some time prior to the bill for divorce Wyatt had sued Rochfort for, 'criminal conversation' (i.e. adultery) with his wife and was awarded damages of £230 which, by 1841 had still not been paid.

When the *habeas corpus* case was brought back to the Court of King's Bench early in 1837, it was stated that Rochfort had, 'lately come over to this country', leaving Mrs Wyatt and her children behind and that he had been arrested for debt and was in the King's Bench prison on two detainers. He was endeavouring to find bail and as soon as he did so he would return to France. The judge in the case concluded that he could not grant an attachment for contempt for not obeying the writ of *habeas corpus* because, 'I do not see how I can say this was a good service [of the writ], having been effected out of the jurisdiction of the Court'.[16] Such were the frustrations, prior to a workable extradition treaty, which confronted the British courts in endeavouring to exert their authority over British subjects abroad.

Further evidence of their impecunious state comes from a series of pathetic letters produced in the House of Lords and sent by Mrs Wyatt to a fellow English resident of Calais, a merchant and banker, Mr John Redshaw Morley of the Rue de Guise.[17] They relate to the hurried departure for Paris in the summer of 1836. The first reads as follows:

I have not personally the Pleasure of knowing you yet, or [to] thank you, and very truly, already for a kind Attention. I hope Mr Addis was properly punctual. I am now going to Paris, and after paying all my little Demands, I find myself looking in vain for 100 Francs more. May I, dare I in fact, a Stranger, entreat Mr Morley to lend it me only till I get to Paris, when Mr Rochfort will return it with the greatest Pleasure, and his hearty Acknowledgements for the service Mr Morley will confer on me. Pray believe me in a great Difficulty, and absolutely dressing to go, the Diligence starts at

Nine; the man is here for the Things, and I minus 100 Francs.
Forgive the Liberty of the Request, the paper, the Writing: and be
assured only of my Thanks and Respect.

E.G. Wyatt

Address me to my Servant, if you please, as Mrs Rochfort.

This appeal is undated but Elizabeth probably set out for
Paris shortly after the date of her passport (29 July).

As her next letter to Morley, dated 19 August, from the
Rue Neuve de Berri, off the Champs Elysées, makes clear, he
had responded positively to her appeal. 100 Francs was not
a vast sum of money, the equivalent of £4 - 2 - 6d sterling, but
nor was it, in those days, negligible.[18] Familiar, as he must
have been, with the financial position of so many of the
British residents of Calais, Morley, whilst he may have been
disappointed, could hardly have been shocked by the
contents of the letter. Their rather startling effrontery is a
different matter. Dickens could surely have made much of
Mrs Wyatt.

My dear Sir,

Had I written you as immediately as I wished a Week even had
not passed without my thanking you, and very sincerely too, for
the kind Obligation you had conferred, and at the same Time have
restored you the amount of it. I have been disappointed in the
Receipt of rather a large Sum of Money, and this alone has
deprived me of the great Pleasure of remitting the Hundred
Francs, which you amiably sent me a few Minutes before my
departure from Calais. By Letters from England I find there will
be some little Delay before I receive the Money I allude to; but I
would make you a Proposal, which if agreeable, I shall immediately
have Pleasure of returning you the 100 Francs, and of receiving
from you another service, which, believe me, I shall appreciate with
much Sincerity.

On the 15th January the Court of Chancery will again pay me
a dividend of £26 - 10s: may I venture to offer you an Order for it,
and to beg, as an additional Service, the Advance of the Balance,
after deducting, as of course, the Discount &c. and the 100 Francs
so very amiably lent me.

I hear from our respected and charming friends the De
Brochets, who dined with us a few Days since, that they are great

Allies of yours, and that now and then you visit Paris. I hope in your next Trip you will give me the Opportunity of personally saying how properly I have valued the Obligation you have already conferred, and how much I shall esteem a Repetition of it, if I may presume to ask it. It is so strange that I never have had the Pleasure of knowing you, and yet that I should have experienced kindness from you.

Mr Troward's Gallantry, too, I shall faithfully remember; I beg to make him my Compliments. Anticipating the Favour of hearing from you, believe me

My dear Sir,
Your obliged
E.G. Wyatt

Again she asks to be addressed as 'Mrs Rochfort'.[19]

The next letter, from the same address, is dated 21 September and makes clear that Morley did not succumb to Mrs Wyatt's request – 'If you will only as readily forgive the Liberty I have taken with you as I forgive you for letting my poor Letters remain so long unanswered'. She again desires that he accepts her order. The final letter, also from Paris, is dated 20 January [1837]. Again, she requests forgiveness:

My dear Sir,
I am confident in the Hope of remitting you my Obligation of 100 Francs during the next few Days and thankful I am to you for the excessively kind Patience you have exercised.

My Honesty has been somewhat tardy of Proof, but you are amiable enough to forgive, and to believe me conscious of the Favour I have received. Pray, my dear Sir, consider me faithfully,

Your obliged
E.G. Wyatt

We never learn whether Morley ever got his 100 Francs back but we do know that Rochfort and Mrs Wyatt did not return to Calais. By 1840 they were living at Ostend, still dodging their creditors. A year later, young Henry Wyatt was a student at Queen's College, Oxford, on his way to becoming an Anglican clergyman. Elizabeth and William were eventually able to return to London although not to live on the income from Rochfort's Irish estates. His mother outlived her peripatetic son by two years.

In the years after the Napoleonic Wars fox-hunting became increasingly fashionable, increasingly written about and increasingly expensive. Young men who inherited fortunes upon which their grandfathers could have lived out their lives in the utmost comfort, began competing for the finest bloodstock and all too often overreached themselves. It is not, therefore, surprising that when, in 1831, Charles James Apperley, the pioneering gentleman hunting correspondent 'Nimrod', was compelled to take up residence in Calais he should meet with several other members of the hunting fraternity, including one of the most celebrated.

Charles James was the 4th of the eight children of Thomas Apperley of Plâsgronow, near Wrexham in Wales. After Rugby school and a couple of years in the light dragoons, he married, in 1801, Elizabeth Wynne of Peniarth, Montgomeryshire. For the next twenty years he and a growing family was to live in a succession of houses in Wales and the Midlands being chiefly dependent upon hand-outs from Elizabeth's family. In 1820, or thereabouts, she left him, taking their children with her, to live at Hampton, Middlesex. Thrown back on his own resources, Apperley began exploiting his most passionate interest by writing for the *Sporting Magazine*. He transformed that journal, if his autobiography is to be believed, from, 'a mere Cockney concern' into the much respected and far more widely-circulated vehicle for the letters of 'Nimrod'. Between 1824 and 1828 he wrote under that pseudonym for the remarkable sum of £1500 p.a.; remuneration which enabled him to keep a stud of first-class hunters and, oddly, to live at Beaurepaire, near Basingstoke, Hants. It was a beautiful house but, as he remarked in his *Hunting Reminiscences* – 'How often have I lamented having resided ten years in that slowest of all counties, Hampshire, instead of pitching my tent northward, whence I could have visited Leicestershire every successive season'.[20]

All went well with Apperley until 1827 when Mr Pittman, the owner of the *Sporting Magazine* died. The new owners refused to raise his salary and the parties entered into a prolonged period of acrimony, Apperley making his final contribution to the paper in 1829. The outcome of the subsequent legal disputes and their expense was that, in 1831, 'I sought the nearest part of France as an asylum'.[21]

Unlike the great majority of such refugees, Apperley appears to have enjoyed his exile. Despite the absence of sport, 'except as exercise', he thought, 'Calais, or its vicinity, one of the most desirable spots in France for him who did not aspire to residence in Paris'. He took a house in the Rue des Thermes, 'which is considered the pleasantest street'.[22] The house was, 'quite new and very comfortable, with three sitting-rooms and five bedrooms, wash-house and', probably a priority with Nimrod, 'stabling for two horses'. He paid £42 to have the house, unfurnished, for three years, a reminder that the presence even of British debtors could have an inflationary effect upon the cost of housing. Apperley, however, must have had cause to regret the deal as, soon after he had moved in, a loud knock on the door may well have caused him to forfeit the greater part of that sum and seek accommodation elsewhere.

The visitor was Apperley's wildly eccentric friend, the huntsman, hell-raiser and former M.P. for Shrewsbury, John Mytton, whose considerable fortune, based on substantial estates in Shropshire and Montgomeryshire, had been squandered upon gifts, gambling, horses and drink. Whether swimming the river Severn, performing extra-ordinary feats of jumping without regard for the safety either of his horse or himself, or riding into his drawing room in full hunting costume on the back of his pet bear, Mytton's behaviour – invariably fuelled by drink – was frequently as extravagant as it was foolhardy.

He had fled his creditors and was staying at Roberts's Royal Hotel. According to Nimrod's *The Life of John Mytton*, the following exchange took place on the doorstep:

'In God's name,' said I, 'what has brought you to France?'

'Why,' he replied, 'just what brought yourself to France… three couple of bailiffs were hard at my brush.'[23]

Apperley was shocked by the sight of his friend – 'There stood before me a round-shouldered, decrepid, tottering old-young man, if I may be allowed such a term… bloated by drink.'

Shortly after this visit Apperley moved to, 'a large old chateau three miles from Calais on the Dunkirk road'.[24] The sporting novelist and creator of Jorrocks, R.S. Surtees, who visited him there, described it as approached by, 'a straight, poplar-planted avenue with a grass-grown courtyard and entered by large old-fashioned gates' and that, 'the usual accompaniments of chateaux in France occupied one end of the building, while the other looked out upon a well-stocked garden'.[25]

Why Nimrod moved out of Calais is not easily accounted for; two competing explanations offering themselves. According to E.D. Cumings's biography, itself based on the writer's own *Life and Times*, the move can be explained by the approach of cholera. That none of his own household contracted the disease he, somewhat idiosyncratically, attributed, 'in great measure to a strict dietary discipline – not a vegetable, not even an apple, being eaten by anyone, and nothing drank but cold, weak brandy and water with meals and a little sound wine afterwards'.[26]

A quite different explanation for the move, however, is told in Nimrod's own life of John Mytton; one that relates to that gentleman's wildly eccentric behaviour. One evening in his room at Roberts's, being much the worse for drink and afflicted by hiccups he resorted to a bizarre treatment which his biographer summarises as follows:

'D——n this hiccup,' said Mytton, as he stood undressed on the floor, apparently in the act of getting into bed; 'but I'll *frighten* it away;' so seizing a lighted candle applied it to the tale of his shirt, and – it being a cotton one – he was instantly enveloped in flames.[27]

Two men in the room at the time managed to extinguish the blaze but then left him to his own devices. The following morning his alarmed valet went to Apperley for assistance:

> Shall I ever forget the scene this morning presented? There lay Mr Mytton, not only shirtless, but sheetless, with the skin of his breast, shoulders and knees of the same colour with newly-singed bacon hog.[28]

Dr Bradley, an English physician resident in Calais, being away from home, Apperley called for Dr Souville, the principal French doctor of the town but, despite his best efforts, Mytton negated them by seeking to alleviate the pain with brandy. A distressing period followed in which, in Nimrod's view, he became increasingly mad. Brother sportsman, including Henry Wyatt and a Mr Vaughton, both of Warwickshire, took turns in standing guard over him. Not always with success:

> He would at this time frequently send for eau de Cologne, under the pretext of using it as perfume, or otherwise externally, on his person. We soon, however, by the quantity consumed, ascertained that he drank it.[29]

His mother and two muscular 'attendants' were summoned from England and took over these duties and, with the approach of spring (of 1832), it was decided that he should be moved from the hotel. Landlords were, however, 'alarmed at the idea of a *gentleman and his keepers*... so, at the request of Mrs Mytton, I consented to hire a chateau and to receive him as an inmate until his recovery was complete'.[30]

The chateau chosen was large enough to allow Mytton and his attendants to occupy apartments separate from Apperley's and he gradually resumed a more regular regimen until, after two months, he was persuaded to return to England and sign away the remainder of his Shropshire property. His *ODNB* biographers claim that he, 'crossed the Channel thrice more before his death' from delirium tremens on 29 March 1834 in the King's Bench prison.[31] He was thirty-eight years old.

Soon after moving to the chateau, Apperley had found himself once more in financial straits which were relieved by an appeal made on his behalf by Surtees who, as we have seen, had visited him there. In the year of Mytton's death things had improved for the journalist. He was released from his debts and in 1836 won back the right to use the pen-name 'Nimrod' enabling him to earn a better living from his writing. He kept two horses and rode or walked daily on the sands. Although the shades of the prison-house had lifted he decided to remain in France where living was comparatively cheap;

Food was not particularly cheap: he did not think there was more than 5 per cent difference in this respect between this part of France and England. The savings were in taxes, rent and wine; the first amounted to only 28 francs a year, and for as many pounds he secured the house to which he moved from the old chateau.[32]

The new house was at St Pierre, alternatively known as the Basse-Ville, situated on the inland side of Calais on the road to St Omer. It had some advantages over the town itself: its taxes were very low and the *octroi*, the municipal duty was avoided so that provisions were cheaper. Although an important focus of the lace-making industry, it also had a *jardin des plantes* and Vauxhall Garden.[33] The house itself was detached and pleasantly situated, 'with three sitting rooms, large garden and paddock, double coal-house, stables etc.'[34] According to Robert Bell Calton, it was, 'a very confortable house, with gardens in the English style on the banks of the canal between Calais and the Basseville.'[35]

Given the fact that he was once more earning good money, the question arises as to why Charles Apperley should have been so concerned to save money. Of course the lesson of John Mytton, whose biography he published in 1836, was a salutary one but there may have been another reason revealed in the St Pierre census of that same year.

Apperley's household was shown to consist of:

Nom	Prénom	Occupation	Age
Apperley	Charles	Rentier	54
Taylor femme Apperley	Sarah		37
Apperley	James		11
Apperley	George		9
Apperley	Harriett		7
Apperley	Adelaide		5
Apperley	Frederick		1
Underwood	Jane	Domestique	19
Agglestone	Elizabeth	Domestique	23 [36]

Which is to say that Charles had a large second family. These were clearly not his wife's children. She had left him c.1820 and she died in 1834. There is no direct reference to this family either in the life edited by E.D. Cuming or in Norman Gash's article in the *ODNB*.[37] The only hint occurs in *My Life and Times* when discussing the cholera epidemic; he there says that of the, 'nine adults and four children under my roof' none contracted the disease.[38]

The apparently irregular nature of his relationship with Sarah may provide another reason why he opted to stay in France until 1843, the year before his death.

Robert Surtees had come to Apperley's aid in 1832 but satirised him cruelly as Pomponius Ego of Calais in his novel *Handley Cross*, presenting him as a conceited show-off, the very opposite of the vulgar, good-natured Jorrocks. There is some accuracy but more exaggeration in this portrayal of a man whose contribution to sporting history was probably only exceeded by that of Surtees himself.

13

'WITH FRENCH PENS AND FRENCH INK'

Arrival in Calais, or perhaps more generally arrival in France, as we have seen, inspired many travelling English men and women to record the experience. A large number of these committed their impressions to print. Robert Southey, in the guise of a Spaniard travelling in England, summarised the situation thus:

> A volume of travels rarely or never, in our days, appears in Spain: in England, on the contrary, scarcely any works are so numerous. If an Englishman spends the summer in any of the mountainous provinces, or runs over to Paris for six weeks, he publishes the history of his travels.[1]

Lieutenant Francis Hall of the Light Dragoons, whose *Travels in Canada and the United States in 1816 and 1817* had already met with some success, nevertheless felt that, 'A man must have considerable literary courage to write 'Travels in France', especially if he begins at Calais'.[2] For one who had spent a considerable amount of time in the backwoods of North America, Hall wrote with a fine urbanity:

> Tis a very moderate assertion to say, that within these ten years past, there have been written as many books of 'Travels in France', as would fill a country gentleman's library. They have swarmed in all forms and sizes, from the humble journalist, who notes down each stage and post-house, takes record of his daily dinners, and fixes literary talons upon each *aubergiste* and *fille-de-chambre* on his road, to the more scientific and exalted tourist, who, soaring above vulgar detail concocts the spiritual essence of his journey, like a rich sauce, from ingredients 'known only to the artist'. The public has thus banqueted on Travels, Agricultural, Philosophical, and Political; on Visits and Visitations, from Six Months to Six Weeks;

on Letters and Observations; on 'Reflections during a Residence' and 'Notes during an Abode'; on 'Walks in, round and about Paris'; on 'Sketches of Scenery' and 'Scenic Delineations' on Journeys, voluntary and forced; on Excursions on Horseback and on Foot; by Old Routes and New Routes and Unusual Routes.

We have met many of these types in the course of this book but in addition to the many and varied travelogue writers there were others inspired, often by the example of Sterne, to attempt writing of a more creative kind.

In 1792 the radical, working-class playwright and novelist Thomas Holcroft published his epistolary novel *Anna St Ives*, sympathetic to the ideas of the French Revolution. Anna, its eponymous heroine – 'Sterne was in my pocket and his gentle spirit was present to my mind' – upon arriving at Calais, is far more critical of her reaction to what she sees than most of her non-fictional fellow countrymen. She writes to her friend Louisa Clifton and asks,

What is there, my dear, in the human mind, that induces us to think everything which is unusual is little less than absurd? Is it prejudice, is it vanity, or is it a short and imperfect view; a want of discrimination? I could have laughed, but that I had a latent sense of my own folly, at the sight of a dozen French men and women, and two or three loitering monks, whom curiosity had drawn together upon the pier head. And what was my incitement to laughter? It was the different cut of a coat. It was a silk bag, in which the hair was tied, an old sword, and a dangling pair of ruffles; which none of them suited with the poverty of the dress, and meagre appearance, of a person who seemed to strut and value himself upon such marks of distinction...

Let us turn our eyes back to the shores we have so lately left: let us examine the trifles we hang about ourselves. How many of them, which characterize and as it were stamp the nation with absurdity, escape unobserved! We see them every day; we have adopted and make them our own, and we should be strangely offended, should any person take the liberty, having discovered the folly of them, to laugh at us.[3]

The fictional Anna is intelligent, rational, enlightened, emancipated. There is in her, perhaps, something of

Holcroft's friend Mary Wollstonecraft.

Anna and her party stay at Dessein's but, although Holcroft had himself visited France back in 1783, the novel betrays no evidence that he had actually stayed at the hotel. In Anna's description there is nothing that could not have been observed by a curious non-resident. Holcroft, the democrat, is not entirely enthusiastic about what was to become known as *l'auberge des Rois*[4]

> We had determined to go to Dessein's.... I was amused with the handbill, stuck up against the walls of this inn, or hotel, as it is called; announcing it to be the largest, the completest, the most magnificent, with a thousand etceteras, in the universe; and recounting not only its numerous accommodations, but the multifarious trades which it contained within its own walls; to all which was added a playhouse. A playhouse it is true there was, but no players; and as for trades, there were at least as many as we wanted. Sir Arthur took over his own carriage; otherwise this first of inns in the universe would not have furnished him with one, but on condition of its being purchased.

Other English novels in which Calais features are as varied as Mrs Johnson's, *Francis the Philanthropist* (1786) Captain Marryat's, *The Naval Officer, or Scenes and Adventures in the Life of Frank Mildmay* (1829) and Barbara Cartland's, *The Heart Triumphant* (1976) but the most famous is surely Dickens's *Little Dorrit* and the chapter in which Arthur Clennam, on the track of the criminal Blandois, visits Miss Wade in the sparse little apartment she shares with Tattycoram. Clennam's grimly anxious mood reflects the Calais he sees – a low, grey, dank town inhabited by, 'French vagabonds and English outlaws', the latter having the air, 'of lounging out a limited round, day after day, which strongly reminded him of the Marchalsea'.[5] Dickens was a Francophile who knew Calais well and his more nuanced attitude to the town is reflected in his wonderful short story *The Calais Night Mail* written in his guise as the Uncommercial Traveller, a nod in the direction of Sterne and his Sentimental, Idle and Inquisitive travellers. As we have seen, to take his mind off the miseries of the crossing Dickens's Traveller sings to himself one of Tom Moore's *Irish Melodies*:

> Rich and rare were the gems she wore,
> And a bright gold ring on her wand she bore;
> But, oh! her beauty was far beyond
> Her sparkling gems or her snow-white wand.

> 'Lady, dost thou not fear to stray,
> So lone and lovely, through this bleak way?
> Are Erin's sons so good or so cold,
> As not to be tempted by woman or gold?'

> 'Sir Knight! I feel not the least alarm,
> No son of Erin will offer me harm:
> For, though they love women and golden store,
> Sir Knight! they love honour and virtue more.'

> On she went, and her maiden smile
> In safety lighted her round the green isle;
> And blest for ever is she who relied
> Upon Erin's honour and Erin's pride.

The Irish poet Thomas Moore is perhaps best known today for his *Irish Melodies* such as *Believe me, if all those endearing young charms; The Last Rose of Summer; The Minstrel Boy* and the favourite of Dickens's Uncommercial Traveller – *Rich and rare were the gems she wore*. He was a man of many parts: poet, biographer, playwright, singer and the star of many a literary salon. In his lifetime it was as the composer of the long oriental romance *Lalla Rookh* (1817) that he won most fame. That success was followed by *The Fudge Family in Paris*, a light-hearted satire on the follies of Restoration France, inspired by a short trip to the French capital which Moore took with his friend Samuel Rogers.[6] It begins with Miss Biddy's amusing impressions of Calais and Dessein's Hotel. Soon after its publication however Moore found himself in severe financial straits and was compelled to seek refuge from his creditors by spending three years in France and Italy. In Venice he met his old friend Byron. They got drunk and Byron gave Moore his Memoirs for publication 'when I am cold'. Moore returned to London incognito (wearing a false moustache!) and sold them to John Murray but failed to prevent them being burned at Murray's Albemarle Street office three days after the news of Byron's death reached England in 1824.[7]

Although Biddy Fudge was no intellectual she may owe something to Anna St Ives. The young Moore had certainly had radical sympathies and the probability is that he had read Holcroft's novel which had been very popular in his student days in the 1790s. Biddy, like Anna, describes Sterne as 'divine' and whilst Anna's 'very first demand had been for pen, ink and paper' Biddy sat down to write, 'A letter from France with French pens and French ink'.[8]

THOMAS MOORE: THE FUDGE FAMILY IN PARIS, 1818
(for footnotes *see* p. 202)
LETTER 1

From Miss Biddy Fudge to Miss Dorothy ——————, of Clonskilty, in Ireland

Amiens

Dear Doll, while the tails of our horses are plaiting,
The trunks tying on, and Papa at the door,
Into very bad French is, as usual translating
His English resolve not to give a *sou* more,
I sit down to write you a line – only think! –
A letter from France, with French pens and French ink,
How delightful! Though – would you believe it, my dear?
I have seen nothing yet *very* wonderful here;
No adventure, no sentiment, far as we've come,
But the cornfields and trees quite as dull as at home;
And, *but* for the post-boy, his boots and his queue,
I might *just* as well be at Clonskilty with you!
In vain, at Dessein's, did I take from my trunk
That divine fellow, Sterne, and fall reading *The Monk!*
In vain did I think of his charming dead Ass,
And remember the crust and the wallet – alas![a]
No monks can be found now for love or for money

(All owing, Pa says, to that infidel Boney);
And, though *one* little Neddy we saw in our drive
Out of classical Nampont, the beast was alive!
By the by, though, at Calais, Papa had a touch
Of romance on the pier, which affected me much.
At the sight of that spot, where our darling *dix-huit*[b]
Set the first of his own dear legitimate feet
(Modelled out so exactly, and – God bless the mark! –
'Tis a foot, Dolly, worthy so *Grand a Monarque*),
He exclaimed, 'Oh mon Roi! And, with tear-dropping eye,
Stood to gaze on the spot – while some Jacobin, nigh,
Muttered out with a shrug (what an insolent thing!)
'Ma foi, he be right – 'tis de Englishman's King;
And dat *gros pied de cochon* – begar, me vil say,
Dat de foot look mosh better, if turned toder way.'
There's the pillar, too – Lord! I had nearly forgot –
What a charming idea! Raised close to the spot;
The mode being now (as you've heard, I suppose)
To build tombs over legs, and raise pillars to toes.[c]
This is all that's occurred sentimental as yet;
Except, indeed, some little flower-nymphs we've met,
Who disturb one's romance with pecuniary views,
Flinging flowers in your path and then bawling for *sous*!
And some picturesque beggars, whose multitudes seem
To recall the good days of the *ancien régime,*
All as rapid and brisk, you'll be happy to learn,
And as thin, as they were in the time of dear Sterne.

Our party consists, in a neat Calais job,
Of Papa and myself, Mr Connor and Bob.
You remember how sheepish Bob looked at Kilrandy,
But Lord! He's quite altered – they've made him a Dandy,
A thing, you know, whiskered, great-coated and laced,
Like an hour-glass, exceedingly small in the waist;
Quite a new sort of creatures, unknown yet to scholars,
With heads so immoveably stuck in shirt collars,
That seats like our music-stools, soon must be found them,
To twirl, when the creatures may wish to look round them!
In short, dear, 'a Dandy' describes what I mean,
And Bob's far the best of the *genus* I've seen;
An improving young man, fond of learning, ambitious,
And goes now to Paris to study French dishes,

Whose names – think, how quick! – he already knows pat,
A la braise, petits pâtés, and – what d'ye call that
They inflict on potatoes? Oh! *maître d'hôtel* –
I assure you, dear Dolly, he knows them as well
As if nothing but these all his life he had ate,
Though a bit of them Bobby has never touched yet;
But just knows the names of French dishes and cooks,
As dear Pa knows the titles of authors and books.

As for Pa, what d'ye think! – mind it's all *entre nous,*
But you know, love, I never keep secrets from you –
Why, he's writing a book – what! A tale? A romance?
No, ye Gods, would it were! – but his Travels in France;
At the special desire (he let out 'other day)
Of his friend and his patron, my Lord Castlereagh,
Who said, 'My dear Fudge – ', I forget th'exact words,
And, it's strange, no one ever remembers my Lord's;
But 'twas something to say, that, as all must allow,
A good orthodox work is much wanting just now,
To expound to the world the new – thingummie – science,
Found out by the – what's-its-name – Holy Alliance,[d]
And prove to mankind that their rights are but folly,
Their freedom a joke (which it *is*, you know, Dolly):
'There's none,' said his Lordship, 'if *I* may be judge,
Half so fit for this great undertaking as Fudge!'

The matter's soon settled – pa flies to *the Row*
(The first stage your tourists now usually go)
Settles all for his quarto – advertisements, praises –
Starts post from the door, with his tablets – French phrases –
'Scott's Visit' of course – in short, everything *he* has
An author can want, except words and ideas: –
And, lo! The first thing in the spring of the year,
Is Phil. Fudge at the front of a Quarto, my dear!

But, bless me, my paper's near out, so I'd better
Draw fast to a close: – this exceeding long letter
You owe to a *déjeûner à la Fourchette,*
Which Bobby would have, and is hard at it yet, –
What's next? Oh, the tutor, the last of the party,
Young Connor: – they say he's like Bonaparte,
His nose and his chin, – which Papa rather dreads,

As the Bourbons, you know, are suppressing all heads
That resemble old Nap's, and who knows but their honours
May think, in their fright, of suppressing poor Connor's?
Au reste (as we say), the young lad's well enough,
Only talks much of Athens, Rome, virtue and stuff;
A third cousin of ours, by the way, poor as Job
(Though of royal descent by the side of Mamma),
And for charity made private tutor to Bob –
Entre nous, too, a papist – how liberal of Pa!ᵉ

This is all, dear – forgive me for breaking off thus;
But Bob's *déjeûner's* done, and Papa's in a fuss.
                                   B.F.
P.S.
How provoking of Pa! He will not let me stop
Just to run in and rummage some milliner's shop:
And my *début* in Paris, I blush to think on it,
Must now, Doll, be made in a hideous low bonnet,
But Paris, dear Paris – oh *there* will be joy,
And romance, and high bonnets, and Madame le Roi!ᶠ

a) In A Sentimental Journey the owner of the Dead Ass addresses the dead
animal with the words, 'And this, said he, putting the remains of a crust into his
wallet, and this, should have been thy portion... hads't thou been alive to have
shared it with me.'

b) 'darling *dix-huit*' i.e. Louis XVIII who returned to France 24 April 1814. La
Colonne Louis XVIII, bearing a bronze plaque of the royal footprint, survives
opposite the Courgain Maritime. The restored monarch spent his first night in his
kingdom at Dessein's hotel. Prior to the Restoration his court-in-exile had been
held at Hartwell House, Bucks. Moore himself was a Whig who thought the French
'shabby dogs' for re-instating the Bourbon monarchy. – L Kelly, *Ireland's Minstrel*,
London 2006.

c) 'To build tombs over legs': Lord Uxbridge (later the Marquis of Anglesey)
had lost his leg at Waterloo. It was buried in the garden of the Brussels surgeon
who amputated it and a 'tomb' raised over it.

d) 'Holy Alliance': a development of the Congress System which Tsar Alexander
in particular was seeking to develop into, 'a sort of ideological cosh for suppressing
revolutions and upholding rulers.' – Boyd Hilton, *A Mad Bad and Dangerous People,
England 1787-1846*, Oxford, 2006.

e) Moore himself was a Catholic.

f) Madame le Roi: a famous mantua-maker in Paris.

Biddy Fudge herself reappeared in Anna Jameson's first
published work, *The Diary of an Ennuyée*, based on her own
first journey to Italy and published in 1826:

Calais, June 21 – What young lady, travelling for the first time on the Continent, does not write a 'Diary'? No sooner have we slept on the shores of France – no sooner are we seated in the gay salon at Dessin's, than we call, like Biddy Fudge, for 'French pens and French ink,' and forth *steps* from its case the morocco-bound diary, regularly ruled and paged, with its patent Bramah lock and key, wherein we are to record and preserve all the striking, profound and original observations – the classical reminiscences – the threadbare raptures – the poetical effusions – in short, all the never-sufficiently-to-be-exhausted topics, sentiment and enthusiasm, which must necessarily suggest themselves whilst posting from Paris to Naples.

Jameson was clearly familiar not only with *The Fudge Family* but also with Marian Starke's *Information and Direction to Travellers on the Continent* in which that lady recommends, 'Bramah locks for writing desks'.[9]

A much more solemn and far less accomplished verse than those of Thomas Moore appeared in the *Gentleman's Magazine* of January, 1828. Its subject, however, was a real life traveller – Joseph Sherwin of Cambridge – who, according to a foot-note to the poem, 'was found dead in his bed at the Hotel Royal, Calais, the morning of 17th July, 1827, in his 41st year'. The lines, written by 'T.N.', were composed, 'in the Protestant Cemetery at Calais on Tuesday Evening, July 31st, 1827'.

Here rests the stranger! here the aching head
Slumbers in peace, amongst the silent dead,
Where gloomy cypress crowns the low grave side,
And cooling night-winds in meanders glide:
Where blooms the rose – the myrtle and beneath
The early violets their sweet odours breathe.
Of man the emblem! they resume their reign,
They live to die, and die to live again!
And hope beneath the newly earth-made mound
'The House appointed' hath poor SHERWIN found!
Alas, poor Sherwin! brief was thy career;
Were Death consigned thy dust to slumber here,
You left your native land, your friends, and home,

With HOPE that promised life for years to come:
Thy peaceful bosom no misgivings gave,
Of an untimely passport to the grave;
When sudden in the arms of ruthless death,
You sunk in silence and resigned your breathe.
Here where no stone 'in uncouth rhyme' rehearse
Thy hapless fate – I pen this simple verse;
Here shall yon star her sacred vigils keep,
And o'er thy grave the silent moonbeam sleep.
Farewell! and at the last eventful day
May life immortal clothe thy mouldering clay.

Being from Cambridge, it might be expected that Sherwin was a member of the University but it appears that he was a working man – a slater,[10] although, apparently, in a considerable way.[11] He had arrived from Margate on the previous Tuesday and seems to have been unaccompanied, his wife having died twelve months earlier.[12] He was never declared bankrupt but it is possible that his debts were catching up with him. Two years before he had advertised, 'To Let, Two houses, containing ten rooms each, built in the most substantial, convenient and ornamental manner' and, 'suitable for the immediate reception of two genteel Families, at a very moderate and reduced rent.'[13] In the meantime there had been a major banking crisis, the most celebrated victim of which was Sir Walter Scott, and Sherwin may have been left with these properties – 'in the most desirable and pleasant' part of Cambridge, on his hands. This, appropriately perhaps, is speculation but what we do know is that, according to his local newspaper, 'he was highly and generally respected, and had retired from business so recently as Christmas last'.[14] He could never have dreamt that his death would command so much space in the *Gentleman's Magazine*.

14

FAREWELL DESSEIN'S!

Especially in the days of sail, English travellers returning home might find themselves detained in Calais by adverse weather; storms or contrary winds or no wind at all. Such a delay might provide the opportunity to reflect upon their travels or, not infrequently, bemoan their misfortune at being kept away from family and friends. A fine Latin example, sometimes said to be etched on a window at Dessein's Inn, has been transcribed with a number of variations.[1] William Jones of Nayland, returning to Calais after a trip to Paris in 1776 and held up by the weather, supplies the earliest transcription of what he calls lines of, 'elegant Latin which were written by an Englishman in like circumstances'.

It has been suggested that they were the work of Samuel Johnson who was there a year before Jones, although his travelling companion, Mrs Thrale, makes no reference to their being delayed – 'we saved out Tide as the phase is by 4 Minutes & all was to our wish'.[2] Jones's translation of the Latin reads as follows (he makes no reference to them being written on glass):

> Expected Eurus, come! thy lingering gale,
> Shall it no more extend the swelling sail?
> The traveller persists for thee to pray,
> Who feels the surfeit of a long delay.
> Mean while descending frequent to the shore,
> His longing eyes his native land explore.
> Across the wave, and blended with the skies,
> He sees the distant hills of Dover rise,
> The tow'ring castle and the extended train
> Of chalky cliffs that crown the watry main.

Though fancy plants him in the favourite land,
His feet still wander on a foreign strand.
Thus on the Stygian bank th' impatient ghost
Spreads forth his arms to gain th'Elysian coast.
His efforts all in vain! he's doomed to stay
While adverse winds and waves obstruct his way.[3]

Twelve years after her trip to Paris with Johnson, Hester
Thrale, now Mrs Piozzi, returning to England after a far
more extensive Continental tour left the following lines at
'our inn':

Over mountains, rivers, vallies,
Here are we returned to Calais;
After all their taunts and malice,
Ent'ring safe the gates of Calais;
While constrained, our captain dallies,
Waiting for a wind at Calais,
Muse! prepare some sprightly sallies
To divert *ennui* at Calais.
Turkish ships, Venetian gallies,
Have we seen since last at Calais;
But though Hogarth (rogue who rallies!)
Ridicules the French at Calais,
We, who walk'd o'er many a palace,
Quite well content return to Calais;
For striking honestly the tallies,
There's little choice 'twixt them and Calais.[4]

She claims that she gave these lines, 'a companion on the
other side of the water' which she left in an apartment of the
Ship Inn at Dover.[5] Her reference to Hogarth is, of course,
to his satirical representation of *Calais Gate*.

Another delayed versifier was Richard 'Conversation'
Sharp who in 1821 addressed the following *Epistle to a Brother:*

How slowly, eager to arrive,
I think the dull postilion drive!
The leagues seem longer, and the *pavé*
Is surely grown more rough and heavy.
Yet haply 'tis in vain I haste,

Dooms as before whole days to waste
Pacing till night on Calais pier,
Invoking winds that will not hear:
While not a packet dares to sail,
Aw'd by the equinoctial gale;
Still looking o'er that white shore
Where I so long to tread once more,
E'en now in thought I spring to land
And grasp o'erjoy'd a brother's hand.[6]

With the introduction and rapid improvement of steam navigation, packet skippers became less dependent upon the direction and strength of the wind, travel became more reliable and travel times were reduced. The opening of a railway connection between London and Dover (in 1844) and between Paris and Calais (in 1848) further cut down the time required to get from one capital to the other, whilst the development of the Folkestone-Boulogne route diverted many passengers away from Calais.

The arrival of the railway also meant that less money was to be made from the sale and hire of carriages. The theatre habitué Charles Hervey who was in Calais in 1849 noted the effect:

A right good hotel is that of worthy Master Dessin, with its trim formal gardens, its apocryphal statues, its white shuttered windows and, alas! its moss-grown courtyard, which now-a-days rarely echoes the sound of any carriage wheels but those of the parti-coloured omnibus jogging periodically to the railway station and back again.[7]

The Calais hoteliers were hard hit and in 1860 Léon Dessin, who had run the great hotel in the Rue Royale since taking it over from his uncle, Louis Quillacq, in 1819, sold the premises to the *municipalité*. He and his wife took over the running of the Lion d'Argent ('Quillacq's') in the Rue Neuve to which he tranferred the name of Dessin.[8]

As the years went by, English writers looked back on the Calais of their youth with nostalgia. Ruskin thought, 'every traveller of thirty years standing must love Calais, the place where he first felt himself in a strange world'.[9] It was his belief that Turner loved it 'excessively'. With the opening of a new theatre early in the twentieth century, a contributor to the *Spectator* gazed sadly at, 'the eyeless façade of the little theatre… where so may Englishmen first heard the thrilling three taps of the mace which still announces the rising curtain on the French stage'.[10] As for Dessein's, it became for a time the town's museum – 'with indian boats, skeletons of birds and fishes, arrows, pictures &c.'[11] In 1880 a writer for the *St James Gazette* put up at the hotel in the Rue Neuve where, 'Madame Dessein, a pleasing old French dame, sat in her parlour and adminsistered' (her husband, Léon, having died three years before after a life of distinguished local service) but all had changed in the Rue Royale:

> I went out betimes to see the old Dessein's in the Rue Leveux, erst Royale [an error – the Rue Leveux was the old Rue de la Comédie at the back of the hotel]. It was pouring with rain and somehow I could not find it. This was set down to forgetfulness, perhaps to confusion from the shower. The trial was made again later but with the same result… At last the news was rudely broken to me. In place of Dessein's was to be seen the shell of an enormous brick building, ready for roofing – a vast communal school, one of M. Ferry's offspring. Dessein's fair gardens, the quaint old hotel, the remise, Sterne's room – all had been levelled, and this precious structure reared in its place. And so there is an end of Dessein's hotel.[12]

The position of the old hotel is today marked by a plaque above a chemist's shop.

The Calais of Sterne and Mrs Thrale, Dorothy and William Wordsworth, Beau Brummell and Harriette Wilson, Thackeray and Dickens has long since disappeared but thanks to what is written by and of them, they can still be seen dining at Dessein's, sauntering about the Place d'Armes or strolling on the sands.

Old Calais lives on.

Thackeray's short-story *Dessein's* appeared in the *Roundabout Papers* which he contributed to the *Cornhill Magazine* in the early 1860s shortly after the hotel had been purchased by the Municipality of Calais for conversion into a museum. Thackeray's moralistic disapproval of Sterne was more thoroughly – and more harshly – expressed in the chapter on 'Sterne and Goldsmith in *The English Humourists of the Eighteenth Century* in which he declares that, 'There is not a page in Sterne's writing but has something that were better away, – a latent corruption, a hint as of an improper presence' and more that is equally damning.[1]

Percy Fitzgerald, although compelled to accept that Thackeray's opinion, 'had much to support it', wrote his biography of Sterne as a defence against Thackeray's more intemperate strictures.

DESSEIN'S
William Makepeace Thackeray

I arrived by the night-mail packet from Dover. The passage had been rough, and the usual consequences had ensued. I was disinclined to travel farther that night on my road to Paris, and knew the Calais hotel of old as one of the cleanest, one of the dearest, one of the most comfortable hotels on the continent of Europe. There is no town more French than Calais. That charming old 'Hotel Dessein,' with its court, its gardens, its lordly kitchen, its princely waiter – a gentleman of the old school, who has welcomed the finest company in Europe – have long been known to me. I have read complaints in *The Times*, more than once, I think, that the Dessein bills are dear. A bottle of soda-water certainly costs – well, never mind how much. I remember as a boy, at the 'Ship' at Dover *(imperante Carolo Decimo)*[2] when, my place to London being paid, I had but 12s left after a certain little Paris excursion (about which my benighted parents never knew anything) ordering for dinner a whiting, a beef-steak, and a glass of negus, and the bill was, dinner 7s., glass of negus 2s., waiter 6d., and only half a crown left, as I was a sinner, for the guard and coachman on the way to London!

And I WAS a sinner. I had gone without leave. What a long, dreary forty hours journey it was from Paris to Calais. Guilt, sir, guilt remains stamped on the memory, and I feel easier in my mind now that it is liberated of this old peccadillo. I met my college tutor only yesterday. We were travelling, and stopped at the same hotel. He had the very next room to mine. After he had gone into his apartment, having shaken me quite kindly by the hand, I felt inclined to knock at his door and say, 'Doctor Bentley, I beg your pardon, but do you remember, when I was going down at the Easter vacation in 1830, you asked me where I was going to spend my vacation? And I said, 'With my friend Slingsby, in Huntingdonshire. Well, sir, I grieve to have to confess that I told you a fib. I had got 20L. And was going for a lark to Paris, where my friend Edwards was staying.' There, it is out. The Doctor will read it, for I did not wake him up after all to make my confession, but protest he shall have a copy of this *Roundabout* sent to him when he returns to his lodge.

They gave me a bedroom there; a very neat room on the first floor, looking into the pretty garden. The hotel must look pretty much as it did a hundred years ago when HE visited it. I wonder whether he paid his bill? Yes: his journey had just begun. He had borrowed or got the money some-how. Such a man would spend it liberally enough when he had it, give generously – nay, drop a tear over the fate of the poor fellow whom he relieved. I don't believe a word he says, but I never accused him of stinginess about money. This is a fault of much more virtuous people than he. Mr Laurence is ready enough with his purse when there are anybody's guineas in it. Still when I went to bed in the room, in HIS room; when I think how I admire, dislike, and have abused him, a certain dim feeling of apprehension filled my mind at the midnight hour. What if I should see his lean figure in the black-satin breeches, his sinister smile, his long thin finger pointing to me in the moonlight (for I am in bed, and have popped my candle out), and he should say, 'You mistrust me, you hate me, do you? And you, don't you know how Jack, Tom and Harry, your brother authors, hate YOU?' I grin and laugh in the moonlight, in the midnight, in the silence. 'O you ghost in black-satin breeches and a wig! I like to be hated by some men,' I say. I know men whose lives are a scheme, whose laughter is a conspiracy, whose smile means something else, whose hatred is a cloak, and I had rather these men should hate me as not.'

'My good sir,' says he, with a ghastly grin on his lean face, 'you have your wish.'

'*Après?*' I say. 'Please let me go to sleep. I shan't sleep any the worse because–'

'Because there are insects in the bed, and they sting you?' (This is only by way of illustration, my good sir; the animals don't bite me now. All the house at present seems to me excellently clean.) 'Tis absurd to affect this indifference. If you are thin-skinned, and the reptiles bite, they keep you from sleep.'

'There are some men who cry out at a flea-bite as loud as if they were torn by a vulture,' I growl.

'Men of the *genus irritabile*, my worthy good gentleman!– and you are one.'

'Yes, sir, I am of the profession, as you say; and I dare say make a great shouting and crying at a small hurt.'

'You are ashamed of that quality by which you earn your subsistence, and such reputation as you have? Your sensibility is your livelihood, my worthy friend. You feel a pang of pleasure or pain? It is noted in your memory, and some day or other makes its appearance in your manuscript. Why, in your last *Roundabout* rubbish you mention reading your first novel on the day when King George IV was crowned.[3] I remember him in his cradle at St. James's, a lovely little babe; a gilt Chinese railing was before him, and I dropped the tear of sensibility as I gazed on the sleeping cherub.'

'A tear–a fiddlestick, MR STERNE,' I growled out, for of course I knew my friend in the wig and satin breeches to be no other than the notorious, nay, celebrated

Mr Laurence Sterne.

'Does not the sight of a beautiful infant charm and melt you, *mon ami*? If not, I pity you. Yes, he was beautiful. I was in London the year he was born. I used to breakfast at the 'Mount Coffee-house.'[4] I did not become the fashion until two years later, when my *Tristram* made his appearance, who has held his own for a hundred years. By the way, *mon bon monsieur*, how many authors of your present time will last till the next century? Do you think Brown will?'

I laughed with scorn as I lay in my bed (and so did the ghost give a ghastly snigger).

'Brown!' I roared. 'One of the most over-rated men that ever put pen to paper!'

'What do you think of Jones?'

I grew indignant with this old cynic. 'As a reasonable ghost, come out of the other world, you don't mean,' I said, 'to ask me a serious opinion of Mr Jones? His books may be very good reading for maid-servants and school-boys, but you don't ask ME to read them? As a scholar yourself you must know that–'

'Well, then, Robinson?'

'Robinson, I am told, has merit. I dare say; I never have been able to read his books, and can't, therefore, form any opinion about Mr Robinson. At least you will allow that I am not speaking in a prejudiced manner about HIM.'

'Ah! I see you men of letters have your cabals and jealousies, as we had in my time. There was an Irish fellow by the name of Goldsmith, who used to abuse me; but he went into no genteel company – and faith! it mattered little, his praise or abuse. I never was more surprised than when I heard that Mr Irving, an American gentleman of parts and elegance, had wrote the fellow's life.[5] To make a hero of that man, my dear sir, 'twas ridiculous! You followed in the fashion, I hear, and chose to lay a wreath before this queer little idol. Preposterous! A pretty writer, who has turned some neat couplets. Bah! I have no patience with Master Posterity, that has chosen to take up this fellow, and make a hero of him! And there was another gentleman of my time,

Mr Thiefcatcher Fielding, forsooth!⁶ a fellow with the strength, and the tastes, and the manners of a porter! What madness has possessed you all to bow before that Calvert Butt⁷of a man? – a creature without elegance or sensibility! The dog had spirits, certainly. I remember my Lord Bathurst praising them: but as for reading his books – *ma foi*, I would as lief go and dive for tripe in a cellar. The man's vulgarity stifles me. He wafts me whiffs of gin. Tobacco and onions are in his great coarse laugh, which choke me, *pardi*; and I don't think much better of the other fellow – the Scots' gallipot purveyor – Peregrine Clinker, Humphrey Random – how did the fellow call his rubbish?⁸ Neither of these men had the bel air, the bon ton, the *je ne scais quoy*. Pah! If I meet them in my walks by our Stygian river, I give them a wide berth, as that hybrid apothecary fellow would say. An ounce of civet, good apothecary; horrible, horrible! The mere thought of the coarseness of those men gives me the *chair de poule*.⁹ Mr Fielding, especially, has no more sensibility than a butcher in Fleet Market. He takes his heroes out of ale-house kitchens, or worse places still. And this is the person whom Posterity has chosen to honor along with me – ME! Faith, Monsieur Posterity, you have put me in pretty company, and I see you are no wiser than we were in our time. Mr Fielding, forsooth! Mr Tripe and Onions! Mr Cowheel and Gin! Thank you for nothing. Monsieur Posterity!'

'And so,' thought I, 'even among these Stygians this envy and quarrelsomeness (if you will permit me the word) survive? What a pitiful meanness! To be sure, I can understand this feeling to a certain extent; a sense of justice will prompt it. In my own case, I often feel myself forced to protest against the absurd praises lavished on contemporaries. Yesterday, for instance, Lady Jones was good enough to praise one of my works. *Très bien*. But in the very next minute she began, with quite as great enthusiasm, to praise Miss Hobson's last romance. My good creature, what is that woman's praise worth who absolutely admires the writings of Miss Hobson? I offer a friend a bottle of '44 claret, fit for a pontifical supper. 'This is capital wine,' says he; 'and now we have finished the bottle, will you give me a bottle of that ordinaire we drank the other day?' Very well, my good man. You are a good judge – of ordinaire, I dare say. Nothing so provokes my anger, and rouses my sense of justice, as to hear other men undeservedly praised. In a word, if you wish to remain friends with me, don't praise anybody. You tell me that the Venus de' Medici is beautiful, or Jacob Omnium[10] is tall. *Que diable!* Can't I judge for myself? Haven't I eyes and a foot-rule? I don't think the Venus IS so handsome, since you press me. She is pretty, but she has no expression. And as for Mr Omnium, I can see much taller men in a fair for twopence.'

'And so,' I said, turning round to Mr Sterne, 'you are actually jealous of Mr Fielding? O you men of letters, you men of letters! Is not the world (your world, I mean) big enough for all of you?'

I often travel in my sleep. I often of a night find myself walking in my night-gown about the gray streets. It is awkward at first, but somehow nobody makes any remark. I glide along over the ground with my naked feet. The mud does not wet them. The passers-by do not tread on them. I am wafted over the ground, down the stairs, through the doors. This sort of travelling, dear friends, I am sure you have all of you indulged.

Well, on the night in question (and, if you wish to know the precise date, it was the 31st of September last), after having some little conversation with Mr Sterne in our bedroom, I must have got up, though I protest I don't know how, and come down stairs with him into the coffee-room of the 'Hôtel Dessein,' where the moon was shining, and a cold supper was laid out. I forget what we had – 'vol-au-vent d'oeufs de Phénix – agneau aux pistaches à la Barmécide,' – what matters what we had?

'As regards supper this is certain, the less you have of it the better.'

That is what one of the guests remarked, – a shabby old man, in a wig, and such a dirty, ragged, disreputable dressing-gown that I should have been quite surprised at him, only one never IS surprised in dr—— under certain circumstances.[11]

'I can't eat 'em now,' said the greasy man (with his false old teeth, I wonder he could eat anything). 'I remember Alvanley eating three suppers once at Carlton House – one night *de petite comité.'*

'*Petit comité,* sir,' said Mr Sterne.

'Dammy, sir, let me tell my own story my own way. I say, one night at Carlton house, playing at blind hookey[12] with York, Wales, Tom Raikes, Prince Boothby, and Dutch Sam the boxer, Alvanley[13] ate three suppers, and won three and twenty hundred pounds in ponies. Never saw a fellow with such an appetite, except Wales in his GOOD time. But he destroyed the finest digestion a man ever had with – always at it.'

'Try mine,' said Mr Sterne.

'What a doosid queer box,' says Mr Brummell.

'I had it from a Capuchin friar in this town. The box is but a horn one; but to the nose of sensibility Araby's perfume is not more delicate.'

'I call it doosid stale old rappee,' says Mr Brummell – (as for me I declare I could not smell anything at all in either of the boxes.) 'Old boy in smock-frock, take a pinch?'

The old boy in the smock-frock, as Mr Brummell called him, was a very old man, with long white beard, wearing, not a smock-frock, but a shirt; and he had actually nothing else save a rope round his neck, which hung behind his chair in the queerest way.

'Fair sir,' he said, turning to Mr Brummell, 'when the Prince of Wales and his father laid siege to our town–'

'What nonsense are you talking, old cock?' says Mr Brummell; 'Wales was never here. His late Majesty George IV. passed through on his way to Hanover. My good man, you don't seem to know what's up at all. What is he talkin' about the siege of Calais? I lived here fifteen years! Ought to know. What's his old name?'

'I am Master Eustace of Saint Peter's,' said the old gentleman in the shirt. 'When my Lord King Edward laid siege to this city–'[14]

'Laid siege to Jericho!' cries Mr Brummell. 'The old man is cracked – cracked, sir!'

'–Laid siege to this city,' continued the old man, 'I and five more promised Messire Gautier de Mauny that we would give ourselves up as ransom for the place.[15] And we came before our Lord King Edward, attired as you see, and the fair queen begged our lives out of her gramercy.'

'Queen, nonsense! you mean the Princess of Wales – pretty woman, *petit nez retroussé*, grew monstrous stout!' suggested Mr Brummell, whose reading was evidently not extensive. 'Sir Sidney Smith was a fine fellow, great talker, hook nose, so has Lord Cochrane, so has Lord Wellington. She was very sweet on Sir Sidney.'[16]

'Your acquaintance with the history of Calais does not seem to be considerable,' said Mr Sterne to Mr Brummell, with a shrug.

'Don't it, bishop? – for I conclude you are a bishop by your wig. I know Calais as well as any man. I lived here for years before I took that confounded consulate at Caen. Lived in this hotel, then at Leleux's.[17] People used to stop here. Good fellows used to ask for poor George Brummell; Hertford did, so did the Duchess of Devonshire. Not know Calais indeed! That is a good joke. Had many a good dinner here: sorry I ever left it.'

'My Lord King Edward,' chirped the queer old gentleman in the shirt, 'colonized the place with his English, after we had yielded it up to him. I have heard tell they kept it for nigh three hundred years, till my Lord de Guise took it from a fair Queen, Mary of blessed memory, a holy woman. Eh, but Sire Gautier of Mauny was a good knight, a valiant captain, gentle and courteous withal! Do you remember his ransoming the–?'

'What is the old fellow twaddlin' about?' cries Brummell. 'He is talking about some knight? – I never spoke to a knight, and very seldom to a baronet. Firkins, my butterman, was a knight – a knight and alderman. Wales knighted him once on going into the City.'

'I am not surprised that the gentleman should not understand Messire Eustace of St. Peter's,' said the ghostly individual addressed as Mr Sterne. 'Your reading doubtless has not been very extensive?'

'Dammy, sir, speak for yourself!' cries Mr Brummell, testily. 'I never professed to be a reading man, but I was as good as my neighbors. Wales wasn't a reading man; York wasn't a reading man; Clarence wasn't a reading man; Sussex was, but he wasn't a man in society. I remember reading your *Sentimental Journey,* old boy: read it to the Duchess at Beauvoir, I recollect, and she cried over it. Doosid clever amusing book, and does you great credit. Birron wrote doosid clever books, too; so did Monk Lewis.[18] George Spencer was an elegant poet, and my dear Duchess of Devonshire, if she had not been a grande dame, would have beat 'em all, by George.[19] Wales couldn't write: he could sing, but he couldn't spell.'

'Ah, you know the great world? so did I in my time, Mr Brummell. I have had the visiting tickets of half the nobility at my lodgings in Bond Street. But they left me there no more cared for than last year's calendar,' sighed Mr Sterne. 'I wonder who is the mode in London now? One of our late arrivals, my Lord Macaulay,[20] has prodigious merit and learning, and, faith, his histories are more amusing than any novels, my own included.'

'Don't know, I'm sure not in my line. Pick this bone of chicken,' says Mr Brummell, trifling with a skeleton bird before him.

'I remember in this city of Calais worse fare than yon bird,' said old Mr Eustace of Saint Peter's. 'Marry, sirs, when my Lord King Edward laid siege to us, lucky was he who could get a slice of horse for his breakfast, and a rat was sold at the price of a hare.'

'Hare is coarse food, never tasted rat,' remarked the Beau. 'Table-d'hôte poor fare enough for a man like me, who has been accustomed to the best of cookery. But rat – stifle me! I couldn't swallow that: never could bear hardship at all.'

'We had to bear enough when my Lord of England pressed us. 'Twas pitiful to see the faces of our women as the siege went on, and hear the little ones asking for dinner.'

'Always a bore, children. At dessert, they are bad enough, but at dinner they're the deuce and all,' remarked Mr Brummell.

Messire Eustace of St. Peter's did not seem to pay much attention to the Beau's remarks, but continued his own train of thought as old men will do.

'I hear,' said he, 'that there has actually been no war between us of France and you men of England for wellnigh fifty year. Ours has ever been a nation of warriors. And besides her regular found men-at-arms, 'tis said the English of the present time have more than a hundred thousand of archers with weapons that will carry for half a mile. And a multitude have come amongst us of late from a great Western country, never so much as heard of in my time – valiant men and great drawers of the long bow, and they say they have ships in armour that no shot can penetrate. Is it so? Wonderful; wonderful! The best armour, gossips, is a stout heart.'

'And if ever manly heart beat under shirt-frill, thine is that heart, Sir Eustace!' cried Mr Sterne, enthusiastically.

'We, of France, were never accused of lack of courage, sir, in so far as I know,' said Messire Eustace. 'We have shown as much in a thousand wars with you English by sea and land; and sometimes we conquered, and sometimes, as is the fortune of war, we were discomfited. And notably in a great sea-fight which befell off Ushant on the first of June – Our Admiral, messire Villaret de Joyeuse,[21] on board his galleon named the *Vengeur,* being sore pressed by an English bombard, rather than yield the crew of his ship to mercy, determined to go down with all on board of her: and to the cry of Vive la Repub– or, I would say, of Notre Dame à la Rescousse, he and his crew all sank to an immortal grave–'

'Sir,' said I, looking with amazement at the old gentleman, 'surely, surely, there is some mistake in your statement. Permit me to observe that the action of the first of June took place five hundred years after your time, and–'

'Perhaps I am confusing my dates,' said the old gentleman, with a faint blush. 'You say I am mixing up the transactions of my time on earth with the story of my successors? It may be so. We take no count of a few centuries more or less in our dwelling by the darkling Stygian river. Of late, there came amongst us a good knight, Messire de Cambronne,[22] who fought against you English in the country of Flanders, being captain of the guard of my Lord the King of France, in a famous battle where you English would have been utterly routed but for the succour of the Prussian heathen. This Messire de Cambronne, when bidden to yield by you of England, answered this, 'The guard dies but never surrenders;' and fought a long time afterwards, as became a good knight. In our wars with you of England it may have pleased the Fates to give you the greater success, but on our side, also, there has been no lack of brave deeds performed by brave men.'

'King Edward may have been the victor, sir, as being the strongest, but you are the hero of the siege of Calais!' cried Mr Sterne. 'Your story is sacred, and your name has been blessed for five hundred years. Wherever men speak of patriotism and sacrifice, Eustace of Saint Pierre shall be beloved and remembered. I prostrate myself before the bare feet which stood before King Edward. What collar of chivalry is to be compared to that glorious order which you wear? Think, sir, how out of the myriad millions of our race, you, and some few more, stand forth as exemplars of duty and honour. *Fortunati nimium!*[23]

'Sir,' said the old gentleman, 'I did but my duty at a painful moment; and 'tis matter of wonder to me that men talk still, and glorify such a trifling matter. By Our Lady's grace, in the fair kingdom of France, there are scores of thousands of men, gentle and simple, who would do as I did. Does not every sentinel at his post, does not every archer in the front of battle, brave it, and die where his captain bids him? Who am I that I should be chosen out of all France to be an example of fortitude? I braved no tortures, though these I trust I would have endured with a good heart. I was subject to threats only. Who was the Roman knight of whom the Latin clerk Horatius tells?'

'A Latin clerk? Faith, I forget my Latin,' says Mr Brummell. 'Ask the parson, here.'

'Messire Regulus, I remember, was his name. Taken prisoner by the Saracens, he gave his knightly word, and was permitted to go seek a ransom among his own people. Being unable to raise the sum that was a fitting ransom for such a knight, he returned to Afric, and cheerfully submitted to the tortures which the Paynims inflicted. And 'tis said he took leave of his friends as gayly as though he were going to a village kermes, or riding to his garden house in the suburb of the city.'[24]

'Great, good, glorious man!' cried Mr Sterne, very much moved. 'Let me embrace that gallant hand, and bedew it with my tears! As long as honour lasts thy name shall be remembered. See this dew-drop twinkling on my check! 'Tis the sparkling tribute that Sensibility pays to Valour. Though in my life and practice I may turn from Virtue, believe me, I never have ceased to honour her! Ah, Virtue! Ah, Sensibility! Oh–'

Here Mr Sterne was interrupted by a monk of the Order of St. Francis, who stepped into the room, and begged us all to take a pinch of his famous old rappee. I suppose the snuff was very pungent, for, with a great start, I woke up; and now perceived that I must have been dreaming altogether. 'Dessein's' of now-a-days is not the 'Dessein's' which Mr Sterne, and Mr Brummell, and I recollect in the good old times. The town of Calais has bought the old hotel, and 'Dessein' has gone over to 'Quillacq's.' And I was there yesterday. And I remember old diligences, and old postilions in pigtails and jack-boots, who were once as alive as I am, and whose cracking whips I have heard in the midnight many and many a time. Now, where are they? Behold they have been ferried over Styx, and have passed away into limbo. I wonder what time does my boat go?

Ah! Here comes the waiter bringing me my little bill.

APPENDIX 1 – Footnotes

1) W.M. Thackeray, *English Humourists of the Eighteenth Century,* (London, 1867).

2) Charles X , the brother of Louis XVIII, succeeded him in 1824 and was deposed in 1830.

3) The coronation of George IV took place on 19 July 1821. In his essay *A Peel of Bells*, Roudabout Papers 24, Thackeray claimed that on that day he read Jane Porter's *The Scottish Chiefs.*

4) The Mount Coffee-House was in Lower Grosvenor St., London.

5) Washington Irving, *Oliver Goldsmith: a biography,* (New York, 1849).

6) Henry Fielding (1707-1754) – novelist and J.P. for Westminster.

7) Calvert was one of the capital's leading producers of porter, a dark brown bitter beer.

8) Scots' gallipot: Tobias Smollett (1721-1771) – novelist, author of *Roderick Random* (1748). *Peregrine Pickle* (1751) and *Humphrey Clinker* (1771).

9) 'chair de poule': Fr. goosebumps.

10) 'Jacob Omnium': *nom de plume* of the writer Matthew James Higgins (1810-1868), 6ft. 8ins. tall.

11) 'shabby old man': George Bryan 'Beau' Brummell (1778-1840) – see Chap. 11 above.

12) 'blind hookey': card game often used for gambling.

13) Frederick Augustus, Duke of York (1763-1827), the Prince of Wales, later George IV(1762-1830), Tom Raikes (1777-1848), John Scrimpshire Clopton Boothby (1740-1800) and William Arden, Sam Elias (1775-1816), Lord Alvanley – members, with Brummell, of the Carlton House set.

14) Eustache de St. Pierre, leader of the six burghers of Calais.

15) Gautier (Walter) de Mauny (d. 1372), English commander, besieged Calais.

16) Sir William Sidney Smith (1764-1840), admiral: Thomas Cochrane (1775-1860), admiral.

17) Brummell had two rooms overlooking the Rue Royale.

18) Matthew Gregory Lewis (1775-1818), author of *'The Monk'.*

19) George, second Earl Spencer (1758-1834); Georgiana Cavendish, Duchess of Devonshire (1757-1806).

20) Thomas Babington Macaulay (1800-1859), politician, historian and poet.

21) Louis Villaret de Joyeuse (1750-1812), commanded French fleet at battle of Glorious First of June, 1794.

22) Pierre de Cambronne (1770-1842), commander of the Old Guard at Waterloo, famously said – *La garde meurt et ne se rend pas.*

23) Fortunati nimium – fortunate are those who know their own good fortune.

24) Story told by Horace: *Odes, iii, 5* – of Roman general Marcus Atilius Regulus (c.308-c.250BC).

APPENDIX 2

Between 1862-65, his biographer Claire Tomalin estimates that Dickens crossed the Channel, 'at least 68 times at a rough reckoning' *(C. Tomalin, Charles Dickens: a Life*, London, 2011). Most of these trips were probably to visit his lover Nelly Ternan who appears to have been living in France in order to protect Dickens' reputation at home. His first trip abroad had been in 1837, accompanied by his wife, Catherine, and illustrator, Hablot K. Browne. They spent their first night at Rignolle's Hotel, Calais, from where he wrote to John Forster to say that, 'We arrived here in great state this morning – I very sick, and Missus very well.'[1] Next day they took a barouche to, 'some gardens where the people dance, and where they were footing it most heartily – especially the women who in their short petticoats and light caps look uncommonly agreeable'.[2] His love affair with France had begun.

The Calais Night Mail, wonderfully evocative of a rough crossing, although not published until 1861, when it appeared in '*The Uncommercial Traveller*', looks back on the days when Dessein's was still, 'the best of inns'.

THE CALAIS NIGHT MAIL
Charles Dickens

It is an unsettled question with me whether I shall leave Calais something handsome in my will, or whether I shall leave it my malediction. I hate it so much, and yet I am always so very glad to see it, that I am in a state of constant indecision on this subject. When I first made acquaintance with Calais, it was as a maundering wretch in a clammy perspiration and dripping saline particles, who was conscious of no extremities but the one great extremity, sea-sickness – who was a mere bilious torso, with a mislaid headache somewhere in its stomach – who had been put into a horrible swing in Dover Harbour, and had tumbled giddily out of it on the French coast, or the Isle of Man, or anywhere. Times have changed, and now I enter Calais self-reliant and rational. I know where it is beforehand, I keep a look out for it, I recognise its landmarks when I see any of them, I am acquainted with its ways, and I know – and I can bear – its worst behaviour.

Malignant Calais! Low-lying alligator, evading the eyesight and discouraging hope! Dodging flat streak, now on this bow, now on that, now anywhere, now everywhere, now nowhere! In vain Cape Grinez, coming frankly forth into the sea, exhorts the failing to be stout of heart and stomach: sneaking Calais, prone behind its bar, invites emetically to despair. Even when it can no longer quite conceal itself in its muddy dock, it has an evil way of falling off, has Calais, which is more hopeless than its invisibility. The pier is all but on the bowsprit, and you think you are there – roll, roar, wash! – Calais has retired miles inland, and Dover has burst out to look for it. It has a last dip and slide in its character, has Calais, to be especially commanded to the infernal gods. Thrice accursed be that garrison-town, when it dives under the boat's keel, and comes up a league or two to the right, with the packet shivering and spluttering and staring about for it!

Not but what I have my animosities towards Dover. I

particularly detest Dover for the self-complacency with which it goes to bed. It always goes to bed (when I am going to Calais) with a more brilliant display of lamp and candle than any other town. Mr and Mrs Birmingham, host and hostess of the Lord Warden Hotel, are my much esteemed friends, but they are too conceited about the comforts of that establishment when the Night Mail is starting.[3] I know it is a good house to stay at, and I don't want the fact insisted upon in all its warm bright windows at such an hour. I know the Warden is a stationary edifice that never rolls or pitches, and I object to its big outline seeming to insist upon that circumstance, and, as it were, to come over me with it, when I am reeling on the deck of the boat. Beshrew the Warden likewise, for obstructing that corner, and making the wind so angry as it rushes round. Shall I not know that it blows quite soon enough, without the officious Warden's interference?

As I wait here on board the night packet, for the South-Eastern Train to come down with the Mail, Dover appears to me to be illuminated for some intensely aggravating festivity in my personal dishonour. All its noises smack of taunting praises of the land, and dispraises of the gloomy sea, and of me for going on it. The drums upon the heights have gone to bed, or I know they would rattle taunts against me for having my unsteady footing on this slippery deck. The many gas eyes of the Marine Parade twinkle in an offensive manner, as if with derision. The distant dogs of Dover bark at me in my misshapen wrappers, as if I were Richard the Third.[4]

A screech, a bell, and two red eyes come gliding down the Admiralty pier with a smoothness of motion rendered more smooth by the heaving of the boat. The sea makes noises against the pier, as if several hippopotami were lapping at it, and were prevented by circumstances over which they had no control from drinking peaceably. We, the boat, became violently agitated – rumble, hum, scream, roar, and establish an immense family washing-day at each paddle-box. Bright patches break out in the train as the doors of the post-office vans are opened, and instantly stooping figures with sacks upon their backs begin to be beheld among the piles, descending as it would seem in ghostly procession to Davy Jones's Locker. The passengers come on board; a few shadowy Frenchmen, with hatboxes shaped like the stoppers of gigantic case-bottles; a few shadowy Germans in immense fur coats and boots; a few shadowy Englishmen prepared for the worst and pretending not to expect it. I cannot disguise from my uncommercial mind the miserable fact that we are a body of outcasts; that the attendants on us are as scant in number as may serve to get rid of us with the least possible delay; that there are no night-loungers interested in us; that the unwilling lamps shiver and shudder at us; that the sole object is to commit us to the deep and abandon us. Lo, the two red eyes glaring in increasing distance, and then the very train itself gone to bed before we are off!

What is the moral support derived by some sea-going amateurs from an umbrella? Why do certain voyagers across the Channel always put that article, and hold it up with a grim and fierce tenacity? A fellow-creature near me – whom I only know to BE a fellow-creature, because of his umbrella: without which he might be a dark bit of cliff, pier or bulk-head – clutches that instrument with a desperate grasp, that will not relax until he lands at Calais. Is there any analogy, in certain constitutions, between keeping an umbrella up, and keeping the spirits up? A hawser thrown on board with a flop replies, 'Stand by! Stand by, below!' 'Half a turn a head!' 'Half a turn a head!' 'Half speed!' 'Half speed!' 'Port!' 'Port!' 'Steady!' 'Steady!' 'Go on!' 'Go on!'

A stout wooden wedge driven in at my right temple and out at my left, a floating deposit of lukewarm oil in my throat, and a compression of the bridge of my nose in a blunt pair of pincers, – these are the personal sensations by which I know we are off, and by which I shall continue to know it until I am on the soil of France. My symptoms have scarcely established themselves comfortably, when two or three skating shadows that have been trying to walk or stand, get flung together, and two or three shadows in tarpaulin slide

with them into corners and cover them up. Then the South
Foreland lights begin to hiccup at us in a way that bodes no
good.

It is about this period that my detestation of Calais knows
no bounds. Inwardly I resolve afresh that I never will forgive
that hated town. I have done so much before, many times,
but that is past. Let me register a vow. Implacable animosity
to Calais everm——— that was an awkward sea, and the
funnel seems of my opinion, for it gives a complaining roar.
The wind blows stiffly from the Nor-East, the sea runs high,
we ship a deal of water, the night is dark and cold, and the
shapeless passengers lie about in melancholy bundles, as if
they were sorted out for the laundress; but for my own
uncommercial part I cannot pretend that I am much
inconvenienced by any of these things. A general howling,
whistling, flopping gurgling and scooping, I am aware of,
and a general knocking about of Nature; but the impressions
I receive are very vague. In a sweet faint temper, something
like the smell of damaged oranges, I think I should feel
languidly benevolent if I had time. I have not time, because
I am under a curious compulsion to occupy myself with the
Irish melodies.

'Rich and rare were the gems she wore,' is the particular
melody to which I find myself devoted.[5] I sing it to myself in
the most charming manner and with the greatest expression.
Now and then, I raise my head (I am sitting on the hardest
of wet seats, in the most uncomfortable of wet attitudes, but
I don't mind it,) and notice that I am a whirling shuttlecock
between a fiery battledore of lighthouse on the French coast
and a fiery battledore of a lighthouse on the English coast;
but I don't notice it particularly, except to feel envenomed
in my hatred of Calais. Then I go on again, 'Rich and rare
were the ge-ems sh-e-e-e wore, And a bright gold ring on her
wa-and she bo-ore, But O her beauty was fa-a-a-a-r beyond' –
I am particularly proud of my execution here, when I
become aware of another awkward shock from the sea, and
another protest from the funnel, and a fellow-creature at the
paddle-box more audibly indisposed than I think he need

be – 'Her sparkling gems, or snow-white wand, But O her beauty was fa-a- a-a-a-r beyond' – another awkward one here, and the fellow creature with the umbrella down and picked up – 'Her spa-a-rkling ge-ems, or her Port! port! steady! steady! snow-white fellow-creature at the paddle-box very selfishly audible, bump, roar, wash, white wand.'

As my execution of the Irish melodies partakes of my imperfect perceptions of what is going on around me, so what is going on around me becomes something else than what it is. The stokers open the furnace doors below, to feed the fires, and I am again on the box of the old Exeter Telegraph fast coach,[6] and that is the light of the for ever extinguished coach-lamps, and the gleam of the hatches and paddle-boxes is THEIR gleam on cottages and haystacks, and the monotonous noise of the engines is the steady jingle of the splendid team. Anon the intermittent funnel roar of protest at every violent roll, becomes the regular blast of a high pressure engine, and I recognise the exceedingly explosive steamer in which I ascended the Mississippi when the American civil war was not, and when only its causes were.[7] A fragment of mast on which the light of a lantern falls, and end of rope, and a jerking block or so, become suggestive of Franconi's Circus at Paris where I shall be this very night mayhap, (for it must be morning now), and they dance to the self-same tune as the trained steed Black Raven. What may be the speciality of these waves as they come rushing on, I cannot desert the pressing demands made upon me by the gems she wore, to inquire, but they are charged with something about Robinson Crusoe, and I think it was in Yarmouth Roads that he first went a seafaring and was near foundering (what a terrific sound that word had for me when I was a boy!) in his first gale of wind. Still, through all this, I must ask her (who WAS she I wonder!) for the fiftieth time, and without ever stopping. Does she not fear to stray, So lone and lovely through this bleak way, And are Erin's sons so good or so cold, As not to be tempted by more fellow-creatures at the paddle-box or gold? Sir Knight I feel not the least alarm, No son of Erin will offer me harm, For though they love fellow-creature with umbrella down again and golden store, Sir Knight they what a tremendous one love honour and virtue more: For though they love Stewards with a bull's eye bright, they'll trouble you for your tickets, sir – rough passage tonight!

I freely admit it to be a miserable piece of human weakness and inconsistency, but I no sooner become conscious of those last words from the steward than I begin to soften towards Calais. Whereas I have been vindictively wishing that those Calais burghers who came out of their town by a short cut into the History of England, with those fatal ropes round their necks by which they have since been towed into so many cartoons, had all been hanged on the spot, I now begin to regard them as highly respectable and virtuous tradesmen.[8] Looking, about me, I see the light of Cape Grinez well astern of the boat on the davits to leeward and the light of Calais harbour undeniably at its old tricks, but still ahead and shining. Sentiments of forgiveness of Calais, not to say of attachment to Calais, begin to expand my bosom. I have weak notions that I will stay there a day or two on my way back. A faded and recumbent stranger pausing in a profound reverie over the rim of a basin, asks me what kind of place Calais is? I tell him (Heaven forgive me!) a very agreeable place indeed – rather hilly than otherwise.

So strangely goes the time, and on the whole so quickly – though still I seem to have been on board a week – that I am bumped, rolled, gurgled, washed and pitched into Calais Harbour before her maiden smile has finally lighted her through the Green Isle, When blest for ever is she who relied, On entering Calais at the top of the tide. For we have not to land to-night down among those slimy timbers – covered with green hair as if it were the mermaids' favourite combing place – where one crawls to the surface of the jetty, like a stranded shrimp, but we go steaming up the harbour to the Railway Station Quay. And as we go, the sea washes in and out among piles and planks, with dead heavy beats and in quite a furious manner (whereof we are proud) and the lamps shake in the wind, and the bells of Calais striking One seems to send their vibrations struggling against troubled air, as we have come struggling against troubled water. And now, the sudden relief and wiping of faces, everybody on board seems to have had a prodigious double-tooth out, and to be this very instant free of the Dentists's hands. And now we all know for the first time how wet and cold we are, and how salt we are; and now I love Calais with my heart of hearts!

'Hotel Dessin!' (but in this one case it is not a vocal cry, it is but a bright lustre in the eyes of the cheery representative of that best of inns). 'Hotel Meurice!' 'Hotel de France!' 'Hotel de Calais!' 'The Royal Hotel, Sir, Angaishe ouse!' 'You are going to Parry, Sir?' 'Your registrair froo, Sir?' Bless ye, my Touters, my commissionaires, bless ye, my hungry-eyed mysteries in caps of a military form, who are always here, day or night, fair weather or foul, seeking inscrutable jobs which I never see you get! Bless ye, my Custom House officers in green and grey; permit me to grasp the welcome hands that descend into my travelling-bag, one on each side, and meet at the bottom to give my charge of linen a peculiar shake up, as if it were a measure of chaff or grain! I have nothing to declare, Monsieur le Douanier, except that when I cease to breathe, Calais will be found written on my heart.[9] No article liable to local duty have I with me, Monsieur l'Officier de l'Octroi,[10] unless the overflowing of a breast devoted to charming town should be in that wise chargeable. Ah! see at the gangway by the twinkling lantern, my dearest brother and friend, he once of the Passport Office, he who collects the names! May he be forever changeless in his buttoned black surtout, with his note-book in his hand, and his tall black hat, surmounting his round, smiling, patient face! Let us embrace my dearest brother. I am yours à tout jamais – for the whole of ever.

Calais up and doing at the railway station, and Calais down and dreaming in its bed; Calais with something of 'an ancient fish-like smell' about it,[11] and Calais blown and sea-washed pure; Calais represented at the Buffet by savoury roast fowls, hot coffee, cognac, and Bordeaux; AND Calais represented everywhere by flitting persons with a monomania for changing money – though I never shall be able to understand in my present state of existence how they live by it, but I suppose I should, if I understand the currency question – Calais EN GROS, and Calais EN DETAIL, forgive one who has deeply wronged you – I was not fully aware of it on the other side, but I meant Dover.

Ding, ding! To the carriages, gentlemen the travellers. Ascend then, gentlemen the travellers, for Hazebrouke, Lille, Douai, Bruxelles, Arras, Amiens, and Paris! I, humble representative of the uncommercial interest, ascend with the rest. The train is light to-night, and I share my compartment with but two fellow-travellers; one, a compatriot in an obsolete cravat, who thinks it is a quite unaccountable thing that they don't keep 'London time' on a French railway, and who is made angry by my modestly suggesting the possibility of Paris time being more in their way; the other a young priest, with a very small bird in a very small cage, who feeds the small bird with a quill, and then puts him up in the network above his head, where he advances twittering to his front wires, and seems to address me in an electioneering manner. The compatriot (who crossed in the boat, and whom I judge to be some person of distinction, as he was shut up, like a stately species of rabbit, in a private hutch on deck) and the young priest (who joined us at Calais) are soon asleep, and then the bird and I have it all to ourselves.

A stormy night still; a night that sweeps the wires of the electric telegraph with a wild and fitful hand; a night so very stormy, with the added storm of the train-progress through it, that when the Guard comes clambering round to mark the tickets while we are at full speed (a really horrible performance in an express train, though he holds on to the open window by his elbows in the most deliberate manner) he stands in such a whirlwind that I grip him fast by the collar, and feel it next to manslaughter to let him go. Still, when he is gone, the small, small bird remains at his front wires feebly twittering to me – twittering and twittering, until, leaning back in my place and looking at him in drowsy fascination, I find that he seems to jog my memory as we rush along.

Uncommercial travels (thus the small, small bird) have lain in their idle thriftless way through all this range of swamp and dyke, as through many other odd places; and about here, as you very well know, are the queer old stone farm-houses, approached by drawbridges, and the windmills that you get at by boats. Here, are the lands where the women hoe and dig, paddling canoe-wise from field to field, and here are the cabarets and other peasant-houses where the stone dove-cotes in the littered yards are as strong as warders' towers in old castles.[12] Here, are the long monotonous miles of canal, with the great Dutch-built barges garishly painted, and the towing girls, sometimes harnessed by the forehead, sometimes by the girdle and the shoulders, not a pleasant sight to see. Scattered through this country are mighty works of VAUBAN,[13] whom you know about, and regiments of such corporals as you heard of once upon a time, and many a blue-eyed Bebelle.[14] Through these flat districts, in the shining summer days, walk those long, grotesque files of young novices in enormous shovel-hats, whom you remember blackening the ground checkered by the avenue of leafy trees. And now that Hazebroucke slumbers certain kilometres ahead, recall the summer evening when your dusty feet strolling up from the station tended hap-hazard to a Fair there, where the oldest inhabitants were circling round and round a barrel-organ on hobby-horses, with the greatest gravity, and where the principal show in the Fair was a Religious Richardson's[15] – literally, on its own announcement in great letters, THEATRE RELIGIEUX. In which improving Temple, the dramatic representation was of 'all the interesting events in the life of our Lord, from the Manger to the Tomb;' the principal female character, without any reservation of exception, being at the moment of your arrival, engaged in trimming the external Moderators (as it was growing dusk), while the next principal female character took the Money, and the Young St John disported himself upside down on the platform.

Looking up at this point to confirm the small, small bird in every particular he has mentioned, I find he has ceased to twitter, and has put his head under his wing. Therefore, in my different way I follow the good example.

APPENDIX 2 – Footnotes

1) J. Hartley, J. (ed,), *The Selected Letters of Charles Dickens*, O.U.P., Oxford, 2015

2) J. Hartley. *op. cit.*

3) The Lord Warden Hotel, Dover – built by the South Eastern Railway was opened in 1853 – next to the Town Station and adjacent to the Admiralty Pier at which the Cross-Channel steamers berthed.

4) See opening soliloquy of Shakespeare's *Richard III* spoken by Gloucester (later Richard III): 'I, that am curtailed of this fair proportion.../That dogs bark at me, as I halt by them.'

5) One of Thomas Moore's *'Irish Melodies'*: 'Rich and rare were the gems she wore, And a bright gold ring on her wand she bore.'

6) The *Telegraph* coach, the fastest from the South-West took 17 hrs to reach London from Exeter. It did not long survive the arrival of the railway in 1844.

7) Dickens made an extensive tour of the United States in 1842. In *American Notes* he describes a voyage down the Ohio from Louisville to Cairo and then up the Mississippi to St Louis.

8) In 1347, during the One Hundred Years War, Edward III of England laid siege to Calais. After a long siege Edward offered to spare the town if six of its leading citizens surrendered themselves with nooses about their necks. They did so but on the intervention of Edward's queen, Phillipa of Hainault, their lives were spared. Rodin's famous statue of the burghers stands in front of Calais Town Hall.

9) In 1558 the England lost Calais its last continental foothold. The English queen, Mary Tudor, claimed that when she died 'Calais' would be found written on her heart.

10) The official responsible for collecting the tax on certain goods entering the town.

11) The words of Trinculo upon meeting Caliban in *TheTempest*, Act. II, Sc. II – 'What have we here – a man or a fish? – dead or alive? A fish, he smells like a fish; a very ancient fish-like smell; a kind of not of the newest Poor John.'

12) Dickens described this rail journey in greater detail in another *All the Year Round* essay – 'In the French Flemish Country' – see J. Edmondson, *Dickens on France*, Northampton, Mass., 2007.

13) Sébastien le Prestre de Vauban (1633-1707), great French military engineer. Built great fortresses all round France, including that at Calais.

14) Bebelle: the little girl who appears in Dickens's short story, *His Boots*, see Edmondson, 2007.

15) Richardson's: the kind of travelling theatre popularised in England by the showman John Richardson (1767?-1837).

APPENDIX 3

In 1836 the radical journalist and novelist George W.M. Reynolds (1814-1874), his literary speculations in Paris having failed, declared himself bankrupt and returned to London. He was a prolific writer whose sensational stories were hugely popular. Although forgotten today, he was more widely read than his contemporaries Dickens and Thackeray. His novel *Grace Darling: heroine of the Fern Islands,* (1839) includes this description (in Chap. XXI) of the English at Calais:

The English at Calais are a remarkably singular race of beings. The generality of them have been obliged to leave their native land for ever, in consequence of the inhumanity of sheriffs' officers and policemen, who would endanger their safeties under the paltry pretext of debts or rogueries. Arriving in Calais with nothing, they usually possess nothing whilst they are there, save the bad opinion of the towns-folk – a species of leasehold property which they only abandon with their lives. In their habits they are for the most part hebdomadal – that is to say, weekly clean shirts, weekly objections to pay the bills that pour in, and a dinner once a week. In reference to the replenishment of their wardrobes they are triennial; but eternity is scarcely an emblem of their predilection for lying. They get-up at mid-day, and if they have any breakfast, they eat it; and, if not, they hasten to see whether they cannot obtain an invitation to partake of one. Having satisfied their hunger – some way or another – they take a walk upon the pier, ogle the fish-girls, watch the steam-boats coming in, laugh at the particulars of the previous night's debauch, and acquire a famous appetite without having exactly made any arrangements for their dinners. This walk brings on three o'clock, and then a lounge in the Grande Place wiles away another hour. There they stand, at the corner of the bankers' houses at the bottom of the Rue du Havre, with their hands in their pockets, large clubs under their arms, their hats cocked over their right ears, and probably one with a great coat on in the summer, and another with white trousers in winter. There they stand, I say; and there they discuss the scandal of the place – how Miss Such-an-One was seen walking late at night in the Basseville with the handsome post-office clerk – how Mrs So-and-So drinks – how Dr This forged a bill upon Mr Morley, the banker – and how Captain That winked at his daughter's running away with a very notorious person residing in Brussels.

APPENDIX 4

DOVER-CALAIS POST OFFICE PACKET FARES, 1828 *(M. STARKE)*

....

Ladies, Gentlemen & Female Servants	10s 6d*
Men Servants	5s
4-Wheel Carriage	£3-3s
Horses	£3-3s

---

* *This was half the amount which the MP Richard Boyle Bernard paid in 1814. He attributed the high price to the heavy post dues at Calais which even for small packet boats amounted to £14.*[52]

LONDON-CALAIS STEAM PACKET FARES, 1828 *(M. STARKE)*

....

Chief Cabin	£1-13s
Fore Cabin	£1-2s-6d
Children under 12	Half price
Servant with Family	As Fore Cabin
Horses	£3-3s
Dogs	5s
4-Wheel Carriage	£4-4s
2-Wheel Carriage	£2-2s

Bibliographical Notes

Chapter 1 – The Shock of Abroad

1   Typical, perhaps, was the journey of William Smith Jnr., author of *A Yorkshireman's Trip to Rome in 1866,* who left Charing Cross at 7.15 in the morning and reached Paris by 6.15 in the evening. At Calais, 'our steamer came alongside one of the long wooden piers... we soon collected together our luggage... and giving up our tickets to an official, walked on to the pier, and we were immediately surrounded by a score of touters, to whose vociferations we lent no ear, but elbowing through them as best we could, made for the railway station, distant about half a mile.'

2   Joseph Addison, Richard Steele & Others, *The Spectator,* No. 15, (ed. C. Gregory Smith) Vol. 1, London, 1945. Addison wrote: 'When I was in *France* I used to gaze with great Astonishment at the Splendid Equipages, and Party-coloured Habits, of that Fantastick Nation'.

3   M. Wordsworth, *Mary Wordsworth's Travel Journal,* 11 July 1820-23 Dec. 1820 (DCMS92) – entry for 11 July 1820.

4   Boyd Alexcander (ed.) *Life at Fonthill, 1807-1822... from the Correspondence of William Beckford,* London, 1957.

5   Nares's autobiography, Merton Coll: Oxford E. 2, 42, pp. 90-2 – quoted in J. Black, *The Grand Tour in the Eighteenth Century,* Stroud, 1992.

6   E. Mavor (ed.) *The Grand Tours of Katherine Wilmot: France 1801-3 and Russia 1805-7,* London, 1992.

7   J.M. Colles (ed.) *The Journal of John Mayne during a Tour of the Continent after the Fall of Napoleon, 1814,* London, 1909.

8   H. Paget Toynbee (ed.) *Walpole's Letters, Vol. 1, 1735-1748,* London, 1903.

9   J. Greig (ed.) *The Farington Diary, Vol. II, (1802-1804)* London, 1923.

10   Although Ian Campbell Ross suggests that *Henry* Errington is a more likely model for Mundungus – see *Laurence Sterne: a Life,* London, 2002 and Dessin informed an American tourist in 1776 that Father Lorenzo never existed – *The American Wanderer through Various Parts of Europe*

by a Virginian, Dublin, 1783.

11 Robert Bell Calton, *Annals and Legends of Calais*, London, 1852.

12 L.P. Curtis (ed.) *Letters of Laurence Sterne*, Oxford, 1935.

13 J. Uglow, *Hogarth; a Life and a World*, London, 1997.

14 Wilbur L. Cross, *The Life and Times of Laurence Sterne*, New Haven, 1929. It is not clear where this story came from. Cross gives no source and it is not to be found in Fitzgerald's earlier biography.

15 Tom Davies's bookshop was the very place in which, two years before, according to Boswell, 'I was fortunate enough to be introduced to the illustrious subject of this work' – *The Life of Johnson*, Oxford, 1961.

16 W. Cole (ed. F.G. Stokes) *A Journal of my Journey to Paris in the Year 1765*, London, 1931.

17 L .P. Curtis (ed.) *op. cit.*

18 P. Fitzgerald, *The Life of Sterne, Vol. 2*, London, 1896.

19 F. Reynolds, *Life and Times of Frederic Reynolds, Written by Himself*, London, 1826.

20 C. Borde, *Calais et la Mer, 1814-1914*, Paris, 1997.

21 R.B. Calton, *op. cit.*.

22 G. Leveson Gower & I. Palmer (eds.) *Hary-o: The Letters of Lady Harriet Cavendish*, London, 1940.

23 Agreed by the British Parliament under 6 & 7 Vic. c.75.

24 With the passage by the British Parliament of the Extradition Acts 1870 - 33 & 34 Cic. c.52 and 1873 - 36 & 37 Vic. c.60 – James Fitzjames Stephen, *The Criminal Law of England*, London, 1883.

25 I. Kelly, *Beau Brummell: the Ultimate Dandy*, London, 2005.

26 A. Young (ed. C. Maxwell) *Travels in France during the years 1787, 1788 & 1789*, Cambridge, 1950.

27 P. Thicknesse, *A year's Journey through France and part of Spain*, Bath, 1777.

Chapter 2 – 'What a cursed thing it is to live in an island!'

1 Remarkably the distance recorded by the French team, led by Jean Dominique Cassini, and their British colleagues, led by William Roy, differed by only 7 feet, R. Hewitt, *Map of a Nation*, London, 2010. The distance given in L. Hebert & G. Dupont, *An Actual Survey and Itinerary of the Road from Calais to Paris*, London, 1814, is 26 miles 58 yards.

2 Dawson Turner, *An Account of a Tour in Normandy*, London, 1820.

3 I am grateful to Martin Lloyd for pointing out that, 'internal control did not really begin to relax until the railways had spread sufficiently to make the attempt to control movements of population ineffective'. See P. Piazza, *Histoire de la Carte Nationale d'Identité*, Paris, 2004.

4 H. Peckham, *The Tour of Holland... Description of Paris*, London, 1772. Etienne-François de Choiseul was the Minister of Foreign Affairs.

5 Quoted in P.W. Clayden, *Rogers and his Contemporaries, Vol. 1*, London, 1889.

6 L. Sterne, *A Sentimental Journey*, London, 1768.

7 M. Lloyd, *The Passport: the History of Man's Most Travelled Document*, Canterbury, 2012.

8 P. Piazza, *op.cit.*

9 S. Scharma, *Citizens: a Chronicle of the French Revolution*, London, 1989.

10 R. Mullen & J. Munson, *The Smell of the Continent*, London, 2009.

11 R. Twiss, *A Trip to Paris in July & August 1792*, London, 1793.

12 R. Twiss, *op. cit.*.

13 R. Twiss, *op.cit.* 'The disturbances in Paris of 10 August' refers to the massacre of the King's Swiss Guards at the Tuileries.

14 M. Lloyd, *op. cit.*.

15 Suffolk Record Office – HA519/133.

16 J. Fennell, *An Apology for the Life of James Fennell*, New York, 1814.

17 J. Fennell, *op. cit.*.

18 M. Lloyd, *op. cit.*.

19 NRO Bul 4/194 610x9. A handwritten endorsement also indicates that Bulwer stayed at the Hotel du Lyon d'Or, Dunkerkque.

20 'A Gentleman of York' A Tour of France in 1818, *Gentleman's Magazine Vol. 90, Pt. 1*, 1820. Mariana Starke recommended the use of circular exchange notes, 'exempt from the deduction of one per cent to which common letters of credit are subject', M. Starke, *Information & Direction for Travellers on the Continent,* 6th ed. London, 1828.

21 R. Sharp, *Letters and Esasys in Prose and Verse,* London, 1834.

22 *The Universal Songster: a Museum of Mirth, Vol. 1,* London, 1825.

23 Rowland E. Prothero (ed.)   *Private Letters of Edward Gibbon, Vol. 2,* London, 1896.

24 Lord Sheffield, *The Miscellaneous Works of Edward Gibbon Esq., with Memoirs of his Life and Writings, Vol. 2,* Letters, London, 1814.

25 F.W. Blagdon, *Paris as it was and as it is,* London, 1803.

26 W.O. Henderson, *Industrial Britain under the Regency,* London, 1968.

27 R. Jessup, *Man of many Talents: an informal biography of James Douglas, 1753-1819,* Chichester, 1975.

28 K. Morgan, *Jabez Fisher: an American Quaker in the British Isles,* Oxford, 1992.

29 P. Hawker, *The Diary of Colonel Peter Hawker, 1802-1853,* London, 1988.

30 Letter to H.R.H. Princess Elizabeth in P. Hughes (ed.) *The Journals and Letters of Fanny Burney, Vol. VIII,* Oxford, 1980.

31 P. Hughes (ed.) *op. cit.*.

32 Lady Theresa Lewis, *Extracts of the Journals and Correspondence of Miss Berry from the Year 1783, Vol. II,* London, 1866.

33 'A Gentleman of York', *op.cit.*

34 M. Baillie, *A Tour upon the Continent in the Year 1818, through parts of France, Italy, Switzerland & the Borders of Germany,* London, 1819.

35 J.T. Norgate (ed.) *Paris and the Parisians, in the Year after Waterloo,* London, 1887. Norgate refers to Troubridge as, 'Sir Thomas', a name and title also employed by Barbara Luttrell in her biography of Cornelia Knight – *The Prim Romantic,* London, 1965 – who was also of the party. However, as Sir Thomas Troubridge, Nelson's friend, had been lost in the Indian Ocean in 1807, this must have been his son, Sir Edward Thomas Troubridge.

36 K. Morgan, *op. cit..*

37 Quoted in A. Bell, *Sydney Smith: a Biography,* Oxford, 1980.

38 Anon., 'A Trip to Paris in August and September 1815', *New Monthly Magazine, 1 May 1816,* No. 28, Vol. V.

39 F. Austin, *The Clift Family Correspondence, 1792-1846,* Sheffield, 1991.

40 Countess of Blessington, *The Idler in Italy, Vol. 1,* London, 1839.

41 W. Scott, *Journal of Sir Walter Scott from the Original Manuscript at Abbotsford,* New York, 1890.

42 C. Borde, *Calais et la Mer, 1814-1914,* Paris, 1997.

43 B.L. Add MSS. 56544/5/6/7.

44 W. Roberts, *A Short Account of a Visit to Paris made in 1821,* Winterthur library, Doc. 1351.

45 The Seventh Duke of Wellington, *Wellington and his Friends,* London, 1965.

46 John M. Cobbett, *Letters from France,* London, 1825.

47 P. Straffa (ed.) *The Works and Correspondence of David Ricardo: Journal of a Tour on the Continent,* Cambridge, 1973.

48 C. Borde, *op. cit..*

49 H.P. White, *A Regional History of the Railways of Southern England,* London, 1961.

50 *The Times,* 24 June 1844.

51 N. Gash, *The Life of Sir Robert Peel after 1830,* London, 1986.

52 R. B. Bernard, *A Tour through some Parts of France, Switzerland, Savoy, Germany & Belgium during the Summer & Autumn of 1814,* London, 1815.

53 J. Ruskin, *Praeterita,* London, 1889.

Chapter 3 – 'A Dozen Dirty Civil Hands'

1   C. Demotier, *Annales de Calais, depuis les temps les plus reculées jusqu'à nos jours,* Calais, 1856.

2   A. Sorel, *L'Europe et la Révolution Française,* Paris, 1903.

3   J.G. Lemaistre, *A Rough Sketch of Modern Paris,* London, 1803.

4   'ragged regiment of Terence': a reference to Terence's comedy *The Eunuch.*

5   J.G. Lemaistre, *op. cit..*

6   Lady T. Lewis, *Extracts from the Journal and Correspondence of Miss Berry for the Years from 1783, Vol. 2,* London, 1865.

7   L. Gibbs (ed.) *The Diary of Fanny Burney,* London, 1966.

8   M. Baillie, *A Tour upon the Continent in the Summer of 1818,* London, 1819.

9   *London Weekly Times,* 23 Sept. 1827.

10   A.B. Granville, *St Petersburgh: a Journal of Travels to and from the Capital,* London, 1828.

11   N. Pinkney, *Travels through the South of France and in the Interior of the Provinces of Provence and Languedoc in the years 1807 and 1808,* London, 1809.

12   M. Wordsworth, *Mary Wordsworth's Journal* (DCMS 92) www.days.com/diaries/wordsworth.pdf

13   F.W. Blagdon, *Paris as it was and as it is,* London, 1803.

14   Frances Trollope, *Paris and the Parisians,* London, 1836. This story provides the title of one of the most readable of recent historical travel books – R. Mullen & J. Munson, *The Smell of the continent: the British discover Europe,* London, 2009.

15   V. de Villiers, *Itinéraire descriptif ou description routière et pittoresque de la France et de l'Italie,* Paris, 1816 and quoted in C. Borde, *op. cit.*

16   *Murray's Handbook for Travellers on the Continent, being a Guide through Holland, Belgium, Prussia and North Germany,* London, 1836.

17   W. Pinkney, *op. cit..*

18   J. Dean Paul, *Journal of a Party of Pleasure to Paris in the Month of August, 1802,* London, 1802.

19   Edmund John Eyre, *Observations made at Paris during the Peace,* Bath, 1803.

20 Dawson Warren, *The Journal of a British Chaplain in Paris during the Peace Negotiations of 1802*, London, 1913.
21 W. Wright, *A Narrative of the Situation and Treatment of the English arrested by order of the French Government at the commencement of hostilities*, London, 1803.
22 J.T. Norgate (ed.) *Paris and the Parisians in the Year after Waterloo*, London, 1887.
23 Lady T. Lewis, *op. cit.*.
24 Edmund John Eyre, *op. cit.*.
25 Murray's Handbook, *op. cit.*
26 'A Gentleman of York' – A Tour of France in 1818, *Gentleman's Magazine Vol. 90, Pt. 1,* 1820.
27 H.E. Litchfield (ed.) *Emma Darwin: a Century of Family Letters*, Cambridge, 1904.
28 H.E. Litchfield, *op. cit.*
29 Countess of Blessington, *The Idler in Italy, Vol.* 1, London, 1839.

Chapter 4 – 'In Ease and even Splendour'
1 M. Gardiner (Countess of Blessington) *Journal of a Tour through the Netherlands to Paris in 1821*, London, 1822.
2 M. Baillie, *A Tour upon the Continent in the Summer of 1818, through parts of France, Italy, Switzerland and the Borders of Germany*, London, 1819.
3 H.E. Litchfield (ed.) Emma Darwin: *A Century of Family Letters, 1792-1896, Vol. 1*, Cambridge, 1904.
4 M. Tyson & H. Guppy, *The French Journals of Mrs Thrale and Dr Johnson*, Manchester, 1932.
5 M. Tyson & H. Guppy, *op. cit.*
6 I. Macintyre, *Hester: the Remarkable Life of Dr Johnson's 'Dear Mistress'*, London, 2008.
7 L. P. Curtis, *Letters of Laurence Sterne*, Oxford, 1935.
8 F.G. Stokes (ed.) *Journal of My Journey to Paris in the Year 1765*, London, 1931.
9 F.G. Stokes (ed.) *op. cit.*
10 M. Brayne (ed.) *Harry Peckham's Tour,* Stroud, 2008.
11 M. Brayne, *op. cit.*
12 E.S Roscoe & H. Clergue (eds.) *George Selwyn: His Letters*

and His Life, London, 1899.

13 Anon. 'Journal of a Tour through France and Part of Italy in the Course of Last Winter and Spring' in *The Scots Magaazine*, January 1803, Edinburgh, 1803.

14 *Damiens Conversations Lexicon*, Leipzig, 1834.

15 A. Hugo & C.V. Monin, *France pittoresque: ou description pittoresque, topographique et statistique*, Paris, 1835.

16 Quoted in N. Pevsner, *A History of Building Types*, London, 1976.

17 *Gentleman's Magazine*, London, 1797.

18 C. Lloyd & R.C. Anderson (eds.) *A Memoir of James Trevenen*, Navy Record Society, 1959.

19 R.B. Calton, *Annals and legends of Calais*, London, 1852.

20 A. Young, *The Autobiography of Arthur Young with selections from his Correspondence*, London, 1898.

21 C. Maxwell (ed.) *Arthur Young: Travels in France during the Years 1787, 1788 & 1789*, Cambridge, 1950.

22 *F. Marlin, Voyages d'un Français depuis 1775 jusqu à 1807, Tome 1*, Paris, 1817.

23 F. Marlin, *op. cit.*

24 A. Barbeau (ed.) *La France et Paris sous le Directoire: lettres d'un voyageuse anglaise*, Paris, 1888.

25 E. Mavor (ed.) *The Grand Tours of Katherine Wilmot: France 1801-3 and Russia 1805-7*, London, 1992.

26 E. Mavor, *op. cit.*

27 E. Mavor, *op. cit.*

28 *Hull Packet*, Issue 905, 15 May 1804, Hull, 1804.

29 H.W. Dickinson, *Robert Fulton: Engineer & Artist – his Life and Work*, London, 1913.

30 W. Pinkney, *Travels through the South of France and the Interior of the provinces of Provence and Languedoc in the years 1807 and 1808*, London, 1809.

31 W. Pinkney, *op. cit.*

32 J.M. Colles (ed.) *The Journal of John Mayne during a Tour of the Continent upon the Re-opening after the Fall of Napoleon in 1814*, London, 1909.

33 J.M. Colles (ed.) *op. cit.*

34 *New Monthly Magazine, No. 28. Vol. V, 1 May 1816*, 'A Trip to Paris in August and September 1816'.

35 *New Monthly Magazine, No. 28*, ibid.

36 E. de Selincourt (ed.) *Journals of Dorothy Wordsworth, Vol. 2*, London, 1952.

37 A.B. Granville, *St Petersburgh: a Journal of travel to and from the Capital*, London, 1828.

38 N. Carter, *Letters from Europe: comprising the Journal of a Tour through Ireland, England, Scotland, France, Italy and Switzerland in the Years 1825, 1826 and 1827*, New York, 1827.

39 J.T. Norgate (ed.) *Paris and the Parisians: the Year after Waterloo*, London, 1887.

40 W.M. Thackeray, 'Notes on a Week's Holiday', in *Roundabout Papers*, London, 1887.

41 Stafford M. Linsley, 'Sopwith, Thomas (1803-1879)' *Oxford Dictionary of National Biography*, Oxford University Press, 2 online ed. 2004.

42 T. Sopwith, *Notes on a Visit to Egypt*, private cirulation, c. 1857.

43 T. Sopwith, *op. cit.*

44 T. Sopwith, *op. cit.*

45 T. Sopwith, *op. cit.*

46 *Nord Matin*, 2 July, 1961, *'L'Hôtel Dessin et ses visiteurs célèbres au XVIIIe siècle.*

47 *Nord Matin*, 3 July, 1961, *'L'Hôtel Dessin et ses visiteurs célèbres au XIXe siècle.*

48 E.A. Smith, *George IV*, London, 1999.

49 Lady Knighton ed.) *Memoirs of Sir William Knighton, Vol. 1*, Paris, 1838.

50 Liverpool's refusal to make Knighton a Privy Councillor caused a major rift between him and the King. 'It is really too bad to reflect', wrote Mrs Arbuthnot, 'that all this intriguing and ill-humour is going on because Lord Liverpool refused to admit into the Privy Council a fellow who, fifteen years ago, carried phials and pill-boxes about Plymouth' – F. Bamford and the Duke of Wellington (eds.) *The Journal of Mrs Arbuthnot, Vol. 1*, London, 1950.

51 J.A. Hamilton, 'Knighton, Sir William, first baronet (1776-1836)' rev. Judith Schmid Lewis, *Oxford Dictionary of*

National Biography, Oxford University Press, 2004, online ed. May 2009.

Chapter 5 – Some Fellow Guests

1   W. Jones, *Observations in a Journey to Paris by way of Flanders,* London, 1777.

2   P.B. Nockles, *The Oxford Movement in Context: Anglican High Churchmanship, 1760-1857,* Cambridge, 1994.

3   W. Jones, *op.cit.*

4   Anon, *Britain Triumphant on the Plains of Waterloo,* Burslem, 1816.

5   Andrew O'Reilly, *The Irish Abroad and at Home: at the Court and in the Camp,* New York, 1856

6   Possibly Sir Colin Campbell (1776-1847), who had been at Waterloo and was attached to Wellington's Staff at Paris, 1815-18.

7   There is some disagreement about the Duke's date of birth but it was probably 1 May 1769. He would therefore have been 49 at this time.

8   Among officers his nick-name was 'Beau'; among the men, 'Nosey'.

9   Letter written by a 'Gentleman of York' to a near Relative – *The Gentleman's Magazine,* Jan. to June, 1820, Vol. XC, Pt. 2.

10 N.P. Willis, *Pencillings by the Way,* London, 1942.

11 The party from Brunswick arrived on the previous evening. According to the transcription of a document entitled *A Visit to Paris in September, 1821 by Wiliam Roberts, M.D.,* dated 13 September, 'Dr Lushington and Mrs Wilde arrived this evening at Dessins Hotel on their return to England after attending the Queen's funeral'. This document (Call No. Doc. 1351) is in the Joseph Downs Collection, Winterthur Library, Delaware, U.S.A.

12 M. Gardiner (Countess of Blessington) *Journal of a Tour through the Netherlands to Paris in 1821.* London, 1822.

13 E.A. Smith, *Oxford Dictionary of National Biography,* Oxford, 2004.

14 E.A. Smith, *op. cit.*

15 *Virtus est sola nobiltas* – Virtue alone is Noble.

16 'M. De Lalot... Chateaubriand', eminent French politicians. Thiers was the founder of the *National*.

17 Lord Brougham, who was at this time Lord Chancellor, had been a founder of the *Edinburgh Review*.

18 'Moncieur Bertin de _____' , alludes to Louis-François Bertin, editor of the *Journal des Débats*. There is a fine portrait of him by Ingres in the Louvre.

19 E. Bulwer Lytton, *England and the English*, Paris, 1836.

Chapter 6 – Fricaseed Chicken and Burgundy

1 Sterne's own explanatory note reads – 'All the effects of Strangers (Swiss and Scotch excepted) dying in France, are seized by virtue of this law, though the heir be upon the spot – the profit of these contingencies being farmed, there is no redress' – Gardener D. Stout (ed.) Laurence Sterne, *A Sentimental Journey through France and Italy by Mr Yorick*, Berkeley, 1967.

2 As, for example, on the occasion – 28 August 1783 – when Woodforde dined with the Townshends of Honingham Hall and found, 'most of the things spoiled by being so frenchified in dressing' – H. Edwards (ed.) *The Diary of James Woodforde, Vol. 10 – 1782-1784*, Parson Woodforde Society, 2013.

3 R.L. Winstanley, *The Inner Man: a Modest Inquiry into the Food and Eating Habits of Parson Woodforde and his Contemporaries*, Parson Woodforde Society Quarterly Journal, XVII, 4, 1984.

4 Barbara Ketcham Wheaton, *Savouring the Past: the French Kitchen & Table from 1300 to 1789*, London, 1983.

5 G. Collier, *France on the Eve of the Great Revolution: France, Holland and the Netherlands a Hundred Years ago*, London, 1865.

6 J.K. Laughton, rev. Nicholas Tracy, 'Collier, Sir George (1738-1795)' *Oxford Dictionary of National Biography*, Oxford 2004.

7 Collier, *op. cit.*

8 Sir J. Chetwode of Oakeley, Staffs.

9 Collier, *op. cit.*

10 Sir John Dean Paul, *Journal of a Journey to Paris in the Month of August 1802.* It is not clear what is, 'quite unknown to us'. According to the author of *La Cuisinière bourgeoisie,* published in Paris in 1742 (quoted by Wheaton, *op. cit.*) only Parmesan and Brie were used in cooking, other cheeses were eaten 'au dessert'. In England cheese was eaten after the meat dishes – R.L. Winstanley & P. Jameson (eds.) *The Diary of James Woodforde, Vol. 11 - 1785-1787,* Parson Woodforde Society, 1999 – 'We gave our Company for Dinner some boiled Skaite & fryed Sprats, Ham & Fowls...Radishes & Watercresses with the Cheese' (2 Dec. 1786).

11 M. Tyson & H. Guppy (eds.) *The French Journals of Mrs Thrale & Dr Johnson,* Manchester, 1932. The friar was Father Felix, a former soldier and, Mrs Thrale believed, 'no mean scholar for the books we found open in his cell shewed he had not neglected modern or colloquial knowledge; there was a translation of Addison's Spectators, and Rapin's Dissertation on the contending Parties of England called Whig and Tory. He had likewise a violin and some printed music for his entertainment' – H. Barrows (ed.) Hester Lynch Piozzi, *Observations and reflections made in the Course of a Journey through France, Italy & Germany,* Ann Arbor, 1967.

12 A.M. Broadley (ed.), D, Warren, *The Journal of a British Chaplain in Paris during the Peace Negotiations of 1802,* London, 1913.

13 F. Marlin, *Voyages d'un Français depuis 1775 jusqu'à 1807, Vol. 1,* Paris, 1817.

14 J, & K. Fry, *A Tale of Two Journeys: France and Belgium in the early 1800s,* Disley, 2005. It seems likely that 'à l'oreille' is a misreading of 'à l'oseille' – a veal stew with sorrel.

15 B. Madan, *Spencer and Waterloo: the Letters of Spencer Madan, 1814-16,* London, 1870.

16 B. Madan, *op. cit.*

17 Gloucester CRO D 2002 F1 – and quoted in J. Black, *The Grand Tour in the Eighteenth Century,* Stroud, 1992.

18 J.M. Colles (ed.) *The Journal of John Mayne during a Tour of the Continent upon the Re-opening after the Fall of Napoleon,*

London, 1909.

19 E. Mavor (ed.) *The Grand Tours of Katherine Wilmot: France 1801-3 and Russia 1805-7,* London, 1992.

20 B.K. Wheaton, *op. cit.*

21 F. Reynolds, *The Life and Times of F. Reynolds: written by Himself,* London, 1826.

22 F. Reynolds, *op.cit.*

23 Louis-Sébastien Mercier, *Le Tableau de Paris, Vol. 1, rev.,* Paris, 1873 – quoted in B.K. Wheaton, op. cit.

24 F. Reynolds, *op. cit.*

25 P. Hawker, *The Diary of Colonel Peter Hawker, 1802-1853, Vol. 1,* London, 1988.

26 P. Hawker, *op. cit.*

27 Beatrix Cary Davenport (ed.) *A Diary of the French Revolution by Gouverneur Morris,* New York, 1977.

28 J.T. Norgate (ed.) *Paris and the Parisians: the Year after Waterloo,* London, 1887.

29 *New Monthly Magazine, No. 34, 1834 (3).* A famous example of such an entertainment in literature is Mrs Leo Hunter's fancy-dress breakfast – or *dejeune* – in Charles Dickens's *Pickwick Papers of 1837.*

30 J.G. Lemaistre, *A Rough Sketch of Modern Paris,* London, 1803. The reviewer of this book in the *Edinburgh Review* thought it, 'not easy to imagine a more dull and insipid series of travels ...his calamities are always a bad dinner, or a dear bill, or a sulky landlord'; none of which, however, overtook him at Dessein's.

31 P.W. Clayden, *The Early Life of Samuel Rogers,* London, 1887.

32 Shropshire Archives, letter 811/3.

33 Anon, *Memoirs of a Man of Fashion,* London, 1821.

34 W. Otter (ed.) *Life and Reminiscences of the Rev. Edward Daniel Clarke, Ll. D,* London, 1824.

35 *Gentleman's Magazine, Vol. XC, Pt. 2, 1820* – Letters written by a Gentleman of York to a Near Relative.

36 E. de Selincourt (ed.) *Journals of Dorothy Wordsworth, Vol. 2,* London, 1952.

37 *The Literary Gazette & Journal of Belles Lettres, Arts &*

Sciences for the Year 1826, 'Travels of Peter Pry'.

38 Anita McConnell, 'Kitchiner, William (1776-1827) *Oxford Dictionary of National Biography,* Oxford, 2002.

39 A.B. Granville, *St Petersburgh: a Journal of Travels to and from that Capital,* London, 1828.

40 'Mutton chops with Maintenon Sauce' – Lamb cutlets covered with an 'appareil Maintenon' – a mixture of Onion soubise and Béchamel Sauce bound with egg yolks and incorporating chopped mushrooms. Named after Madame de Maintenon, the morganatic second wife of Louis XIV, reputed to have been a good cook – P. Montagné, *Nouveau Larousse Gastronomique,* Paris, 1960.

41 V. Hugo, *France et Belgique, Alpes et Pyrénées,* Paris, 1842.

42 E.D. Cuming (ed.) *'Nimrod': My Life and Times,* London, 1827.

43 R.H. Stoddard (ed.) *Personal Reminiscences of Chorley, Planché and Young,* New York, 1876.

44 L. Junot (Mme la Duchesse d'Abrantès), *Memoirs de Mme la Duchesse d'Abrantès, ou Souvenirs Historique sur Napoleon, la Révolution, La Directoire et La Restauration,* Paris, 1832.

45 Charles Hervey, 'The Habitué's Notebook', in *The New Monthly Magazine and Humourist, Vol. 85,* 1849.

Chapter 7 – 'Much handsomer when you approach it from the water'

1 M. Brayne (ed.) *Harry Peckham's Tour,* Stroud, 2008.

2 J. Ruskin, *Praeterita,* London, 1885.

3 M. Tyson & H. Guppy (eds.) *The French Journals of Mrs Thrale and Doctor Johnson,* Manchester, 1932.

4 P. Gosse, *Doctor Viper,* London, 1952.

5 E. De Selincourt, *Journals of Dorothy Wordsworth, Vol. 2,* London, 1952.

6 M. Wordsworth, *Travel Journal,* Dove Cottage, DCMS 92; http://www.day-books.com/diaries/wordsworth.pdf.

7 M. Wordswoth, *op. cit.*.

8 L. Hebert & G. Dupont, *An Actual Survey & itinerary of the Road from Calais to Paris….,* Paris, 1814.

9 L. Hebert & G. Dupont, *op. cit.*.

10 W. Jones, *Observations in a Journey to Paris...*, London, 1776.

11 N. Carter, *Letters from Europe...*, New York, 1827.

12 T. Sopwith, *Notes on a Visit to Egypt,* London, 1857.

13 F. Lennel, *Calais par l'Image, Tome 3,* Paris, 1996.

14 R. Bell Calton, *Annals and Legends of Calais....,* London, 1852.

15 R. B. Calton, *op. cit.*

16 J. Ruskin, *op. cit.*

17 M. Brayne (ed.) *op. cit.*

18 E. J. Eyre, *Observations made at Paris during the Peace,* Bath, 1803.

19 E. Planta, *A New Picture of Paris.....,* London, 1828.

20 E. J. Eyre, *op. cit.*

21 J. Albany, *The Englishman's Guide to Calais,* London, 1829.

22 E.J. Eyre, *op. cit.*

23 R.B. Calton, *op. cit.*

24 J. Albany, *op. cit.*

25 E. De Selincourt (ed.) *op. cit.*

26 E. De Selincourt (ed.) *op. cit.*

27 M. Tyson & H. Guppy (eds.) *op. cit.*

28 M. Tyson & H. Guppy (eds.) *op. cit.*

29 S. Johnson, *Prayers and Meditations,* London, 1785.

30 M. Tyson & H. Guppy,(eds.) *op. cit.*

31 A.M. Broadley (ed.) *The Journal of a British Chaplain in Paris during the Peace negotiations of 1802,* London, 1913.

32 J. Ruskin, *op. cit.*

33 P. Fitzgerald, *The Life of Laurence Sterne, Vol. 2,* London, 1896.

34 From *The Mirror of Literature,* Issue 283, 17 Nov. 1827.

35 An Old Contributor, *Blackwoods Magazine,* Vol. 42, CCLXV, 1837.

36 R. B. Calton, *op. cit.*

37 E.J. Eyre, *op. cit.*

38 E, Planta, *op. cit.*

39 W. Roberts, *A Short Account of a Visit to Paris made in 1821,* Winterthur Library, Doc. 1351.

40 R.B. Calton, *op. cit.*

41 From *The Mirror of Literature,* Issue 283, 17 Nov. 1827.

42 From *The Mirror of Literature,* Issue 283, 17 Nov. 1827.

43 J. Albany, *op. cit.*

44 R.B. Calton, *op. cit.*

45 E.D. Cuming (ed.), *My Life and Times by Nimrod,* Edinburgh, 1927.

46 J. Albany, *op. cit.*

47 J. Albany, *op. cit.*

48 From *The Mirror of Literature,* Issue 283, 17 Nov. 1827.

49 J. Ruskin, *op. cit.*

50 R.B. Calton, *op. cit.*

51 R.B. Calton, *op. cit.*

52 http://www.nationalgallery.org.uk/paintings/joseph-mallord-william-turner-calais-pier

53 J. Greig (ed.), *The Farington Diary, Vol. 2, 1802-1804,* London, 1923.

54 *Courier,* 28 April, 1814.

55 F. Lennel, *Calais par l'Image, Tome 3,* Paris, 1996.

56 'T. Brown' (ed.) *The Fudge Family in Paris,* London, 1818.

57 F. Hervé, *How to enjoy Paris in 1842,* London, 1842.

58 E. De Selincourt, *Journals of Dorothy Wordsworth, Vol. 1,* London, 1952.

59 R.B. Calton, *op. cit.*

60 P.W. Clayden, *The Early Life of Samuel Rogers,* London, 1887.

61 http://blogs.kent.ac.uk/specialcollections/tag/tourism/page/3/

62 R.B. Calton, *op. cit.*

63 J. Albany, *op. cit.*

64 *Murray's Handbook for Travellers on the Continent, being a Guide through Holland, Belgium, Prussia and North Germany,* London, 1836.

65 J. Albany, *op. cit.*

66 J. Albany, *op. cit.*

67 J. Albany, *op. cit.*

68 J. Albany, *op. cit.*

69 E. De Selincourt, *Journals of Dorothy Wordsworth, Vol. 1,* London, 1952.

70 W. Wordsworth, *Selected Poems of William Wordsworth*, London, 2005.

71 E. De Selincourt, *Journals of Dorothy Wordsworth, Vol. 1*, London, 1952

72 W. Wordsworth, *op. cit.*

73 C.M. Maclean, *Born under Saturn: a biography of William Hazlitt*, London, 1943.

74 W. Wordsworth, *op. cit.*

75 I. Bryden (ed.) *The Pre-Raphaelites: Writings and Sources, Vol. III* – John Ruskin on 'Pre-Raphaelitism', London, 1998.

76 J. Albany, *op. cit.*

77 K. & M. Allott (eds) *The Poems of Matthew Arnold*, London, 1979.

78 N. Murray, *A Life of Matthew Arnold*, London, 1996.

79 K. & M. Allott (eds) *op. cit.*

Chapter 8 – Un Pièce au Théâtre

1 W. Fawcett (ed.) James Essex, *Journey of a Tour through Part of Flanders and France in August 1773*, London, 1888.

2 C. Demotier, *Annales de Calais, depuis les temps les plus reculés jusqu'à nos jours*, Calais, 1856.

3 T. Holcroft, *Anna St. Ives, Vol. 2, 24*, London, 1792.

4 P. Quennell, *Four Portraits*, London, 1945.

5 John Lord Sheffield, *The Miscellaneous Works of Edward Gibbon Esq., with Memoirs of his Life and Writings, Vol. II*, London, 1814. Lord Coleraine was John Hangar, 2nd Baron Coleraine (1743-94).

6 *Scots Magazine, January 1803*, Anon, Journal of a Tour through France and Part of Italy in the Course of Last Winter & Spring, Edinburgh, 1803.

7 In fact, *Nicodème dans la Lune, ou révolution pacifique*, a 3-act farce by 'Cousin Jacques' (the pen-name of Louis Abel Beffroy de Reigny) which had been first performed in Paris in 1790. Aerostation = ballooning.

8   Ah! ça ira, ça ira, ça ira,
         Le peuple en ce jour sans cesse répète,
         Ah! ça ira, ça ira, ça ira.
         Malgré les mutins tout réussira! etc.

First sung in 1790 it quickly became the most popular song of the Revolution. During the Directory it actually became mandatory to sing it before theatrical performances. In a foot-note Reynolds points out that the, 'old gentleman was not at the head of the whole police of Calais, but the director of a particular detachment – a sort of superior Dogberry.' The incident on which the play was based had taken place on 18 October 1791. At the height of a storm, a fishing boat, the *Saint-Pierre* of Dieppe, heading for the North Sea herring fishery with 34 sailors on board, had been wrecked at the entrance to Calais harbour. Four local fishermen managed to save the lives of 23 of the Dieppe men but a further heroic attempt was unsuccessful and two of the Calaisiens, Gavet and Mareschal, lost their lives – C. Demotier, *op. cit.*

9 F. Reynolds, *Life and Times of Frederick Reynolds*, London, 1827.

10 *Edinburgh Review* for April-July 1806, Vol. VIII, Edinburgh, 1806.

11 J.G. Lemaistre, *A rough Sketch of Modern Paris or Letters on Society, Manners, Public Curiosities and Amusements in that Capital*, London, 1803. This was an earlier book than that which had been so unkindly treated by the Edinburgh reviewer.

12 Sir J.D. Paul, *Journey of a Party of Pleasure to Paris*, London, 1803.

13 William Parsons (1736-1795) – comic actor, very popular in England where he created the part of Sir Fretful Plagiary in Sheridan's *The Critic*.

14 Edmund John Eyre, *Observations made at Paris during the Peace*, Bath, 1803.

15 H. Swinburne (trans. Albert Babeau), *La France et Paris sous le Directoire: lettres d'un voyageuse anglaise suivies d'ectraits des lettres de Swinburne*, Paris, 1888.

16 Swinburne, *op. cit.*

17 P.W. Clayden, *The Early Life of Samuel Rogers*, London, 1887. Rogers appears to think that Eustache and St. Pierre were two of the six burghers who surrendered themselves to

Edward III following the siege of Calais in 1347. In fact Eustache de St Pierre was the leading citizen. The drop-scene was a curtain or canvas dropped near the front of the stage to allow for a scene-change behind.

18 *Scots Magazine, January 1803, op.cit.*

19 *European Magazine, December 1803,* 'A Young Gentleman' *A Portrait of Revolutionary Paris... observed in a late Tour.*

20 T. Frost, *The Lives of the Conjurors,* London, 1876.

21 *Scots Magazine, January 1803, op.cit.*

22 *Scots Magazine, January 1803, op.cit..*

23 W. Pinkney, *Travels through the South of France and the Interior of the Provinces of Provence & Languedoc in the Years 1807 and 1808,* London, 1809.

24 W. Pinkney, *op. cit.*

25 J.G. Alger, *Napoleon's British Visitors and Captives,* London, 1904.

26 Quoted in J. G. Alger, *op. cit.*

27 Hon. R.B. Bernard, *A Tour through some Parts of France, Switzerland, Savoy, Germany and Belgium during the Summer & Autumn of 1814,* London, 1815.

28 Hon. R.B. Bernard, *op. cit.*

29 Hon. R.B. Bernard, *op. cit.*

30 *Les Théâtres (Lois, Reglements, instruction, Salles de Spectacles...) par un Amateur,* Paris, 1817.

31 C. Demotier, *op. cit.* Marie-Catherine de Villedieu's *Manlius* had first been performed in 1662, five year's before Jean Racine's great tragedy. The French adaptation of *Hamlet* was probably that of Jean-François Ducis whose *Abufar* had first been perfomed in 1795. It seems likely that *Iphigénie en Tauride* was Christoph-Willbald Gluck's opera of 1779.

32 S. Watson, *A Journey to the Simplon,* London, 1818. 'Madame Georges' was, in fact, the distinguished tragic actress Marguerite-Joséphine Weimer (1787-1867), usually known as 'Mademoiselle George'.

33 J. G. Alger, *op. cit.*

34 *The Literary Panorama and National Reporter,* October, 1814, London.

35 *The Literary Panorama and National Reporter, op. cit.*

36 *British Neptune,* 14 Sept. 1818.

37 R. Rush, *Narrative of a Residence at the Court of London,* London, 1833.

38 J. Bew, Castlereagh: *Enlightenment, War & Tyranny,* London, 2011.

39 P. Ginistry (ed) *Memoirs d'une danseuse de corde,* Paris, 1907.

40 J. Bew, *op. cit.*

41 Quoted in J. Quérard, *La France litteraire, ou Dictionnaire bibliographique des Savants,* Paris, 1838.

42 See www.calais.fr/histoire/theatre/theatre.htm

43 Plan Cadastral de Calais, 1834.

44 N. Mulard, *Calais au temps de la Dentelle,* Calais, 1968.

45 N. Mulard, *op. cit.*

46 K.D. Reynolds, 'Vining Family (per 1807-1915)' *Oxford Dictionary of National Biography,* Oxford University Press, 2004.

47 J. Albany, *The Englishman's Guide to Calais,* London, 1829.

48 'San Carlos' – a reference to the Teatro di San Carlo, Naples, inaugurated in 1737. It was rebuilt following a fire in 1816. On the re-opening of the theatre Stendhal wrote, 'it dazzles the eye, it enraptures the soul'. It had a capacity of 1,444.

49 The character of Monsieur Calicot, a pretentious fabric salesman, was created by the dramatist Eugène Scribe (1791-1861) for his play *Le Combat aux Montagnes, ou La Folie Beaujon.* Calicot, a true dandy, only sold – and valued – the latest fashions.

50 Marc-Antoine Desaugiers (1772-1827) – composer, dramatist and song-writer, who often collaborated with Scribe.

51 M. Plante had been the leading comic actor in the company since at least 1817, *Les Théâtres...,* *op. cit.*

52 Fronting – in fact Frontin, a roguish valet in Alain-René Le Sage's comedy *Turcaret, ou le Financier* of 1709.

53 Charles-Gabriel Potier (1774-1838) – vaudeville actor on Paris stage.

54 'James' – unsure unless it refers to Dorothy Jordan

(1761-1816) who was also known as, 'Mrs James'; Benjamin Wrench (1778-1843) was a distinguished comic actor on the London stage.

55 'Jocrisse' – a type of foolish valet who appears in many comedies.

56 Joseph-Mira Brunet (1766-1851) – comic actor who spent most of his career at the Thèâtre des Variétes, Paris.

57 Marie-Elizabeth Joly (fl. 1761-98) or her husband(?) Perlet – 'the most celebrated and talented French comedian', 'Anecdotes of the French Stage', *The Gentleman's Magazine & American Monthly Review, Vol. 1*, Philadelphia 1837.

58 See http://www.calais,fr/histoire/theatre/theatre.htm

Chapter 9 – Breakdown, Dentention & 'a little finesse'

1 *E. De Selincourt & Helen Darbishire (eds.), The Poetical Works of William Wordsworth, Vols I - V*, Oxford, 1940-49.

2 P. Thorold, *The British in France: Visitors and Residents since the Revolution,* London, 2008.

3 C. Kennedy, *Narratives of the Revolutionary and Napoleonic Wars,* London, 2013.

4 W. Wright, *A Narrative of the Situation and Treatment of the English arrested by order of the French Government at the commencement of Hostilities etc.,* London, 1803.

5 J.G. Alger, *Napoleon's British Visitors and Captives, 1801-1815,* London, 1904.

6 W. Wright, *op.cit.* According to M. Lewis, *Napoleon and his British Captives,* London, 1962, Wright escaped in a trunk from Le Havre. This is incorrect as a reading of Wright's work makes clear.

7 W. Wright, *op. cit.*

8 W. Wright, *op. cit.*

9 W. Wright, *op. cit.* An iron bath filled with sand was thought to be effective in the treatment of some ailments. Fine Calais sand was regarded as the most suitable for this purpose – A. Lees, *The Cyclopedia: a Universal Dictionary of Arts, Science and Literature,* London, 1819. There is a possibility that Mallison was sent to Valenciennes. M. Lewis, *op. cit.* includes a, 'Mr W.H. Malison (or Malleson)' as being among the civilians detained there. If Lewis is correct, however, he escaped which would have been difficult for a 'cripple'.

10 W. Wright, *op. cit.*
11 W. Wright, *op. cit.*
12 E. Boys, *Narrative of a Captivity, Escape and Adventures in France,* London, 1827.

Chapter 10 – 'A State of Great Destitution'
1 J. Albany, *The Englishman's Guide to Calais,* London, 1829.
2 J.V. Beckett & J.E. Heath, *'When was the Industrial Revolution in the East Midlands?',* Midland History, Vol. XIII, Birmingham, 1988.
3 N. Mulard, *Calais au Temps de la Dentelle,* Calais, 1963. The 1841 Census shows Webster, aged 60, living in the Rue Lafayette, together with his wife Rebecca (née Maltby), aged 52, and son William (30).
4 N. Mulard, *op. cit.*
5 www.archivespasdecalais.fr – *Recensement de Population de St Pierre-dès-Calais:* liste nominative. 1841.
6 A. Vion, *Calais et Saint-Pierre au XIXe Siècle,* Dunkirk, 1982.
7 G. Kelly, *Tulle* 34, November, 1991, Adelaide. *Tulle* is the journal of the Australian Society of the Lacemakers of Calais.
8 N. Mulard, *op. cit.*
9 C. Demotier, *Annales de Calais, depuis les temps les plus reculés jusqu'à nos jours,* Calais, 1856.
10 N, Mulard, *op. cit.*
11 *The Standard,* London, 24 March 1848.
12 C. Borde, *Calais et la Mer (1814-1914),* Paris, 1997.
13 K. Ireland, *The Family History of Hiram Longmire, 1814-1880,* Adelaide, 1972.
14 K. Ireland, *op. cit.*
15 For information on the Bromhead family I thank Stephen Black (private communication).
16 N. Mulard, *op. cit.*
17 N. Mulard, *op. cit.*
18 N. Mulard, *op. cit.*

Chapter 11 – 'No better than a sort of Alsatia'

1   Reproduced in *The Mirror of Literature, Amusement and Instruction*, 17 Nov. 1827, Issue 283. The King's Bench was the debtor's prison in Southwark. Those who could afford to do so purchased 'Liberty of the Rules' which allowed them to live within an area of 3 sq. miles about the prison.

2   Various Authors, *Young Americans Abroad, or Vacations in Europe, Travels in England, France, Holland, Belgium, Prussia and Switzerland*, Boston, 1852.

3   *The Pall Mall Gazette*, City Men, IV – The Chairman, 25 Feb. 1869, Issue 1261.

4   S. Foote, *A Trip to Calais: a Comedy in Three Acts*, (London, 1794).

5   E.W. Sunstein, *Mary Shelley: Romance & Reality*, Baltimore, 1991.

6   M. Shelley, *History of a Six Weeks Tour*, London, 1817.

7   M. Seymour, *Mary Shelley*, London, 2000.

8   *The Derby Mercury*, 25 Sept. 1833.

9   G. Le G. Norgate, 'Pole, William Wellesley – third earl of Mornington (1763–1845)', rev. John K. Severn, *Oxford Dictionary of National Biography*, Oxford University Press, 2004; online edn, Jan 2008.

10   A. Ashby & A. Jones, *The Shrigley Abduction*, Stroud, 2003. The Shrigley Abduction case may have been the inspiration for the story of the proposed elopement from a young ladies' boarding school in Charles Dickens's *The Pickwick Papers* of 1836/7.

11   Ashby & Jones, *op. cit.*

12   Quoted in Ashby & Jones, *op. cit.*

13   Quoted in Ashby & Jones, *op. cit.*

14   Quoted in Ashby & Jones, *op. cit.*

15   Ashby & Jones, *op. cit.*

16   Quoted in R. Mullen & J. Munson, *The Smell of the Continent: the British Discover Europe*, London, 2009.

17   T. A. B. Corley, 'Chudleigh, Elizabeth [married names Elizabeth Hervey, countess of Bristol; Elizabeth Pierrepont, duchess of Kingston upon Hull] (c.1720–1788)', *Oxford Dictionary of National Biography*, Oxford

University Press, 2004; online edn. Jan 2008.

18 Introduction to the 1794 edition of Foote's play *A Trip to Calais*.

19 C.E. Pearce, *The Amazing Duchess: being the Romantic History of Elizabeth Chudleigh*, Vol. 2, London, 1911.

20 Pearce, *op. cit.*

21 Quoted in Pearce, *op. cit.*

22 Quoted in Pearce, *op. cit.*

23 Mavor, *op. cit.*

24 Pearce, *op. cit.*

25 Pearce, *op. cit.*

26 D'Oberkirch, Baroness, *Memoirs of the Baroness d'Oberkirch: written by herself and edited by her grandson, the Count de Montboison*, London, 1852.

27 Pearce, *op. cit.*

28 Mavor, *op. cit.*

29 Mavor, op. cit.

30 PRO, Prob 11/1186.

31 T.A.B. Corley, *op. cit.*

32 K. Williams, *England's Mistress: the Infamous Life of Emma Hamilton*, London, 2007.

33 K. Williams, *op. cit.*

34 R.Bell Calton, *Annals and Legends of Calais with Sketches of Emigré Notabilities and a Memoir of Lady Hamilton*, London, 1852.

35 L. Vernon Harcourt (ed.), *The Diaries and Correspondence of the Rt. Hon. George Rose*, London, 1860.

36 R. Bell Calton, *op. cit.*

37 R. Bell Calton, *op. cit.*

38 R. Bell Calton, *op. cit.*

39 K. Williams, *op.cit.* Williams does, however, contrast the £28 spent on Emma's funeral with the £14,000 spent on Nelson's.

40 Ian Kelly in *Beau Brummell: the Ultimate Dandy*, London (2005) refers to Brummell and his friends as the original 'fashion police'.

41 Kelly, *op. cit.*

42 Letter quoted in Kelly, *op. cit.*

43 H. Wilson, *Memoirs of Hariette Wilson,* London, 1831.

44 Capt. Jesse, *The life of Beau Brummell,* Vol. I, London, 1844.

45 R. Bell Calton, *op. cit.*

46 R. Bell Calton, *op. cit.*

47 R. Bell Calton, *op. cit.*

48 B. Pool (ed.) *The Croker Papers,* London, 1967.

49 T. Raikes, *A Portion of his Journal from 1831-47,* Vol. I, London, 1856.

50 J.H. McCartney (ed.) *The Wits and Beaux of Society by Grace and Philip Wharton,* Vol. II, London, 1890.

51 J.H. McCartney (ed.) *op. cit.*

52 Capt. Jesse, *The Life of Beau Brummell,* Vol. II, London, 1927.

53 Capt. Jesse, *op. cit.*

54 J.F. Tattershall (ed.) *Reminiscences of a Literary Life: Charles Macfarlane, 1799-1858, Author and Traveller,* London, 1917.

55 Capt. Jesse, *op. cit.*

56 P.W. Wilson, *The Greville Diary,* Vol. I, London, 1927 – entry for 6 March 1830.

57 Capt. Jesse, *op. cit.*

58 V.E. Hartley Booth, *British Extradition Law and Procedure,* Alphen a/d Rijn, 1981.

Chapter 12 – The Moustache and Nimrod

1 J.G. Lockhart, *Memoirs of the Life of Sir Walter Scott,* 3 Vols. (Paris, 1838).

2 *The Memoirs of Harriette Wilson written by herself,* 4 vols., (London, 1825).

3 *Memoirs, op. cit.*

4 According to the entry on Wilson in the ODNB, [K.D. Reynolds, Wilson, Harriette, *The Oxford Dictionary of National Biography,* Oxford University Press, 2004, online edition] this took place in 1826 but her most recent biographer Frances Wilson, *The Courtesan's Revenge,* (London, 2003), gives the date as three years previous.

5 F. Wilson, *op. cit.* In fact when she died a number of her old suitors, including Brougham, clubbed together to pay for her funeral.

6   *Journal of the House of Lords,* Vol. 73, (London 1841).

7   *Journal, op. cit.*

8   *Journal, op. cit.*

9   I. Kelly, *Beau Brummell: the Ultimate Dandy,* (London, 2005).

10 www.archivesenligne.pasdecalais.fr.   *Recensement de Population de Calais: liste nominative, 1836*

11 *Journal, op. cit.*

12 F. Wilson, *op. cit.*

13 F. Wilson, *op. cit.*

14   *Reports of Cases argued and determined in the court of King's Bench. From Hilary Term 7th William IV to Michaelmas Term* 1st Vict. 1837, (London, 1839).

15 *Reports, op. cit.*

16 *Reports, op. cit.*

17 John Morley makes a fleeting appearance in George W.M. Reynolds's sensational novel *Grace Darling; the heroine of the Fern islands,* see Appendix 4.

18 The website http://measuringworth.com gives the 2011 equivalent of £4 - 2 - 6d, using the Retail Price Index, as £319.

19 *Journal, op. cit.*

20 E.D. Cuming (ed.) *My Life and Times by Nimrod,* (London, 1827).

21 E.D. Cuming, *op. cit.*

22 E.D. Cuming, *op. cit.*

23 Nimrod, *Memoirs of the Life of the Late John Mytton Esq.,* (London, 1903).

24 E.D. Cuming, *op. cit.*

25 E.D. Cuming, *op. cit.*

26 E.D. Cuming, *op. cit..*

27 Nimrod, *op. cit.*

28 Nimrod, *op. cit.*

29 Nimrod, *op. cit.*

30 Nimrod, *op. cit.*

31 G.R.F. Barker, 'Mytton, John (1796-1834), rev. George C. Barugh, *Oxford Dictionary of National Biography,* Oxford University Press, 2004.

32 E.D. Cuming, *op. cit.*
33 *The Mirror of Literature, Amusement and Instruction*, Vol. XXXII, (London, 1838)
34 E.D. Cuming, *op. cit.*.
35 Robert Bell Calton, *Annals and Legends of Calais*, (London, 1852).
36 www.archivesenligne.pasdecalais.fr. – *Recensement de Population de St Pierre-Lès-Calais: liste nominative, 1836.*
37 Norman Gash, 'Apperley, Charles [Nimrod] 1778-1843, *Oxford Dictionary of National Biography*, Oxford University Press, 2004.
38 E.D. Cuming, *op. cit.*

Chapter 13 – 'With French pens and French ink'
1 R. Southey, *Letters from England*, London, 1807.
2 F. Hall, *Travels in France in 1818*, London, 1819.
3 T. Holcroft, *Anna St Ives*, London, 1792.
4 In 1794 the suspension of Habeas Corpus was followed by the arrest of a group of radicals which included Thomas Hardy, John Horne Tooke, John Thelwall and Holcroft. They were indicted for high treason but the case against them collapsed ignominiously.
5 C. Dickens, *Little Dorrit*, Vol. 2, Chap. 20. See also J. Edmondson, *Dickens on France*, Northampton, Mass., 2007.
6 L. Kelly, *Ireland's Minstrel: a life of Tom Moore – Poet, Patriot and Byron's Friend*, London, 2006.
7 H. Carpenter, *The Seven Lives of John Murray*, London, 2008.
8 *Anna St Ives*, Letter I – 'Expectation is on a tiptoe: my busy fancy has pictured to itself Calais, Montreuil, Abbeville – in short, every place which the book of post roads enumerates, and some of which the divine Sterne has rendered so famous.' Letter XX – 'My very first demand has been for pen, ink and paper'.
9 For Mariana Starke *see* Chapter 2 above.
10 He is so described in a notice which appeared in the *Cambridge Chronicle*, 18 July 1828, requesting his creditors to contact a firm of London solicitors.

11 When the contents of his house, in Brunswick Place, Cambridge, were sold at auction on 26 & 27 September, 1827 they included, 'Modern household furniture, Linen, prints, Pictures, China, Glass and a Grand piano-forte, with additional keys, by Broadwood', *Cambridge Chronicle*, 21 Sept. 1827.

12 *Bury & Norwich Post*, 1 August, 1827.

13 *Cambridge Chronicle*, 1 August 1825.

14 *Cambridge Chronicle*, 27 July, 1827.

Chapter 14 – Farewell Dessein!

1 I am grateful to Dick Bateman for his research into these verses.

2 M. Tyson & H. Guppy, *The French Journals of Mrs Thrale and Doctor Johnson*, Manchester, 1932.

3 W. Jones, *Observations on a Journey to Paris by way of Flanders in the Month of August, 1776*, London, 1777.

4 H. Barrows (ed.) *Hester Lynch Piozzi: Observations and Reflections made in the Course of a Journey through France, Italy & Germany*, Ann Arbor, 1967.

5 H. Barrows (ed.), *op. cit.*

6 R. Sharp, *Letters and Essays in Prose and Verse*, London, 1834.

7 C. Hervey, The Habitué's Notebook in '*The New Monthly Magazine & Humorist*, Vol. 85, pt. 1, 1849.

8 From the website of Les Amis de Vieux Calais – http://lesamisdevieuxcalais.com/amisdu_vieux_calais/site-dico_d.htm

9 J. Ruskin on 'Pre-Raphaelitism' in I. Bryden, *The Pre-Raphaelites & Sources*, Vol. III, London, 1998.

10 *The Spectator*, 7 October, 1911.

11 From *St James's Gazette*, re-printed in *Aberdeen Weekly Journal*, 29 July 1880.

12 From *St James's Gazette, op. cit.*

Sources
Archival and Official
British Library – B.L. Add MSS 56544/5/6/7
Dove Cottage – DCMS92
Gloucestershire Record Office – CRO D 2002 F1
National Archives – PRO Prob 11/1186
Norwich Record Office – NRO Bul 4/194 610
Shropshire Archives – Letter 811/3
Wintherthur Library – Doc. 1351
Journal of the House of Lords, Vol. 73, 1841
Reports of Cases argued and determined in the Court of King's Bench, from Hilary term 7th William IV to Michaelmas Term 1st Victoria 1837, 1839

Books *(Place of publication London unless otherwise stated.)*
Albany, J., *The Englishman's Guide to Calais,* Hurst, Chance, 1829
Alger, J.G., *Napoleon's British Visitors and Captives,* Constable, 1904
Allott, K & M., *The Poems of Matthew Arnold,* Longman, 1979
Alexander, Boyd (ed.) *Life at Fonthill, 1807-1822,* Hart-Davis, 1957
Anon. *Britain Triumphant on the Plains of Waterloo* Burslem 1816.
Anon, *Damiens Conversations Lexicon,* Leipzig, 1834
Anon, *Les Théâtres (Lois, règlements, instruction, Salles de Spectacles...) par un Amateur,* Paris, 1817
Anon, *Memoirs of a Man of Fashion,* 1821
Anon. ('A Virginian') *The American Wanderer through Various Parts of Europe by a Virginian,* J. Robson, 1783
Anon, *The Universal Songster: a Museum of Mirth,* Vol.1, 1825
Anon, *Murray's Handbook for Travellers on the Continent, being a Guide through Holland, Belgium, Prussia and North Germany,* J. Murray, 1836
Apperley, C.J. ('Nimrod') *Memoirs of the Life of the Late John Mytton Esq.,* Methuen, 1903
Ashby, A. & Jones, A., *The Shrigley Abduction,* Sutton, Stroud, 2003

Austin F. (ed.), *The Clift Family Correspondence, 1792-1846*, Cectal, Sheffield, 1991

Baillie, M., *First Impressions on a Tour upon the Continent in the year 1818, through Parts of France, Italy, Switzerland & the Borders of Germany*, J. Murray, 1819

Bamford, F. & Wellington, Duke of, (eds.) *The Journal of Mrs Arbuthnot*, Vol. 1, Macmillan, 1950

Barbeau, A. (ed.) *La France et Paris sous le Directoire: lettres d'un voyageuse anglaise*, Mesnil, Paris, 1888

Barrows, H. (ed.) *Hester Lynch Piozzi: Observations and Reflections made in the Course of a Journey through France, Italy and Germany*, University of Michigan Press, Ann Arbor, 1967

Bell, A., Sydney Smith: a Biography, Oxford University Press, Oxford, 1980

Bernard, R.B., *A Tour through Some Parts of France, Switzerland, Savoy, Germany & Belgium during the Summer and Autumn of 1814*, Longman, 1815

Bew, J., *Castlereagh: Enlightenment, War & Tyranny*, Quercus, 2011

Black, Jeremy, *The Grand Tour in the Eighteenth Century*, Alan Sutton, Stroud, 1992

Blagdon, F.W., *Paris as it was and as it is*, 1803

Blessington, Countess of, *Journal of a Tour through the Netherlands to Paris in 1821*, Longman, 1822

Blessington, Countess of, *The Idler in Italy*, Henry Colburn, 1839

Booth, V.E. Hartley, *British Extradition Law and Procedure*, Sijthoff & Noordhoff, Alphen a/d Rijn, 1981

Borde, C., *Calais et la Mer, 1814-1914*, Presses Universitaires du Septentrion, Paris, 1997

Boswell, J., *The Life of Johnson*, Oxford University Press, Oxford, 1961

Boys, E., *Narrative of a Captivity, Escape and Adventures in France*, Richard Long, 1827

Brayne M. (ed.) *Harry Peckham's Tour*, Nonsuch, Stroud, 2008

Broadley, A.M. (ed.) *Dawson Warren: The Journal of a British Chaplain in Paris during the Peace Negotiations of 1802*, Chapman & Hall, 1913

Bryden, I., *The Pre-Raphaelies: Writings and Sources*, Vol. III, Routledge, 1998

Bulwer Lytton E., *England and the English* Paris 1836

Burke, J. (ed.) W. Hogarth, *An Analysis of Beauty*, Oxford University Press, Oxford, 1955

Calton, R. Bell, *Annals and Legends of Calais*, J.R. Smith, 1852

Carpenter, H., *The Seven Lives of John Murray*, John Murray, 2008

Carter, N., *Letters from Europe: comprising the Journal of a Tour through Ireland, England, Scotland, France, Italy and Switzerland in the Years 1825, 1826 and 1827*, G. & C. Carvill, New York, 1827

Choules, J.O. (ed.) *Young Americans Abroad, or Vacation in Europe: Travels in England, France, Holland, Belgium, Prussia, and Switzerland*, Gould & Lincoln, Boston, 1852

Clayden, P.W., *The Early Life of Samuel Rogers*, Smith Elder, 1887

Clayden, P.W., *Rogers and his Contemporaries*, Vol. I, Smith Elder, 1889

Cobbett, John M., *Letters from France*, Jowett & Mills, 1825

Colles, J.M. (ed.) *The Journal of John Mayne during a Tour of the Continent upon its Re-opening after the Fall of Napoleon, 1814*, Bodley Head, 1909

Collier, G., *France on the Eve of the Great Revolution: France, Holland and the Netherlands a Hundred Years Ago*, Richard Bentley, 1865

Cross, Wilbur L., *The Life and Times of Laurence Sterne*, Yale University Press, New Haven, 1929

Cuming, E.D. (ed.) *'Nimrod': My Life and Times*, Blackwood, 1927

Curtis, L.P. (ed.) *Letters of Laurence Sterne*, Oxford University Press, Oxford, 1935

Davenport, Beatrix Cary (ed.) *A Diary of the French Revolution by Gouverneur Morris*, Harrap, 1939

Demotier, C., *Annales de Calais, depuis les temps le plus reculées jusqu'à nos jours*, Calais, 1856

De Selincourt, E. (ed.) *Journals of Dorothy Wordsworth*, Vol. 2, Macmillan, 1952

Dickins, C., *Little Dorrit,* Bradbury & Evans, 1857

Edmundson, J., *Dickens on France,* Northampton, Mass., Interlink, 2007

Edwards, H. (ed.) *The Diary of James Woodforde,* Vol. 10 (1782-1784), Parson Woodforde Society, 2013

Eyre, Edmund J., *Observations made at Paris during the Peace,* Bath, 1803

Fawcett, W. (ed.) *James Essex: Journey of a Tour through Part of Flanders and France in August 1773,* 1888

Fennell, J., *An Apology for the life of James Fennell,* Benjamin Blom, New York, 1969

Fitzgerald, P., *The Life of Sterne,* Vols. I & II, Downey, 1896

Foote, S., *A Trip to Calais: a Comedy in Three Acts,* J. Parsons, 1794

Frost, T., *The Lives of the Conjurors,* 1876

Fry, J. & K., *A Tale of Two Journeys: France and Belgium in the early 1800s,* Millrace, Disley, 2005

Gash, N., *The Life of Sir Robert Peel after 1830,* Longman, 1986

Gibbs, Lewis. (ed.) *The Diary of Fanny Burney,* J.M. Dent, 1966

Gosse, P., *Doctor Viper: the Querulous Life of Philip Thicknesse,* Cassell, 1952

Granville, A.B., *St Petersburgh: a Journal of Travels to and from the Capital,* 1828

Greig, J. (ed.) *The Farington Diary,* Vol. II (1802-1804), Hutchinson, 1923

Hall, F., *Travels in France in 1818,* 1819

Harcourt, L. Vernon., *The Diaries and Correspondence of the Rt. Hon. George Rose,* Bentley, 1860

Hawker P., *The Diary of Colonel Peter Hawker, 1802-1853,* Greenhill, 1988

Hébert L. & Dupont G., *An Actual Survey and Itinerary of the Road from Calais to Paris,* printed by Schulze & Dean, 1814

Henderson, W.O., *Industrial Britain under the Regency,* Frank Cass, 1968

Hervé, F., *How to enjoy Paris in 1842,* 1842

Holcroft, T., *Anna St Ives,* 1792

Hughes P. (ed.) T*he Journals and Letters of Fanny Burney,* Vol. VIII, Oxford University Press, Oxford, 1980

Hugo, A. & Monin, C.V. *France pittoresque: ou déscription pittoresque, topographique et statistique,* Paris, 1835

Hugo, V., *France et Belgique, Alpes et Pyrenées,* Paris, 1842

Ireland, K., *The Family History of Hiram Longmire, 1814-1880,* Adelaide, 1972

Jesse, Capt., *The Life of Beau Brummell,* Vol. 1, Saunders & Otley, 1844

Jessup R., *Man of Many Talents: an Informal Biography of James Douglas, 1753-1819,* Phillimore, Chichester, 1975

Johnson, S., *Prayers and Meditations,* G.Strahan, 1785

Jones, W., *Observations in a Journey to Paris,* 1776

Junot, L. (Madame la Duchesse d'Abrantès), *Mémoires de Mme la Duchesse d'Abrantès, ou Souvenirs historique, sur Napoléon, la Révolution, la Directoire et la Restauration,* Paris, 1832

Kelly, I., *Beau Brummell: the Ultimate Dandy,* Hodder & Stoughton, 2005

Kelly, L., *Ireland's Minstrel: a Life of Thomas Moore – Poet, Patriot and Byron's Friend,* I.B. Tauris, 2006

Kennedy, C., *Narratives of the Revolutionary and Napoleonic Wars,* Palgrave Macmillan, Basingstoke, 2013

Knighton, Lady, *Memoirs of Sir William Knighton,* Vol. 1, A.& W. Galignani, Paris, 1838

Lees, A., *The Cyclopedia: a Universal Dictionary of Arts, Sciences and Literature,* 1819

Lemaistre, J.G., *A Rough Sketch of Modern Paris,* J. Johnson, 1803

Lennel, F., *Calais par l'Image,* Tome 3, Téméraire, Paris, 1996

Leveson-Gower G. & I. Palmer (eds.) *Hary-O: The Letters of Lady Harriet Cavendish,* John Murray, 1940

Lewis, M., *Napoleon and his British Captives,* Allen & Unwin, 1962

Lewis, Lady Theresa, *Extracts of the Journal and Correspondence of Miss Berry from the Year 1783,* Vol. II, Longmans, 1866

Litchfield, H.E. (ed.) *Emma Darwin: a Century of Family Letters,* Cambridge University Press, Cambridge, 1904

Lloyd, C. & Anderson, R.C. (eds.) *A Memoir of James Trevenen,* Navy Record Society, 1959

Lloyd, M., *The Passport: the History of Man's Most Travelled Document,* Queen Anne's Fan, Canterbury, 2012

Lockhart, J.G., *Memoirs of the Life of Sir Walter Scott,* A. & W. Galignani, Paris, 1838

Macfarlane, C., *Reminiscences of a Literary Life,* Murray, 1917

Macintyre, I., *Hester: the remarkable Life of Dr Johnson's 'Dear Mistress',* Constable, 2008

Maclean, C.M., *Born under Saturn: a biography of William Hazlitt,* Collins, 1943

Madan, B. (ed.) *Spencer and Waterloo: the Letters of Spencer Madan, 1814-16,* L.S. & P., 1970

Marlin, F., *Voyages d'un Français depuis 1775 jusqu'à 1807* Tome I, Paris, 1817

Mavor, E. (ed.) *The Grand Tours of Katherine Wilmot: France 1801-3 and Russia 1805-7,* Weidenfeld & Nicolson, 1992

Maxwell, C (ed.) A. Young, *Travels in France during the Years 1787, 1788 & 1789,* Cambridge University Press, Cambridge

McCartney, J.H. (ed.) *Wits and Beaux of Society by Grace and Philip Wharton,* Vol. 2, J.W. Jarvis, 1890

Montagné, P., *Nouveau Larousse Gastronomique,* Larousse, Paris, 1960

Montbrison, Count of. (ed.) *Memoirs of the Baroness d'Oberkirch,* 1852

Moore, T ('T. Brown') *The Fudge Family in Paris,* Longman Hurst, 1818

Morgan K., *Jabez Fisher: an American Quaker in the British Isles,* Oxford University Press, Oxford, 1992

Mulard, N., *Calais au temps de la Dentelle,* Les Cahiers de Vieux Calais, Calais, 1968

Mullen R. & Munson J., *The Smell of the Continent,* Macmillan, 2009

Murray, N., *A Life of Matthew Arnold,* Hodder & Stoughton, 1996

Nockles P. B. *The Oxford Movement in Context: Anglican High Churchmanship, 1760-1856,* Cambridge 1994

Norgate J. (ed.) *Paris and the Parisians in the Year after Waterloo,* London Literary Society, 1887

O'Reilly, A. *The Irish Abroad and at Home: at the Court and in the Camp,* New York, 1856

Otter, W. (ed.) *Life and Remains of the Revd. Edward Daniel Clarke, Ll.D,* 1824

Paul, J. Dean., *Journal of a Party of Pleasure to Paris in the Month of August, 1802,* T. Cadell, 1802

Pearce, C.E., *The Amazing Duchess: being the Romantic History of Elizabeth Chudleigh,* Vol. 2, Stanley Paul & Co., 1911

Peckham, H., *The Tour of Holland, Dutch Brabant, the Austrian Netherlands and Parts of France: in which is included a Description of Paris,* G. Kearsly, 1772

Pevsner, N., *A History of Building Types,* Thames & Hudson, 1976

Piazza, P., *Histoire de la Carte Nationale d'Identité ,* Odile Jacob, Paris, 2004

Pinkney, N., *Travels through the South of France and in the interior of the provinces of Provence and Languedoc in the years 1807 and 1808, 1809*

Pool. B. (ed.) *The Croker Papers,* Batsford, 1967

Prothero, Rowland E. (ed.) *Private Letters of Edward Gibbon,* Vol. 2, J. Murray, 1896

Quennell, P., *Four Portraits,* Collins, 1945

Quérard, J., *La France litteraire, ou Dictionnaire bibliographiques des Savants,* Firmin Didot, 1838

Raikes, T., *A Portion of his Journal from 1831-47,* Vol. 1, Longmans, 1856

Reynolds, F., *Life and Times of Frederic Reynolds,* Henry Colburn, 1826

Reynolds, G.W.M., *Grace Darling: the Heroine of the Fern Islands.* G. Henderson, 1839

Roscoe, E.S. & Clergue. (eds.) *George Selwyn: His Letters and his Life,* T.F. Unwin, 1899

Ross, Ian Campbell, *Lawrence Sterne – a Life,* Oxford University Press, Oxford, 2002

Rush, R., *Narrative of a Residence at the Court of London,* S.Bentley, 1833

Ruskin, J., *Praeterita,* G. Allen, Orpington, 1889

Scharma, S., *Citizens: a Chronicle of the French Revolution,* Penguin, 1989

Scott, Sir Walter, *Journal of Sir Walter Scott from the Original Manuscript at Abbotsford*, D. Douglas,   Edinburgh, 1890

Seymour, M., *Mary Shelley*, John Murray, 2000

Sharp, R., *Letters and Essays in Prose and Verse*, E.Moxon, 1834

Sheffield, Lord (ed.) *The Miscellaneous Works of Edward Gibbon, Esq., with Memoirs of his Life and Writings, Vol. 2, Letters*, J. Murray, 1814

Shelley, M., *History of a Six Weeks Tour*, T. Hookham, 1817

Simmons, J. (ed.) *Robert Southey: Letters from England*, Cresset Press, 1951

Smith, C. Gregory (ed.) *The Spectator by Joseph Addison, Richard Steele, & Others*, Vol. 1, J.M. Dent, 1945

Smith, E.A., 'Caroline (1768-1821)' *Oxford Dictionary of National Biography*, Oxford, 2004

Smith, E.A., George IV, Yale University Press, 1999

Smith, W., *A Yorkshireman's Trip to Rome in 1866*, Longmans, 1866

Sorel, A., *L'Europe et la Révolution Française*, Paris, 1903

Starke, M., *Information and Direction for Travellers on the Continent*, 6th ed., J. Murray, 1828

Sterne, L. ('Yorick') *A Sentimental Journey*, T. Becket & P.A. de Hondt, 1768

Stoddard, R.H. (ed.) *Personal Reminiscences of Chorley, Planché and Young*, Scribner, New York, 1876

Stokes, F.G. (ed.) *A Journal of my Journey to Paris in the Year 1765*, Constable, 1931

Stout, Gardener D., *A Sentimental Journey through France and Italy by Mr Yorick*, University of California Press, Berkeley, 1967

Straffa P. (ed.) *The Works and Correspondence of David Ricardo: Journal of a Tour on the Continent*, Cambridge University Press, Cambridge, 1973

Sunstein, E.W., *Mary Shelley: Romance and Reality*, Johns Hopkins, Baltimore, 1991

Thackeray, W.M., 'Notes on a Week's Holiday' in *Roundabout Papers*, Collins, 1887

Thicknesse, P., *A Year's Journey through France and Part of Spain*, Bath (printed), 1777

Thorold, P., *The British in France: Visitors and Residents since the Revolution*, Continuum , 2008

Toynbee, H. Paget (ed.) *Walpole's Letters*, Vol. I, Clarendon Press, Oxford, 1903

Trollope, F., *Paris and the Parisians*, A. & W. Galignani, Paris, 1836

Turner, Dawson, *An Account of a Tour in Normandy*, J & A. Arch, 1820

Twiss, R., *A Trip to Paris in July & August 1792*, W. Lane, 1793

Tyson M. & Guppy, H. (eds.) *The French Journals of Mrs Thrale and Dr Johnson*, Manchester University Press, Manchester, 1932

Uglow, J., *Hogarth: a Life and a World*, Faber & Faber, 1997

Vion, A. *Calais et St Pierre au XIXe Siècle* Dunkirk, 1982

Watson, S., *A Journey to the Simplon*, 1818

Wellington, Seventh Duke of., *Wellington and his Friends*, Macmillan, 1965

Wheaton, Barbara Ketcham, *Savouring the Past: the French Kitchen and Table from 1300 to 1789*, Chatto & Windus, 1983

White, H.P., *A Regional History of the Railways of Southern England*, Phoenix House, 1961

Williams, K., *England's Mistress: the Infamous Life of Emma Hamilton*, Arrow, 2007

Willis, N. P. *Pencillings by the Way*, London 1942

Wilson, F., *The Courtesan's Revenge*, Faber & Faber, 2003

Wilson, H., *Memoirs of Hariette Wilson*, Stockdale, 1831

Wilson, P.W. (ed.) *The Greville Diary*, Vol. 1, Heinemann, 1927

Wordsworth, W., *Selected Poems of William Wordsworth*, Methuen, 2005

Wright, W., *A Narrative of the Situation and Treatment of the English arrested by order of the French Government at the commencement of hostilities*, J. Badcock, 1803

Young, A., *The Autobiography of Arthur Young with Selections from his Correspondence*, Smith, Elder, 1898

Newspapers & other publications

Aberdeen Weekly Journal, 29 July 1880

Blackwood's Magazine, 42, CCLXV, 1837

British Neptune, 14 Sept., 1818

Bury & Norwich Post, 1 August 1827

Cambridge Chronicle, 1 Aug. 1825, 27 July 1827, 21 Sept. 1827, 18 July 1828

Courier, 28 April, 1814

Derby Mercury, 25 Sept. 1833

Edinburgh Review, April-July 1806, Vol. VIII, 1806

European Magazine, December, 1803

Gentleman's Magazine, for the years 1797, 1820

Gentleman's Magazine & American Monthly Review, Vol. 1, Philadelphia, 1837

Hull Packet, 905, 15 May, 1804

Literary Gazette & Journal of Belles Lettres, Arts & Sciences for the Year 1826

Literary Panorama and National Reporter, October, 1814

London Weekly Times, 23 Sept. 1827

Midland History, Vol. XIII, 1988

Mirror of Literature, 283, 17 Nov. 1827

Mirror of Literature, Amusement and Instruction, Vol. XXXII, 1838

New Monthly Magazine, No. 28, Vol. 5, 1816

New Monthly Magazine, No. 34, Vol. 3, 1834

New Monthly Magazine, No. 85, 1849

Nord Matin, 2 & 3 July, 1961

Pall Mall Gazette, Issue 1261, 25 Feb. 1869

Quarterly Journal of the Parson Woodforde Society, XVII, 4, 1984

The Scots Magazine, January 1803

The Spectator, 7 oct. 1911

The Standard, London 24/3/1848

The Times, 24 June, 1844

Online *Oxford Dictionary of National Biography,* OUP 2004

Barker, G.R.F., 'Mytton , John (1796-1834)' rev. George C. Barugh,

Corley, T.A.B., 'Chudleigh, Elizabeth [married names Elizabeth Hervey, countess of Bristol; Elizabeth Pierrepoint, duchess of Kingston-upon-Hull] (c.1720-1788)'

Gash, N., 'Apperley, Charles [Nimrod] 1778-1843'

Hamilton, J.A., 'Knighton, Sir William, first baronet (1776-1836), rev. Judith Schmid Lewis

Laughton, J.K., 'Collier, Sir George (1738-1795)' rev. Nicholas Tracy

Linsley, Stafford M., 'Sopwith, Thomas (1803-1879)'

McConnell, Anita, 'Kitchiner, William (1776-1827)

Norgate, G. Le G., 'Pole, William Wellesley, third earl of Mornington (1763-1845)' rev. John K. Severn

Reynolds, K.D., 'Wilson, Harriette (1786–1845)' OUP Sept 2010

Reynolds, K.D., 'Vining Family (per 1807-1915)'

Smith, E.A., 'Caroline (1768-1821)' OUP, online edition 2004

Websites
http://blogs.kent.ac.uk/specialcollections/tag/tourism/page/3/
www.calais.fr/histoire/theatre/theatre.htm
www.lesamisduvieuxcalais.com/amisdu_vieux_calais/sitedico_d.htm
www:measuringworth.com
http://www.nationalgallery.org.uk/paintings/Joseph-mallord-william-turner-calais-pier

Image Credits
Cover *Calais Sands, at low tide, Poissards collecting bait* by J.M.W. Turner, ©Bury Art Gallery, Greater Manchester, UK.
Plates
1. *Calais Gate, or O, the Beef of Old England* by William Hogarth, ©Private Collection Ken Walsh/Bridgeman Images.
2. *An Inn Yard in Calais*, ©Trustees of the British Museum.
3. William Bulwer's Passport, courtesy of Norfolk Record Office, BUL 4/194 610 X9.
4. *To Calais*, satirical print made by George Cruikshank, ©Trustees of the British Museum.

5. From William Clarkson Stanfield, *Coastal Scenery,* Calais, engraved by W. Finden ©Tate, London, 2015.

6. J.M.W. Turner, *Calais Pier,* ©National Gallery, London, UK,/Bridgeman Images.

7. *Arriving at Calais,* ©Universal History Archive/UIG/ Bridgeman Images.

8. *Mrs Thrale and Her Daughter Hester* [Queeney] by Sir Joshua Reynolds, ©Beaverbrook Art Gallery, Fredericton, N.B., Canada/Bridgeman Images.

9. *The Passport Office, Calais,* ©Bibliothèque Historique de la Ville de Paris, Paris, France Archives Charmat/Bridgeman Images.

10. 'Routes de Calais à Paris', Dessin's hotel, Calais – courtesy of Norfolk Record Office, BUL 4/194 610 X9

11. *Elizabeth, Duchess Dowager of Kingston,* engraved by Thomas Taylor ©National Portrait Gallery.

12. *'Nimrod'* [Charles James Apperley], engraved by E. Finden from portrait by Daniel Maclise, ©National portrait Gallery.

13. *The Désobligeant,* illustration from a Victorian edition of *A Sentimental Journey,* courtesy of Look & Learn.

14. An Englishman's Bill for his stay at Dessin's, Wiltshire & Swindon Archives, 415/430.

15. *Margaret, Countess of Blessington* by Sir Thomas Lawrence, ©Wallace Collection, London.

16. *Robert Webster,* artist unknown ©Musée des Beaux-Arts de Calais.

17. *Sample of lace from Webster's Factory,* Calais © Cité Internationale de la Dentelle et de la Mode de Calais

18. *Débarquement d'Anglais à Calais pour Paris,* ©Trustees of the British Museum.

19. *Le Départ,* ©Trustees of the British Museum.

Illustrations
1. Plan of Calais from the plan cadastral, James Thornely.
2. *Laurence Sterne,* engraving by Edward Fisher of portrait by Sir Joshua Reynolds, author's collection.
3. Plan of Calais and St. Pierre with fortifications, James Thornely.
4. *Nôtre Dame, Calais,* Private Collection photo ©Liszt Collection/ Bridgeman Images
5. *Madame Saqui,* Harry H. Beard Collection, given by Isobel Beard, © Victoria and Albert Museum, London.
6. *Sarah Ann Bromhead,* photograph courtesy of Stephen Black, Australia.

INDEX